MONTGOMERY COLLEGE LIBRARY
GERMANTOWN CAMPUS

Essentials
of
Grammar

LANGUAGE, THOUGHT, AND CULTURE: *Advances in the Study of Cognition*

Under the Editorship of: E. A. HAMMEL
DEPARTMENT OF ANTHROPOLOGY
UNIVERSITY OF CALIFORNIA
BERKELEY

Michael Agar, Ripping and Running: A Formal Ethnography of Urban Heroin Addicts

Brent Berlin, Dennis E. Breedlove, and Peter H. Raven, Principles of Tzeltal Plant Classification: An Introduction to the Botanical Ethnography of a Mayan-Speaking People of Highland Chiapas

Mary Sanches and Ben Blount, Sociocultural Dimensions of Language Use

Daniel G. Bobrow and Allan Collins, Representation and Understanding: Studies in Cognitive Science

Domenico Parisi and Francesco Antinucci, Essentials of Grammar

In preparation

Elizabeth Bates, Language and Context: The Acquisition of Pragmatics

Eugene S. Hunn, Tzeltal Folk Zoology: The Classification of Discontinuities in Nature

Ben G. Blount and Mary Sanches, Sociocultural Dimensions of Language Change

Essentials of Grammar

Domenico Parisi
Francesco Antinucci

Instituto di Psicologia del CNR
Rome, Italy

Translated by
Elizabeth Bates

ACADEMIC PRESS   New York   San Francisco   London
A Subsidiary of Harcourt Brace Jovanovich, Publishers

The authors thank Elizabeth Bates of the Department of Psychology at the University of Colorado, Boulder, Colorado, for her able assistance in translating and revising this work, which was originally published in 1973 under the title *Elementi di Grammatica* by Boringhieri of Turin, Italy.

COPYRIGHT © 1976, BY ACADEMIC PRESS, INC.
ALL RIGHTS RESERVED.
NO PART OF THIS PUBLICATION MAY BE REPRODUCED OR TRANSMITTED IN ANY FORM OR BY ANY MEANS, ELECTRONIC OR MECHANICAL, INCLUDING PHOTOCOPY, RECORDING, OR ANY INFORMATION STORAGE AND RETRIEVAL SYSTEM, WITHOUT PERMISSION IN WRITING FROM THE PUBLISHER.

ACADEMIC PRESS, INC.
111 Fifth Avenue, New York, New York 10003

United Kingdom Edition published by
ACADEMIC PRESS, INC. (LONDON) LTD.
24/28 Oval Road, London NW1

Library of Congress Cataloging in Publication Data

Parisi, Domenico.
    Essentials of grammar.

    (Language, thought, and culture series)
    Translation of Elementi di grammatica.
    Bibliography: p.
    Includes index.
        1.   Grammar, Comparative and general.   2.   Semantics.
I.   Antinucci, Francesco, joint author.   II.   Title.
P151.P3313   418   75-32033
ISBN 0–12–544650–0

PRINTED IN THE UNITED STATES OF AMERICA

> Quoniam quidem intelligere et scire contigit
> in omni scientia ex cognitione principiorum...
>
> TOMMASO DI ERFURT
> *De modis significandi sive Grammatica speculativa*, 1.

Contents

FOREWORD ... ix

1 Grammar as a Model of Linguistic Competence ... 1

2 The Nucleus ... 15

3 Adverbials ... 32

4 Componential Analysis ... 41

5 Nominals ... 86

6 The Performative ... 110

7 Presuppositions ... 124

8 The Mapping Mechanism ... 134

9 A Comparison with Traditional Grammar ... 162

GLOSSARY	175
BIBLIOGRAPHY	177
INDEX	179

Foreword

Anyone who has tried seriously to describe the meanings of the words and sentences in his language, by using ordinary language, knows how easy it is to get trapped in the circularities and vaguenesses of the language used in the description. Anyone who has tried to construct a formal grammar of a language knows how complex a task it is to link up with that grammar the principles by which the meanings of sentences can be shown to be related to the meanings of their constituent words. There is a pressing need, obvious to people who have faced both of these problems, for some model or conceptual framework in whose terms it is possible to represent everything that can be known about word meanings and sentence meanings and which can at the same time be integrated with a theory of the grammatical organization of sentences and the grammatical functions of words.

One effort to provide such a model is the movement in modern linguistics that has come to be called generative semantics. The workers in this movement can be described as having (1) a commitment to a particular model for the representation of meaning, a model whose details differ from one worker to the next but which largely depends on the meaning-analysis potential of the predicate calculus; (2) a commitment to the discovery of a simple set of principles for relating semantic representations with facts about grammatical form and the structural organization of sentences; (3) a commitment to the discovery of the set of (psychologically real) primitive concepts in terms of which the model can operate; (4) the practice of careful introspective analysis of chosen words in the model's terms; (5) a willingness to extend the explanatory scope of the model to facts and problems not envisioned from the beginning; and, sometimes, (6) an eagerness to look for evidence of the truth or workability of the model in the experience of language comprehension or in the data of language acquisition.

In the technical and pedagogical literature of linguistics, the generative semantics model is presented either through modern logic or through traditional methods of analysis within linguistics. Since the model is technically neither an instance of nor an application of logic and since its intellectual style, vocabulary, form of argument, and the scope of its subject matter are so strikingly different from traditional concerns in linguistic semantics, the necessity of approaching it on either of these two avenues has always seemed unfortunate. The book that Domenico Parisi and Francesco Antinucci have written identifies a version of the generative semantics model, developing it in its own terms and with no intellectual prerequisites in either linguistics or formal logic. The authors have concentrated on making the notations intelligible, making the style of analysis familiar, and demonstrating the applicability of the model to a large number of semantic domains. The readers of this book will learn their way around in the vocabulary of change, causation, location, and movement, in the analysis of adverbs and negation, and in the study of speech acts and presuppositions—all timely and critical areas in modern semantic theory.

This book offers a direct and nontechnical introduction to issues in the theory of grammar and the theory of semantics. It will acquaint its readers with a feeling for the nature of semantics as a subject matter and will give them enough training in the technical apparatus and enough exposure to the method of analysis to enable them to begin carrying out semantic analyses of their own. Where the novices' analyses are successful, they will enjoy the excitement of discovery; where they are unsuccessful, they will have reasons to read other, more technical works in this rapidly advancing field. In either case they will profit from having read through this book.

CHARLES J. FILLMORE
Department of Linguistics
University of California
Berkeley, California

Grammar as a Model of Linguistic Competence

To introduce the reader to the argument of this book the best approach seems to be to explain its title: *Essentials of Grammar.*

Let us begin with the term **grammar.** Some clarification is necessary, since the use that we will make of this term is somewhat different from the definitions we all learned in school.

Among the activities of which the human organism is capable is included the ability to communicate by means of language: to speak and to understand others when they speak. The science that studies language is a science of living organisms, and as such it must necessarily be considered a branch of biology. Furthermore, language is listed among those activities of the organism that are defined as "higher processes"—activities under the control of its central nervous system, among the complex, global processes located in the brain. Hence, ideally, language should be the object of study of the so-called "neurosciences": neuroanatomy, neurophysiology, the biochemistry of the nervous system, and so forth. However, the current state of these sciences is not such as to permit making a detailed study based on direct observation of the structures that make language possible. We do know, for example, that for most individuals linguistic functions are located in the left cerebral hemisphere and that particular areas of that hemisphere seem to be especially important for these functions. But our knowledge does not go much beyond this. Even though constant progress is being made in our knowledge of the cerebral structures involved in language, this knowledge is still minimal in comparison with the enormously complex activities of speaking and understanding. This may be due in part to the fact that, at the level of cerebral structure, language is neither strictly localized nor connected with gross anatomical, histological, and physiological differences, but involves

1

instead some type of complex and dynamic organization at the functional level (see Luria, 1967; Lenneberg, 1967). Unfortunately, at this functional level there are no neurological models for such complex activities as language. Hence, at this point in scientific history, the sciences that can explain most about the nature of language are not the neurosciences, but rather psychology and linguistics (although these too must be viewed as fundamentally biological sciences.) **Psycholinguistics**—the field that radically unites psychology and linguistics—differs from the neurosciences as follows: The neurosciences make a direct study of the material structures (tissues, cells, electrical activity, anatomical and physiological connections) that carry out man's higher functions; their empirical data are direct observations of these material structures, and their models and theories focus on their nature and function. By contrast, psycholinguistics does not set out to study directly the cerebral structures responsible for language functions. Its empirical data are, instead, the ultimate results of the linguistic functions carried out in the brain: the production and understanding of sentences, the judgments that the speaker of a language can make concerning sentences in his language (this point is elaborated further on), and so forth. On the basis of such data, psycholinguists elaborate models and theories of the kind of system that may underlie these events. This system probably does not coincide directly with the brain. A psycholinguistic model of language is not intended to be a direct model of the cerebral functions and structures responsible for language. Psycholinguistic models say nothing about the material characteristics of the system, the "hardware" that carries out language. However, psycholinguistic models can at least tell us this: Whatever the cerebral structures responsible for language, they must have an organization that can carry out functions as described by the psycholinguistic model. Hence, psycholinguistics describes the "software" for the language machine, and as such constitutes the first step toward a biological theory of language. Insofar as it is adequate, such a model permits us to describe the nature of a fundamental human activity. Furthermore, given an adequate psycholinguistic model, the neuroscientist will know what to look for in studying the cerebral structures and functions responsible for language.

We will give the name **linguistic competence** to the system, present in some material form in the human brain, which permits man to speak and to understand others when they speak. The term **grammar** refers in turn to the psycholinguistic model that reconstructs such a system. Therefore, grammar is a model of linguistic competence. But what do we mean by the term **model**? Given a certain set of phenomena, the scientist constructs a **model** when he elaborates a unified group of concepts with which he can represent, in all essential aspects, each of these phenomena and all of their interrelations. Hence, a model is a simplified, symbolic representation of a certain set of phenomena. It permits us to "understand" these phenomena, by showing us their reciprocal connections and revealing to us otherwise hidden regularities. In other words, a model permits us to explain, predict, and perhaps eventually control the phenomena under study.

This conception of grammar as a scientific theory of the set of phenomena called language—that is, as a model of the linguistic competence underlying these phenomena—has some important consequences. The first is that for a grammar, as for every scientific theory, the problem of empirical verification assumes major importance. Every aspect of the model must be justified by reference to a set of empirical events whose explanation requires the introduction of that aspect into the model.

At this point we should clarify the fundamental empirical data for a model of language, in our view: They are the judgments that speakers of a language can make regarding sentences in that language. To illustrate, let us consider the following two sentences:

(1)   *John thinks that it would be better to leave right away.*
(2)   **The table thinks that it would be better to leave right away.*

The first sentence is comprehensible, and it is easy to imagine "normal" circumstances in which someone might pronounce it. The second sentence is, instead, less comprehensible, and it is difficult to imagine circumstances in which it might be uttered.[1] We **feel** that in sentence (2) there is something that we do not fully understand (for example, how a table manages to think), so that in order to give the sentence a meaning we must make a special use of the word *table* or perhaps of the word *think* (an extended, metaphorical use, etc.). This is not the case for sentence (1), which has a normal usage and poses no problems for comprehension. We can, then, say that sentence (1) is acceptable and sentence (2) is not acceptable (or that it is less acceptable, or acceptable only in particular circumstances). The acceptability of (1) and the nonacceptability of (2) constitute one type of empirical data for psycholinguistics.

Let us examine some other examples of acceptable and unacceptable sentences. Some acceptable sentences are

(3)   *Mary is leaving.*
(4)   *John gave her the books.*
(5)   *John and I washed the windows.*

[1] Unacceptable sentences are marked with an asterisk.

Some unacceptable sentences are

(6) *Mary am leaving.
(7) *John gave she the books.
(8) *John and washed I the windows.

Furthermore, sentence (3) can be considered completely acceptable, whereas the sentence

(9) ?John and me washed the windows.

can be acceptable for some speakers, perhaps less so than sentence (5), but certainly more than (8), which is entirely "out." The acceptability of (3), (4), and (5), the unacceptability of (6), (7), and (8), and the relative acceptability of (9) are all empirical facts to be accounted for in a psycholinguistic theory.

Now consider the sentence

(10) Frank must have left because the windows are closed.

As it is written, this sentence is ambiguous. In other words, it can have more than one interpretation. The first interpretation could be paraphrased as something like "I think that the reason Frank left is because the windows are closed." According to this interpretation, Frank is a person who cannot stand to be in a room with closed windows, and hence the fact that the windows were closed forced Frank to leave. But there is a second possible interpretation for (10), which might be paraphrased as "I think that Frank has left, and the reason why I reached that conclusion is that the windows are closed." In this second case, the fact that the windows are closed is the reason why the speaker believes that Frank has gone—perhaps because Frank usually closes the windows before he leaves. In this interpretation, we know nothing about Frank's own reasons for leaving.

Although sentence (10) has two interpretations as used here, there is rarely any ambiguity when the sentence is used in concrete communication— because of the context, or because of the way in which the sentence is pronounced. With regard to context, we usually have enough information about Frank, or about the events that have preceded the speaker's statement, to prefer one of the two interpretations automatically. With regard to pronunciation, the speaker usually tends to pause slightly before *because* when he has the second interpretation in mind (a pause usually indicated in writing with a comma), and the words that follow also often have a different intonation. Nevertheless, without these small differences in sound, sentence (10) has two interpretations, two meanings. This is also an empirical fact.

Grammar as a Model of Linguistic Competence

Similarly, the sentence

(11) *I only ate a few pieces of candy.*

has two interpretations, one in which I ate a few pieces of candy and nothing else, and another in which the number of pieces of candy that I ate were very few, while I also ate a banana split and two boxes of popcorn. By contrast, the sentence

(12) *I only ate the candy.*

a sentence that seems quite similar, has only one interpretation: that I ate candy and nothing else. The fact that sentence (11) has two interpretations and sentence (12) has only one is an empirical fact.

Now consider these two sentences:

(13) *Frank kept Harold from leaving.*
(14) *Harold didn't leave.*

These stand in a particular relationship to one another, a relationship that we call **entailment**. To assert sentence (13) entails being ready to assert sentence (14) as well. One cannot assert that Frank kept Harold from leaving and then say that Harold left.

We find similar relationships holding among these pairs of sentences:

(15) *I saw Harold's children.*
(16) *Harold has children.*

and

(17) *Frank left.*
(18) *I know that Frank left.*

One cannot assert (15) and (17) without being prepared at the same time to assert (16) and (18), respectively. Hence, the facts that (13) entails (14), (15) entails (16), and (17) entails (18), are also empirical data.

Notice that the relationship that ties these pairs of sentences is unidirectional. For example, (13) entails (14), but not vice versa. To assert that Frank kept Harold from leaving entails asserting that Harold stayed, but to assert that Harold stayed does not entail asserting that Frank kept him from leaving. However, there are other pairs of sentences in which the truth relation is reciprocal, and the speaker judges the two sentences to mean more or less the same thing. In this case we say that two sentences paraphrase each other.

Hence

(19) Frank has stopped smoking.

paraphrases

(20) Frank doesn't smoke anymore.

in that (a) the assertion of (19) entails the assertion of (20), and, reciprocally, the assertion of (20) entails the assertion of (19); (b) the speaker judges (19) and (20) to be similar in meaning. In the same way, the following two sentences paraphrase each other:

(21) Frank ate the apple.
(22) The apple was eaten by Frank.

When two sentences are paraphrases of one another, then it is also true that if one of the sentences is rendered unacceptable, we can automatically predict that the other will be unacceptable as well. Thus, insofar as the sentence

(23) *The rock has stopped thinking.

is unacceptable, automatically the sentence

(24) *The rock doesn't think anymore.

is unacceptable. Similarly, if the sentence

(25) *Frank sleeps the living room.

is unacceptable, then the sentence

(26) *The living room is slept by Frank.

is also unacceptable.

In addition to the reciprocal entailments just described, there are other, less stringent kinds of paraphrase relations. We can say that a sentence is a paraphrase of another even when it is not the case that one entails the other. The two sentences

(27) Frank is sleeping.
(28) It is Frank who is sleeping.

are paraphrases. Yet, although the assertion of (28) entails the assertion of (27), it is not necessarily the case that the assertion of (27) entails the assertion of (28). There is a special kind of focus in *It is Frank who is sleeping* that is not present in the sentence *Frank is sleeping*. Nevertheless, (27) and

(28) are quite similar in meaning, and the condition established above still holds insofar as anything that renders one of the sentences unacceptable automatically renders the other unacceptable as well. Hence if

(29) *The rock thinks.*

is unacceptable, we can rest assured that

(30) **It is the rock that thinks.*

is also unacceptable, and vice-versa. In either case, we can conclude that the fact that (19) is a paraphrase of (20), (21) of (22), and (27) of (28) are all empirical data.

These are concrete examples of the basic empirical data with which a linguistic model must deal. They consist of the judgments that speakers can make regarding the acceptability or unacceptability of sentences, of the different interpretations that a single sentence can have, of the entailment and paraphrase relations holding among sentences, and so forth. The first task of a model of language is to explain these facts, or as we said earlier, to demonstrate reciprocal connections and uncover underlying regularities. In essence, the model is a scientific theory from which these facts can be deduced. A model must explain why one sentence is acceptable and another is not, or whether sentences are acceptable only in particular circumstances. It must explain why a given sentence has only one interpretation while another has two or more, and in the latter case, it must furnish a representation of the various meanings of the single sentence and it must show the reciprocal relations among these representations. Finally, it must explain why two sentences are paraphrases of one another by furnishing a representation of the meaning of each sentence such that the similarities and the differences are quite clear. When he explains these facts, the psycholinguist constructs a model of the "software" system which, if programmed into the speaker's brain, should permit that speaker to produce, understand, and make linguistic judgments about sentences.

We have seen that the basic empirical data of a model of language are the judgments of speakers. These are the basic data, because they offer the most direct access to the fundamental mechanisms of linguistic competence, and because there are at present no other sources of data that permit a study of linguistic competence in all its richness, detail, and breadth. But the judgments of speakers are not the only empirical data available to psycholinguists. Other sources of data are the acquisition of linguistic competence by children, historical changes within languages, the phenomena of degeneration that are observed in certain language disturbances, the data obtainable in the laboratory through the use of experimental procedures, the many phenomena regarding differences in linguistic competence among individuals and groups, and so forth. An adequate psycholinguistic model of language must be able to account for all these data.

This view of grammar as a scientific theory has other consequences beyond the fundamental need for empirical justification. Between two grammars—that is, two alternative theories—we must be able to choose which grammar best serves the function of explanation, which model can handle the largest number of phenomena with the smallest number of theoretical constructs, within a coherent, unified system. Another function of a model is to show the connections between those phenomena that it was constructed to explain and other, different but related phenomena. For linguistic competence, which is an area of mental activity, this means that an adequate psycholinguistic model should be capable of making connections with models of perception, memory, learning, thought, and social abilities, thereby serving as part of a general model of mental processes.

In this book, then, the reader will find a grammar, in the sense of a model or scientific theory of linguistic competence, considered as part of man's mental capacity. As noted earlier, this use of the term **grammar** is somewhat different from the standard definition. In standard usage, the term "grammar" either corresponds to nothing very specific, just some form of reflection on language, or else, in its schoolroom usage, it refers to the study of linguistic norms, of the "correct" use of language. In this second definition grammar is not a theory of what people do but a set of prescriptions about what they *should* do. Obviously, this second definition has little to do with the purpose of this book. One might ask, then, why we continue to use the term "grammar" at all, given that it has denotations that we reject. The answer covers three points. First, our way of conceiving grammar is not really new. It can be found, albeit in a rather different form, in a fundamental tradition of linguistic study called universal or philosophical grammar, an approach that has never really been "surpassed" by so-called modern or scientific linguistics. Hence, our use of the term has an historical justification. Second, in the more recent field of generative linguistics, pioneered by Noam Chomsky, the term "grammar" is once again being used in the sense outlined here. As the ideas of Chomsky and his followers gain wider circulation this definition of "grammar" is also becoming better known. Given the overall similarities in approach, it is no accident that generative linguistics is often compared with the much older tradition of universal or rationalist grammar. On the other hand, the general outlines of our own model are, in fact, derived in large measure from recent generative linguistics—which explains our coinci-

Grammar as a Model of Linguistic Competence

dental preference for this view of grammar.[2] Finally, our choice of the term "grammar" rather than some other term lies also in a deliberate decision to try to influence the prevailing use of the word, rendering it more creditable, and perhaps modifying at the same time the "schoolroom" approach that is responsible for lay usage of the term.

If grammar is a model of linguistic competence, it should be divided into parts that correspond to natural divisions within linguistic competence itself. To speak means to formulate thoughts which one intends to communicate and to produce physically the sounds to which, according to a precise set of rules, those thoughts correspond. This correspondence between sound and thought means that the listener should be able, upon receiving the sounds, to reconstruct the thoughts that the speaker intended to communicate. If the sounds produced by the speaker are not the appropriate ones (i.e., if they do not correspond according to a precise set of rules to the speaker's thoughts), the listener will either be unable to reconstruct anything on the basis of those sounds, or he will reconstruct thoughts different from the one's that the speaker intended to convey. In either case, communication has failed.

If this is the essential structure of linguistic competence, a grammar should include these fundamental divisions:

(a) A model or way of representing the meaning of each sentence that the speaker of a given language knows how to produce or understand;

(b) A model of the sounds uttered with that sentence;

(c) A model of the mechanism that, given a meaning, matches it to the appropriate set of sounds, and vice-versa.

The grammar presented in this book does not pretend to be a complete model of language. It contains fairly detailed information about point (a), the

---

[2] Given the limits of the present work, we did not try to detail background and bibliographic references for individual point of comparison between our model, Chomsky's model, and the writings of many of Chomsky's students. However, many of the specific proposals that have been incorporated in our model find their origin in the work of some linguists who developed a particular approach to language (known as Generative Semantics) within the framework of generative linguistics. Therefore, we list below only those works that are directly relevant to the points to be discussed in the book.

Chapters 2 and 3: Fillmore (1968); Lakoff (1970)
Chapter 4: Lakoff (1972); McCawley (1968)
Chapter 5: Bach (1968); McCawley (1970)
Chapter 6: Ross (1970); Searle (1969)
Chapter 7: Fillmore (1971); Grice (1975); Gordon and Lakoff (1971)

representation of the meanings of sentences (Chapters 2–7). But it furnishes only bare general outlines and examples regarding point (c), the mechanism that makes meanings into sound and vice-versa. And it provides nothing whatsoever regarding (b), the phonetic or sound system.

Having clarified what we mean by "grammar" and what, in our view, are its principal subdivisions, let us turn to another aspect of the title of this book. The reader may ask why, given that the linguistic material used in our presentation is taken entirely from the English language, we have entitled the book *Essentials of Grammar* rather than *Essentials of English Grammar*. Obviously, the ability to communicate through language assumes different forms according to regions and human groups. There are a vast number of different languages. Within any individual language (for example English) we find idiosyncratic aspects possessed only by that language and no other. However, there are also universal aspects shared by all human languages. These universal aspects reflect aspects of the capacity for speech characteristic of the species as a whole. Indeed, it is likely that at least some of these have a biological basis, part of the genetic inheritance with which all children are born (see Lenneberg, 1971). The idiosyncratic aspects of individual languages are, instead, tied to the history of the group who speaks that language, and must be acquired by children in the course of language learning. One can choose to study either the universal or the unique aspects of language, but either course is possible **only** through the study of particular languages. Since there is no "universal" language, even the study of linguistic universals must be based on empirical data from individual languages. Nevertheless, it is clear that one can confront the study of a given language from two different approaches, one aimed at the study of those aspects that render that language different from all others and the other aimed at "using" the individual case to gain access to underlying, presumably universal aspects of the human capacity for language.

It must also be stressed that the study of and acquaintance with a particular language could not progress at all if it were not based on some knowledge of universal aspects of language. If a particular language is only one possible realization of the underlying universal capacity, it is likely that we would not get very far in its study if we did not already have as a starting point some assumptions about universal characteristics that define language. In this sense, the study of universals has a logical priority with respect to the study of individual languages.

At this point it should be clear why we have entitled this book *Essentials of Grammar* rather than *Essentials of English Grammar*. The primary goal of the book is to present a model of linguistic universals, a universal grammar—or more simply, a grammar. This approach leaves us open to the risk of influence from the particular characteristics of the language on which the analysis is based (in this case English), masking the underlying universals shared by all languages. This difficulty is found frequently in traditional grammars, which are greatly influenced by the particular characteristics of Latin and Greek. We hope we have been more successful in avoiding this problem, although obviously we cannot be certain. The test will lie in applying our grammar—which pretends to be universal—to different languages, perhaps quite distant from English. If we can obtain the same results regarding the naturalness of the representations, the ability to capture underlying regularities, and the overall explanatory power of the model, then we can be more confident that our theory models something more universal than English grammar. If our model fails this test—i.e. it cannot be applied equally to other languages—then it is not valid for English either, at least in the sense intended here. Only a truly universal grammar can capture the fundamental mechanisms underlying any particular language.

Both universal and idiosyncratic aspects are, obviously, tightly interwoven within any language. One of the advantages of a universal approach is that it helps us to untangle this interaction, furnishing hypotheses about where to look, within the language mechanism, for universal versus particular characteristics. We noted earlier that any language necessarily contains three systems: one which constructs meanings, another which formulates sequences of sounds, and a third system which establishes the connections between sound and meaning. The second system, which processes incoming sounds (reception) and creates outgoing sounds (production), is not treated in this book. Hence, we do not pretend to offer hypotheses about its universal or idiosyncratic aspects. However, with regard to the other two systems, we are prepared to advance some precise hypotheses. The system which permits the speaker and the listener to process meanings (in both understanding and speaking) is essentially universal. The individual mechanisms of which that system consists are common to all languages. This means that, at least in principle, the meanings of sentences in all the languages of the world should be representable with these mechanisms. Most of this book (Chapters 2–7) is devoted to the description of mechanisms for representing meaning: predicate, argument, nucleus, adverbial, nominals, nouns, noun modifiers, subordinate sentential structures, performatives, and presuppositions. The question is quite different for the system which, given a meaning structure, permits the selection of appropriate sounds, and vice-versa. It is within this system, which we will call the **projection** or **mapping mechanism** (Chapter 8), that the fundamental differences between particular languages are found. In short, languages will differ above all in the means used to express universal meanings.

The mapping rules of various languages, although based on common principles, differ from one language to another. Hence, it is necessarily the case that Chapter 8, which briefly describes some possible mapping rules for English, is more "English" than all the other chapters, in the sense that if the grammar were to make use of linguistic material from, say, Italian or Latin or Turkish, Chapter 8 would differ a great deal more from the current version than would any of the other chapters. Nevertheless, this chapter is intended more as an illustration of the general characteristics or universals required for mapping rules, rather than a detailed presentation of the mapping rules of English.

It should now be clear what we mean by the linguistic notion of grammar, and that we will be speaking of grammar in general rather than English grammar. This leaves out only one aspect of our title, the notion of **essentials.** The reason for the choice of this term is simple. Ours is not a complete grammar, but rather an effort to present what we feel are the foundations, the essential elements, of a complete grammar.

This last comment brings us to a discussion of the limits of this work, limits which are several and varied. We have already noted that of the three fundamental divisions of linguistic competence, one is not discussed at all in this book (i.e., phonetics), and another is presented only in terms of its most general characteristics (i.e., the mapping mechanism). But even within the one division that is examined in greatest detail (the representation of sentence meanings), there are many problems yet to be confronted. We will offer hypotheses about the kinds of concepts and mechanisms (largely of a universal character) which should permit an exhaustive and satisfying representation of the meaning of sentences. We will try to demonstrate how these concepts and mechanisms can be applied to represent (and thereby explain) a series of aspects of sentence meaning. However, there are a great many aspects of meaning to which this analysis has not been applied. Furthermore, in some cases the definitions that we have given to certain concepts and mechanisms leave much to be desired. Finally, with regard to empirical verification of the model, this model obviously has the provisional status of all scientific theories. It is valid only to the degree that no better substitutes are available. This is true for individual aspects of the theory as well as for its fundamental characteristics and assumptions. Our model may have an adequate empirical basis (in the sense outlined earlier), but much further verification is indispensable. Finally, because of limitations of space, the model is presented in this book without the full array of facts and data which are already available to sustain it. The few data presented are all in the form of speaker judgments, and for other data of the same type we can only refer the reader to other works. However, it is useful to note that the model has been applied, with good results, to the study of the development of language in the first years of life, providing further empirical support in this field as well.[3]

One further important limitation of this book must be noted. We have spoken and will speak of linguistic competence in the singular, assuming a uniformity within language. Such uniformity does not exist. Even assuming, as we do, a universal basis to linguistic competence, obviously no linguistic competence, as present in the brain of one human being, is identical to the version present in the brain of another—nor even within the same person at different points in time. Language contains a realm of differences—social, **dialectal** (variations among subgroups), **idiolectal** (variations among given individuals) and **diachronic** (variations across the history of a language or of an individual). As far as our grammar describes a single type of linguistic competence and neglects the differences, this is one more limitation. We maintain, nevertheless, that the extension and application of our grammar to the study of linguistic diversity is both possible and necessary. In fact, this seems to us to be the only correct way to confront the study of linguistic diversity, using an adequate model of the fundamental and universal linguistic mechanisms as a framework for the study of variations.

We will conclude by summarizing for the reader in a series of points what we consider to be the most important general characteristics of the grammar presented in this book:

(1) The grammar is conceived as a scientific model of linguistic competence. Insofar as linguistic competence is considered a part of man's cognitive competence, the science concerned with language—whether it is called linguistics, or the psychology of language, or psycholinguistics—is part of a science of the mind, intended as the system of higher functions of the human organism. Hence, the grammar poses problems and advances hypotheses concerning the relations between linguistic competence and the cognitive competence of which it is a part.

(2) A grammar is a theory of linguistic competence which must be verified empirically. On the one hand, this means that research should be carried out with the simplest, most coherent, and explanatory theory available that also permits connection with a general theory of the mind. On the other hand, research must be aimed at validating empirically every single aspect of the grammar.

[3] Antinucci and Parisi, 1973 and 1975; Parisi and Antinucci, 1974.

(3) The principal source of empirical data are judgments that speakers of a language can make concerning various characteristics of the sentences of their language. But there are other types of empirical data which a grammar must also consider and explain, e.g., acquisition of language by children, historical change, etc.

(4) The grammar operates according to a separation between meanings and the means for expressing them (in sounds or otherwise), and is committed to furnishing an adequate representation of both. Moreover, the grammar requires a system of rules that connect the two systematically.

(5) The grammar furnishes both a model of the meaning of words and a model of the meaning of sentences, and indicates the relations between these two types of meaning.

(6) The grammar also includes the **pragmatic** or contextual aspects of a grammar, the systematic mechanisms that regulate the concrete **use** of language and not only its **structure**. In fact, we assume that such pragmatic mechanisms are a systematic part of the structure of language.

(7) The model presented here pretends to identify universal aspects of language—a pretension which also requires a good deal of empirical justification. A model based on linguistic universals improves our understanding of individual languages (for example, English), while it can, at the same time, be extended to the study of other languages. Finally, universals may correspond to fundamental mental mechanisms, which may in turn reflect innate principles of the organization of the human mind.

(8) It should be possible to extend the model to the study of many other aspects of language beyond those discussed here. Furthermore, the model should be applicable within several practical fields, e.g., language disorders, linguistic education, machine models of natural language. Such applications of the model would permit more systematic research within those fields, while at the same time providing further empirical tests for the grammar itself.

The Nucleus

In the preceding chapter we stated that a grammar should be subdivided according to the fundamental divisions of linguistic competence: (a) a representation of the meaning of sentences, (b) a representation of the sound form of sentences, and (c) a representation of the mechanism that connects meaning with sound. We will begin with the problem of choosing a representation for the meaning of a sentence. Given the enormous complexity of this problem, it will be necessary to proceed gradually, considering some simpler sentences first and then passing on to more complex forms. Also, we will consider the various aspects of the meaning of a sentence one at a time.

Our starting point will be to examine the usefulness of a set of notions that have been treated in traditional grammar under the name **parsing**, which includes the analysis of sentences in terms of subject, predicate, and complements. As we shall see, these traditional notions will either be abandoned or radically changed within our analysis.

To start off, consider the sentence

(1)   *The house is burning.*

According to traditional grammar *the house* is the subject and *is burning* is the predicate. Now consider a second sentence:

(2)   *John is burning the house.*

In this sentence, the subject is now *John*, and *the house* has become the object complement. Hence, according to a traditional parsing, *the house* has two distinct roles in (1) and (2): It is the subject in (1) and the object complement in (2). Yet we know that at the level of meaning, the role of *the house* with respect to *burning* is the same in (1) and (2). In short, in both cases the house is what is burned. We can test this by substituting for *house* something which cannot be burnt, e.g., *the hypotenuse*. Since *burning* must necessarily be attributed to a material substance, and a hypotenuse is certainly not a material substance, this substitution leads to an interesting result. Both the sentences

(3) *The hypotenuse is burning.
(4) *John is burning the hypotenuse.

become meaningless. The reason why the sentences are meaningless is independent of the fact that *hypotenuse* is either the subject or the object complement of *burn*. What is crucial to the interpretation of these sentences is the semantic role of *the hypotenuse* with respect to *burning*, a role which is identical in sentences (3) and (4). The categories of subject and object complement are simply not relevant.

Another case in which the concepts of subject and complement fail to capture semantic relations is found with active sentences and their corresponding passive forms. For example, in the two sentences

(5) Mary broke the glass.
(6) The glass was broken by Mary.

Mary always has the role of the one carrying out the action of breaking, and *the glass* always has the role of that which is broken. Yet from the viewpoint of traditional analysis, *Mary* is the subject in (5) and the agent complement in (6), and *the glass* is the object complement in (5) and the subject in (6).

In this case as well, if we violate a restriction that the predicate imposes on the subject in (5), a corresponding violation occurs automatically between the predicate and the agent complement in (6). For example, both of the following sentences automatically become meaningless:

(7) *Sadness broke the glass.
(8) *The glass was broken by sadness.

In the sentences presented so far, there is a single semantic role for an element that is treated in two different ways in traditional grammar, e.g., first as the subject and then as the object complement as in (1) and (2). Let us now examine some sentences in which different semantic roles are classified within a single category by traditional logical analysis, or parsing. Consider, for example

(9) Carl is sad.
(10) The film is sad.

Carl and *the film* are the subjects of their respective sentences. But the

The Nucleus

semantic relationship between *Carl* and *is sad* in (9) is quite different from the relation between *the film* and *is sad* in (10). For example, (9) could be paraphrased with

(11)   *Carl feels sad.*

while obviously it is not possible to paraphrase (10) with the corresponding sentence

(12)   **The film feels sad.*

Clearly, the semantic roles of *Carl* and *the film* in (9) and (10) are quite distinct. Carl is the one who feels sadness, while the film is that which causes sadness to be felt. To define them in both cases as subjects does not permit us to capture this difference.

A confirmation of this comes from the fact that *Carl* and *the film* cannot be conjoined or compared if the predicate is *to be sad*. One cannot say

(13)   **Carl and the film are sad.*
(14)   **Carl is sadder than the film.*

since conjunction and comparison both require that the things which are conjoined or compared have the same semantic role with respect to the predicate. Thus, while (14) is not acceptable, (15) and (16) are:

(15)   *Carl is sadder than Mary.*
(16)   *The film is sadder than the book.*

What must we conclude from these examples? That there are semantic relations, holding between the predicate and the other elements present in the sentence, which are not captured with the traditional concepts of subject, object complement, indirect object complement, etc. We will now examine whether it is possible to give the meaning of the sentence a new representation in which these concepts are unnecessary. This will require, first of all, stripping the sentence subject of the privilege accorded to it in traditional grammar, treating it instead by the same standard as other complements. At this point, let us introduce the concept of **argument**, which will indicate any of the various elements of a sentence that are set in relation to one another by the predicate—regardless of the traditional classification of these elements as subject or complement. We suggest that a sentence is basically formed of a predicate and one or more arguments. This structure can be given a graphic representation. For example, if the predicate of a sentence has only one argument, we have the representation

(17)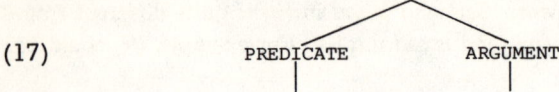
PREDICATE   ARGUMENT

(The abbreviations PRED and ARG will be used for PREDICATE and ARGUMENT.) Sentence (1), in which the predicate *burn* has only one argument *house,* will be represented as

(18)
PRED   ARG
is burning   the house[1]

If the predicate has two arguments, as is the case in sentence (5), we have instead

(19)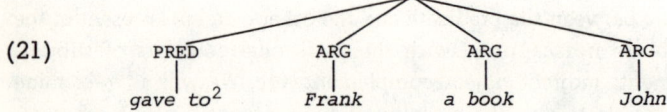
PRED   ARG   ARG
broke   Mary   the glass

There are also predicates with three arguments, such as *give* in the sentence

(20)   *Frank gave a book to John.*

which has the representation

(21)
PRED   ARG   ARG   ARG
gave to[2]   Frank   a book   John

As should be evident, the order in which we write the various elements of a sentence within these representations does not correspond to the order in which these elements appear in the sequence of sounds. We need not be surprised by this fact. (18), (19), and (21) are representations of the meaning

---

[1] We will write English words and sentences in italics but not the basic linguistic elements that appear just below the graphic representations, since these elements are already a first approximation to an abstract representation of meaning.

[2] We noted that the predicate is that which places arguments in relation to one another. *To* in (20) contributes to the expression of such a relation, and hence forms part of the predicate.

of their respective sentences; that is to say, of the conceptual nature of what we are saying. They represent the semantic relations among the various elements in the sentence, relations quite distinct from the temporal relations (i.e., what comes first, what comes second, etc.) present in the directly observable sequence of sounds. Naturally, the semantic relations and the temporal relations present in the sound sequence are connected to one another by what in the previous chapter were called **mapping rules**. But this is another complex mechanism, and will be treated in Chapter 8.

On the other hand, if the order in which we have written the various arguments in (19) and (21)[3] is not a temporal order, this does not mean that the various arguments of the sentence can change position at will within such representations. The place occupied by each argument is very relevant. For example, in (19) the first argument of *broke* is the one who carries out the action of breaking, while the second argument is the thing which is broken. Thus, if instead of writing (19), we were to write

(22)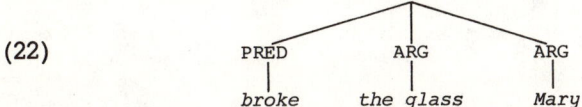

—that is, if we changed the position of the arguments—we would have a representation not of (5), but of a new sentence:

(23) **The glass broke Mary.*

which incidentally is a meaningless sentence. It violates the restriction imposed by *broke* on that which is broken, the restriction that this thing must not be an animate being.

The same holds for (21). The first argument of *give* is the one who carried out the action of giving, the second argument is the thing given, and the third is the one who receives. If we were to exchange the positions of Frank and John, we would obtain the representation of another sentence:

(24) *John gave a book to Frank.*

In general, we can say that each argument of a predicate, which we distinguish from the other arguments by virtue of its position in the graphic representation, has a precise semantic role with respect to the predicate.

---

[3] Since (18) has only one argument, the problem does not arise. The position of the predicate is never a problem, since, by convention, we will always write it in the first position from the left.

So far we have examined one-, two-, and three-place predicates all of which are, according to traditional grammar, verbs. In other sentences the predicate might also be that, which in traditional grammar, would be classified as an adjective or a noun. For example, predicates with one or two arguments that are classified as adjectives in traditional grammar are *Irish* and *similar*, respectively, in

(25)   *Frank is Irish.*
(26)   *Frank is similar to John.*

These sentences have the following representations:

(27)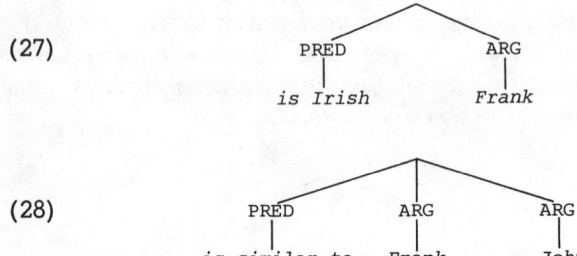

(28)

Similarly, certain uses of what are traditionally called nouns, particularly when they occur without the article, can be used as predicates that attribute something to another noun, as in

(29)   *Frank is vice president of Smith & Co.*

which would be represented as

(30)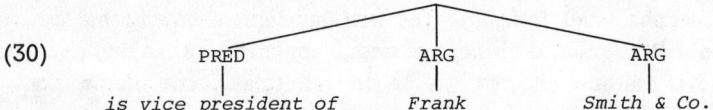

Even so-called prepositions can be predicates, a possibility which is not predicted by traditional grammar. For example, the sentences

(31)   *The book is on the table.*
(32)   *This ticket is for Peter.*

have the following representations:

(33)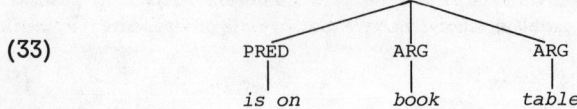

(34)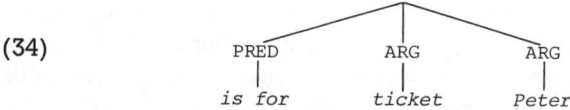

It is true that in English prepositions and adjectives that serve as semantic predicates generally are accompanied by the verb *to be*. There is reason to believe, however, that this is an accident of English structure. There are other languages, for example Russian, in which relations like the one expressed in sentence (29) are linked by nothing resembling a verb. This would tend to support our intuition that, for example, *is vice president* or *is on* represent predicates regardless of the way those terms are classified in traditional grammar. What is essential is for the predicate to be an attribute of something (when the predicate has only one argument) or a relation between two or more things (when the predicate has two or more arguments). Examples of attributes are *to burn* in (1), *to be Irish* in (25). Examples of relations are *to break* in (5), *to be similar to* in (26), *to be on* in (31). From this point of view, it is only secondary that the predicates appear as verbs, adjectives, nouns, or prepositions. In the sentences seen so far, we generally recognize a verb as a predicate by the form of the word itself (e.g., the endings on verbs in the finite mode). For adjectives, nouns, and prepositions— at least in English—we recognize the predicate by an element detached from the word, in this case the copula.

We noted earlier that each argument has a well-determined semantic role with respect to its predicate. At this point it should also be clear that each predicate has a determined number of arguments. That number depends on the semantic nature of the predicate. To establish how many arguments a particular predicate has, there is no choice but to engage in a detailed analysis of the meaning of that predicate. In fact, the meaning of a predicate is nothing more than the particular relationship which it establishes among a fixed number of arguments. The arguments are those elements which the meaning of the predicate necessarily requires. *To be Irish* is a predicate which cannot be conceived without something which is Irish. Hence it is a predicate with one argument. *To be on* requires, instead, two arguments, an object which is located and its location. *To give* requires three arguments, the giver, the receiver, and the thing given.[4]

In determining how many arguments a given predicate has it is necessary to proceed with great caution, only after an exhaustive analysis of the

---

[4] The case of *burn*, which appeared once with one argument and another time with two arguments, is nevertheless no exception to the rule that every predicate has a fixed number of arguments. See Chapter 4 on this point.

meaning of that predicate. One or two sentences in which the predicate is used are not sufficient to establish the number of arguments, since the superficial form of a sentence often does not provide an adequate idea of its semantic structure.

Consider, for example, the predicate *to be tall*. In the sentence

(35) Mark is tall

this predicate seems to have only one argument, *Mark*. Nevertheless in the sentence

(36) Mark is taller than Peter

to be tall seems to have two arguments, *Mark* and *Peter*. It is true that in (36) the predicate appears to be *is taller than* rather than *to be tall*, and therefore obviously expresses a relationship between two things. But if we reflect a little, we realize that the predicate in sentence (35) is not *to be tall*, but rather *is taller than*. Just as in (36) we compare Mark and Peter, in the same way in (35) we compare Mark with norms concerning the height of persons. This comparison leads us to conclude that Mark is taller than that norm. Hence the meaning of both (35) and (36) can be represented as

(37)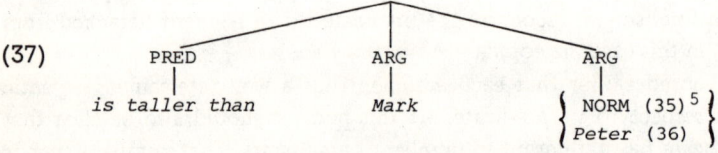

It frequently happens that one or more arguments of a predicate are not specified in the semantic structure of a particular sentence, and hence are not expressed in the sequence of sounds. If, for example, we say:

(38) Louis is eating.

we appear to have a predicate with one argument, while in reality *is eating* has two arguments, as in the sentence

(39) Louis is eating the strawberries.

The difference is that the second argument, that which is eaten, remains unspecified in (38). Hence, the representation of (38) and (39) is actually

---

[5] We will write NORM in capitals because it represents an abstract semantic element rather than a word. On this point, see Chapter 4.

The Nucleus   23

(40)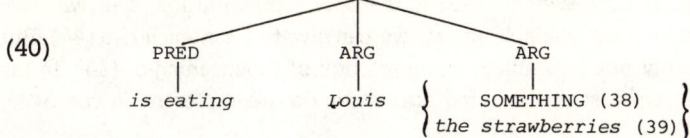

Similarly, *received* is a predicate with three arguments, even though in the sentence

(41)   *George received a letter.*

the third argument is not specified. Sentence (41) and the sentence

(42)   *George received a letter from Barbara.*

have the same representation, i.e.,

(43)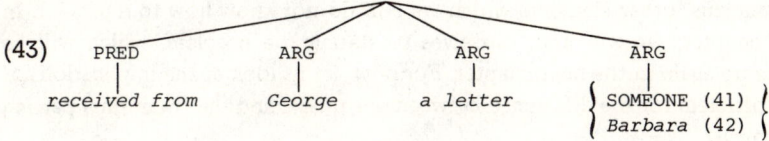

There is a more general reason why the surface form of a sentence is not a reliable indicator of the number and kinds of arguments for each predicate. This last reason poses an interesting problem and permits us to clarify another important difference between our model of sentence meaning and traditional parsing approaches. The problem is as follows. Consider the sentence

(44)   *Mary knits the sweater in the living room.*

Knits is a relationship between Mary and the sweater, but we cannot claim that it expresses an intrinsic relationship between Mary, the sweater, and the living room. If we analyze the meaning of *knit* we find that it requires someone who knits and something that is knit. But it is not absolutely necessary to specify where the knitting takes place. Hence, *knits* would be a predicate with only two arguments, representable as

(45)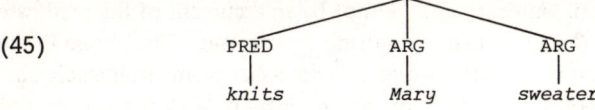

The problem is now evident. (45) is the only representation that, with the mechanisms we have available so far, we can give to a sentence like (44). But (45) is certainly not a complete representation of the meaning of (44). *In the living room* remains unaccounted for. How do we represent *in the living room?*

The problem is a general one. For example, in

(46) Mary broke the glass this afternoon.

we know how to represent only one part, similar to representation (19). *Broke* is a predicate with two arguments, filled in this sentence by *Mary* and *the glass*. *This afternoon* is not an argument of *broke* and therefore remains outside the representation.

In fact, what we are able to represent so far is only one small part of a sentence, the predicate and its arguments. We will call this essential part of every sentence the **nucleus.** But the majority of sentences have, in addition to the nucleus, other elements which we still do not know how to represent. In this chapter, we will limit ourselves to stating the problem, which will be taken up again in the next chapter. For now, let us look at the implications of this problem for the difference between our model and the traditional parsing approach.

In sentence (44), *in the living room,* according to traditional grammar, would be a locative complement. But consider now the sentence

(47) Mary put the sweater in the living room.

In contrast with *knits, put* is a predicate with three arguments. We cannot talk about someone putting something without indicating where that thing is put. But it is possible to say that someone knit something without indicating where the knitting took place. Thus, the representation for (47) would be

(48)
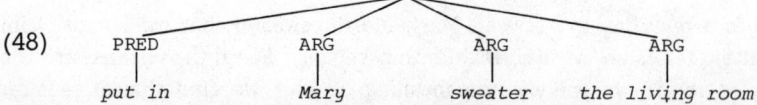

A comparison between sentences (47) and (44) permits the formulation of a general principle: the same phrase (as it would be called in traditional analyses) can be an argument of the predicate in one sentence (and hence part of the nucleus of that sentence) and yet not be an argument of the predicate in another sentence (hence remaining outside the nucleus). The phrase *in the living room* would always be classified as a locative complement in traditional analyses. But it serves as an argument of the predicate in (47), forming part of

The Nucleus

the nucleus, while it is outside the nucleus in (44). We must underline this point, since one might think that there is a one-to-one correspondence between traditional analyses and our proposal, namely subject, object complement, and indirect object complement are always part of the nucleus, whereas all the remaining complements are always outside of it. Examples like (44) and (47) show that this is not the case.

Other examples can be offered. Take the sentences

(49)　　　　Carolyn threw the ball into the garden.
(50)　　　　Carolyn threw the ball in the garden.

In the old parsing model *in the garden* and *into the garden* have the same traditional logical role as locative complements. But in (49) the phrase *into the garden* completes the directional meaning of the three-place predicate *throw*. Like *put*, which requires an agent, a thing which is put, and a place where the thing is put, *throw* in (49) describes an effort by Carolyn to change the location of the ball such that the ball ends up in the garden. The representation of (49) would be

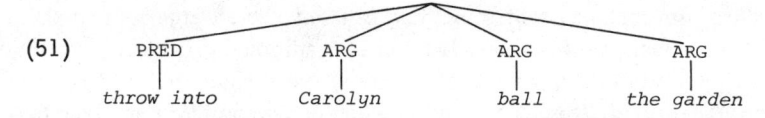

(51)　　　PRED　　　　ARG　　　　ARG　　　　ARG
　　　　throw into　　Carolyn　　 ball　　 the garden

In (50), on the other hand, the phrase *in the garden* does not tell us the intended terminal location of the ball (which is left unspecified), but rather the place where the action of Carolyn throwing the ball took place. Hence, the nucleus of (50) would be represented as

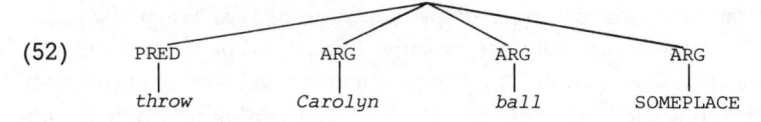

(52)　　　PRED　　　　ARG　　　　ARG　　　　ARG
　　　　 throw　　　Carolyn　　　ball　　 SOMEPLACE

in which *in the garden*, like *in the living room* in sentence (44), remains outside the nucleus.

Sentences (47) and (51) illustrate the fact that traditional locative complements can serve as arguments of the nucleus. A wide variety of other elements can also serve as arguments of the nucleus, intrinsic to the meaning of a given predicate:

(53)　　　　The court sentenced him to three years.
(54)　　　　I payed John three dollars.
(55)　　　　The contest will last a week.

In these sentences *three years, three dollars,* and *a week* are all arguments of their respective predicates. These three sentences have the following representations:

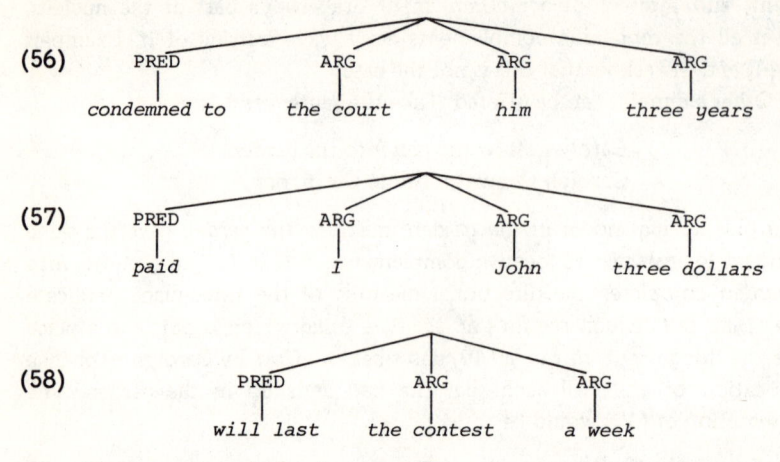

(56)
```
         PRED         ARG          ARG          ARG
     condemned to  the court       him       three years
```

(57)
```
         PRED         ARG          ARG          ARG
         paid          I           John      three dollars
```

(58)
```
                     PRED          ARG          ARG
                  will last    the contest     a week
```

Hence, we conclude that something can serve as an argument of the nucleus independently of its classification in traditional grammars, just as several of the traditional grammatical categories (verb, noun, adjective, etc.) can also serve as predicates. The criterion whereby we consider something to be the argument of a predicate is that it is necessarily required to complete the meaning of that predicate. Since predicates differ greatly from one another, it is natural that we find among the arguments of predicates traditional complements of every type.

In keeping with the plan proposed at the beginning of this chapter, we have so far considered only very simple sentences, and we have provided the means for representing only the essential nucleus of these sentences, the predicate with its arguments. In the next chapter we will take up the problem of representing elements outside the nucleus. Nevertheless, even in this chapter, restricting ourselves to an analysis of the nucleus, we can examine a further complication in the simple sentences considered so far.

Note this rather different sentence:

(59) *Frank hopes that John is sleeping.*

The apparent complexity of this sentence need not overwhelm us. It can, in fact, be analyzed entirely in terms of the concepts introduced so far. It is simply a matter of recognizing one of the most important characteristics of language—the principle of **recursion.**

The Nucleus

In sentence (59) there is a predicate *hope*, which has two arguments. The first argument is *Frank* and the second is *that John is sleeping*. What is new about this sentence? Simply that there is a predicate that takes a whole sentence as one of its arguments—or more accurately, the predicate takes a **sentential structure** as an argument. Hence, in (59) *hopes* expresses a relation uniting two arguments: the one who has the hope (*Frank*) and the content of that hope (*that John is sleeping*). (59) has a representation something like

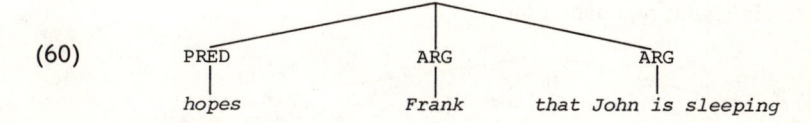

(60)
```
            PRED        ARG              ARG
             |           |                |
           hopes        Frank     that John is sleeping
```

But if we examine the second argument of (59)—the phrase *that John is sleeping*—we notice immediately that this argument is a sentential structure, a structure which in its own right consists of a predicate with arguments. In this case, the predicate is *is sleeping*, and there is only one argument *John*. Hence, a more detailed representation for (59) would be

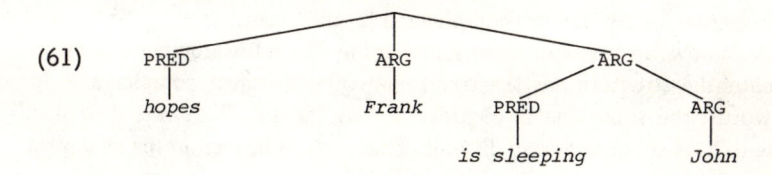

(61)
```
       PRED       ARG              ARG
        |          |             /     \
      hopes      Frank         PRED     ARG
                                |        |
                            is sleeping  John
```

This representation demonstrates a very important fact. The structure formed by a predicate and its arguments occurs twice. First, we have the predicate *hopes* with its two arguments, *Frank* and *that John is sleeping*. Second, we have the predicate *is sleeping* with its argument *John*. But note further that these two structures are in a very precise relation to one another. The second structure, formed by the predicate *is sleeping* and its argument *John*, taken as a whole, is nothing other than one of the arguments of the first structure, formed by the predicate *hopes*. Hence, the second structure is part of the first, or to be more precise, the second sentential structure is **embedded** in the first. This is the recursivity of language just mentioned. The same structure (in this case the predicate–argument structure) can recur twice in the same sentence, yet the second structure remains part of the first. We will call a sentential structure embedded as an argument in another sentential structure the **subordinate clause**. The sentential structure within which it is embedded is called the **main clause**.

But recursivity does not stop here. The sentence

(62)   Mary told me that Frank hopes that John is sleeping.

demonstrates that the predicate–argument structure can recur three times. In sentence (62), we have first of all a predicate *told* with three arguments: *Mary*, *me*, and *that Frank hopes that John is sleeping*. Then we have the predicate *hope* with two arguments: *Frank* and *that John is sleeping*. Finally, we have the predicate *is sleeping* with only one argument, *John*. Thus (62) has the following representation:

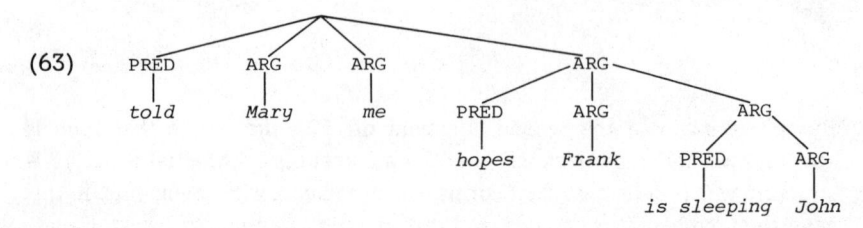

(63)
```
        PRED    ARG    ARG         ARG
         |       |      |           |
        told    Mary    me    PRED  ARG         ARG
                               |     |           |
                              hopes Frank  PRED  ARG
                                           |     |
                                      is sleeping John
```

Perfectly correct sentences can be constructed in which the predicate–argument structure recurs four, even five times. The only difficulty is that such sentences can become too complicated to understand.

Until now we have examined sentences in which the argument made up of a sentential structure has the traditional role of object complement. In other words, the subordinates considered thus far are all objects. But it is possible to have subordinates in different roles, as can be seen in the examples

(64)   That Kathleen left for Kansas City surprised me.
(65)   That John will agree to the project is unlikely.
(66)   Frank asked me if Clara would return.

which have the following representations:

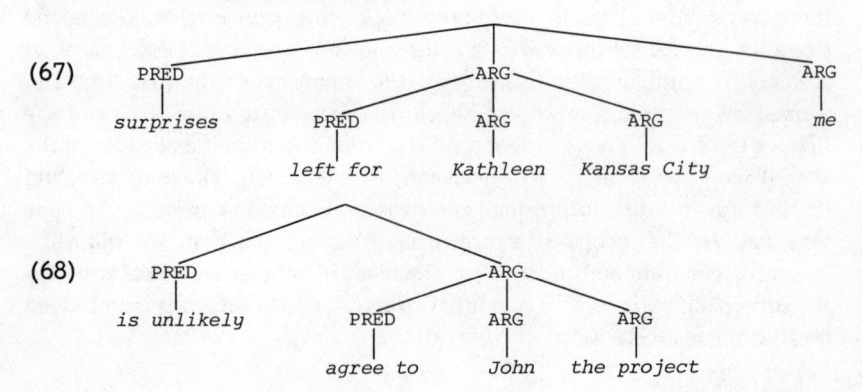

(67)
```
      PRED                    ARG                     ARG
       |                       |                       |
    surprises     PRED        ARG         ARG         me
                   |           |           |
                left for   Kathleen   Kansas City
```

(68)
```
      PRED              ARG
       |                 |
   is unlikely    PRED  ARG        ARG
                   |     |          |
                agree to John   the project
```

The Nucleus

(69)
```
        PRED        ARG      ARG         ARG
         │           │        │         ╱    ╲
       asked       Frank      me      PRED    ARG
                                       │       │
                                   would return Clara
```

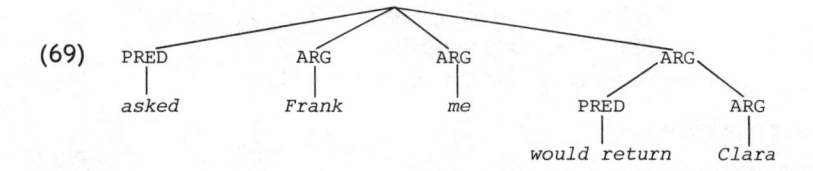

All these subordinates are explicit, in that their predicate is expressed as a verb in the finite mode. But there are also implicit subordinates, such as the case in which the predicate of the subordinate is expressed as an infinitive verb. Consider, for example, the sentence

(70) *Frank promised you to be silent.*

Here we have a predicate *promised* with three arguments: *Frank, you,* and *be silent*. But the third argument, *to be silent*, is in turn also a sentential structure consisting of a predicate *to be silent* and its single argument *Frank*. These implicit subordinates are characterized by the fact that one of their arguments is identical to one of the arguments of the main clause in which they are embedded. Because of this identity, the argument of the subordinate need not be expressed. But we can always recover this deleted argument. Thus while in sentence (70) the unexpressed argument of *to be silent* is *Frank,* in another sentence

(71) *Frank begged you to be silent.*

the unexpressed argument of *to be silent* is *you* and not *Frank*. Sentences (70) and (71) will therefore have the representations

(72)
```
       PRED       ARG      ARG        ARG
        │          │        │        ╱   ╲
     promised    Frank     you     PRED   ARG
                                    │      │
                                 be silent Frank
```

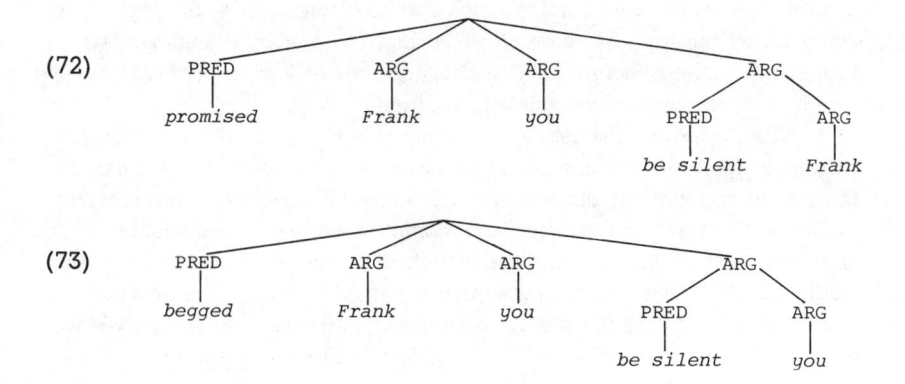

(73)
```
       PRED       ARG      ARG        ARG
        │          │        │        ╱   ╲
      begged     Frank     you     PRED   ARG
                                    │      │
                                 be silent  you
```

Implicit subordinates can also have varied semantic roles with respect to the predicate. Thus the sentences

(74)   John's smoking marijuana bothers me.
(75)   Bill forced him to withdraw.
(76)   Grace prevented Claude from working.

have the representations

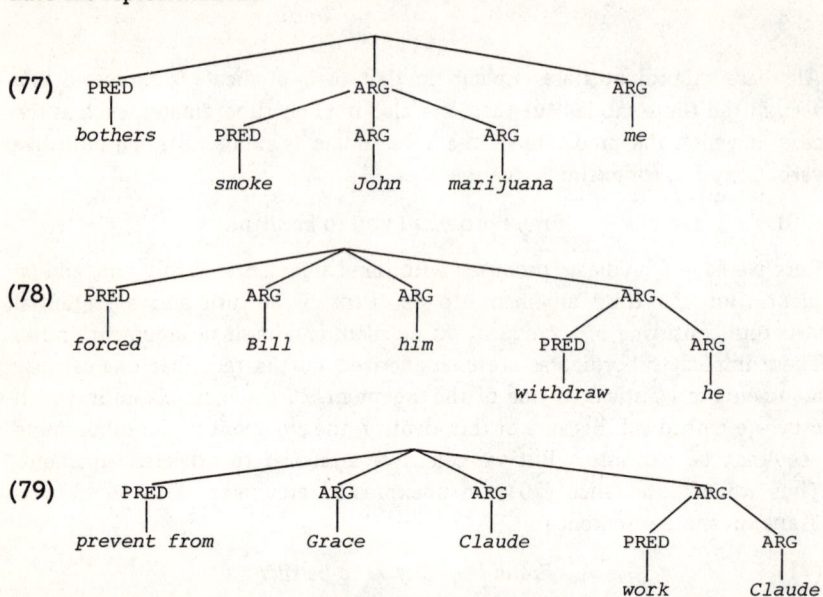

(77)
```
        PRED         ARG                    ARG
         |         / | \                     |
       bothers  PRED ARG  ARG                me
                 |   |    |
               smoke John marijuana
```

(78)
```
       PRED   ARG   ARG        ARG
        |     |     |         /   \
      forced Bill  him      PRED   ARG
                             |      |
                          withdraw  he
```

(79)
```
       PRED      ARG    ARG        ARG
        |         |      |        /   \
   prevent from Grace  Claude   PRED  ARG
                                 |     |
                                work  Claude
```

In this chapter we have explored the nature of the nucleus that is necessary for all sentences. This nucleus is a structure formed by a predicate and the arguments (one or more) which that predicate intrinsically requires to complete its meaning. We have also seen that the predicate–argument structure is a recursive structure, in that the argument of a given predicate can in turn be a second predicate–argument structure.

With regard to the relation between this model of the sentence and parsing analyses, we can conclude that there are some substantial differences. If we want to represent the semantic relations holding within a sentence, the traditional concepts of subject and complement are not adequate. It is necessary, first of all, to consider the subject as one of the arguments of the predicate, on the same plane as the other arguments. Hence, up to this point a notion like that of **subject** has not been useful, and we can set it aside. As we will see later on, at another level this notion will become relevant once again, and we will introduce it at that point. Nevertheless, it will still be considerably modified with respect to its traditional use. With regard to the notion of complement, we have seen that the traditional parsing approach classifies as **complements** both elements within the nucleus (arguments of the predicate) and elements outside the nucleus. Furthermore, if we examine particular complements we find that any given category—for example, locative or duration complements—can serve as the argument of a nucleus in one sentence and as an element outside the nucleus in another. Hence, it seems appropriate to eliminate the notion of complement entirely, since it serves no apparent purpose within the grammar being developed here.

The fact that the predicate—argument structure is recursive allows us to pass quite naturally from the syntax of simple clauses to the syntax of complex sentences. When one of the arguments of the nucleus is also a sentential structure, then we have a sentential structure embedded in the nucleus, or more briefly, a nuclear subordinate. Subordinates include what are traditionally called subject subordinates, object subordinates, indirect interrogatives, etc. But even here there is something new with respect to the old parsing models. First, as we have done at the level of subject and object complement, we will also cease to speak of subjective or objective clauses, substituting instead the general term **nuclear subordinate**. Furthermore, nuclear subordinates include not only the traditional subjective and objective clauses, but also embedded sentences serving a wide variety of semantic roles with respect to the nuclear predicate.

Adverbials 3

In the preceding chapter we outlined a way of representing the nucleus of a sentence. The nucleus is made up of a predicate and its arguments. There can be only one argument, or there can be more than one. If there is only one argument, the predicate is a property or attribute of that argument. If there are two or more arguments, the predicate is a relationship among these arguments. Therefore, for each predicate used within a sentence, there is a well-determined number of arguments that it requires. The very meaning of the predicate determines the number and kinds of arguments that it will have. If the predicate is *sleep,* it is sufficient to conceive of someone who sleeps to form a nucleus; thus *sleep* has only one argument. If the predicate is *hope,* we need someone who hopes and something that is the object of that hope; hence *hope* is a predicate with two arguments. And so forth.

As we already mentioned in the last chapter, this analysis leaves a problem of representation unsolved. We have a way to represent those arguments present in the sentence which serve as the arguments of the nucleus. But elements are frequently present in sentences which are not required by the intrinsic nature of the predicate, and thus remain outside the nucleus. How shall these elements be represented?

Consider once again the two sentences

(1)   *Mary put the sweater in the living room.*
(2)   *Mary knit the sweater in the living room.*

In the first sentence we have a predicate that expresses a relationship between *Mary, the sweater,* and *the living room*—in this case, the predicate *put.* A concept like *put* requires three arguments: one who puts, something that is put, and a location where it is put. Thus, as we saw earlier, the representation of (1) is

Adverbials

```
(3)        PRED         ARG          ARG              ARG
            |            |            |                |
          put in        Mary      the sweater    the living room
```

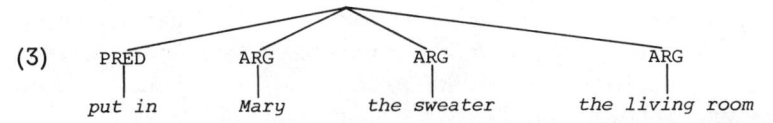

The solution is quite different for *knit* in (2). A concept like *knit* requires only two arguments: someone who knits, and something that is knit. One cannot say that *to knit* is a relationship between one who knits, something that is knit, and a place where the knitting occurs. Thus *knit* is a predicate with two arguments, and the representation of (2) is

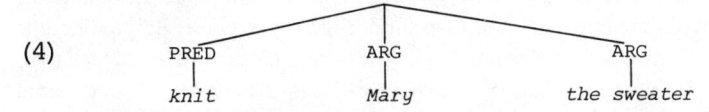

```
(4)              PRED            ARG               ARG
                  |               |                 |
                knit             Mary          the sweater
```

But this is clearly not a complete representation of sentence (2). Let us examine more closely the element in (2) which remains outside the representation, *in the living room*.

Instead of expressing a third argument of *knit*, thus completing the meaning of the nucleus, *in the living room* seems to refer to the nucleus as a whole. In sentence (2) we carry out two operations. First, we construct the nucleus, formed by the predicate *knit* and its two arguments *Mary* and *the sweater*. Then, with a second operation, we take this nucleus *Mary knit the sweater* and place it in relation to *in the living room*. Thus, it is as if we said "Mary knit the sweater," and this took place "in the living room." *In the living room*, in sentence (1), serves to complete the meaning of the nucleus, which is otherwise only half-finished. In sentence (2), on the other hand, *in the living room* appears as an unnecessary adjunct to the nucleus.

What is precisely the nature of the relationship between *in the living room* and the nucleus in sentence (2)? We have said that in this sentence we carry out two operations: we build a nucleus and then we place it in relation to *in the living room*. But *in the living room* is formed by at least two elements, *in* and *the living room*. If we propose that *in* is a predicate with two arguments, and that in sentence (2) these arguments are *Mary knit the sweater* and *the living room*, then we have found a way to represent the entire sentence (2). The representation is the following:

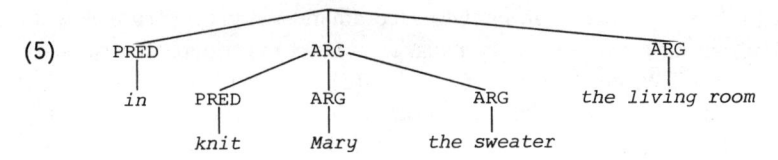

```
(5)     PRED          ARG                        ARG
         |             |                          |
         in     PRED      ARG       ARG      the living room
                 |         |         |
                knit      Mary   the sweater
```

With this representation we capture the two facts that characterize *in the living room* in sentence (2). First, it is outside the nucleus. Second, sentence (2) expresses a relation between the nucleus, taken as a whole, and *in the living room*.

Obviously, if we want to give sentence (2) a representation like (5), we must expand our concept of a predicate. At the outset we considered only the predicate of the nucleus, that is something which is usually expressed in English with a verb in the finite mode. But we immediately found extensions of this concept, so that the term **predicate** was applied also within sentential structures embedded as arguments of the nucleus, that is to predicates of nuclear subordinates. When a nuclear subordinate is explicit, its predicate is expressed as a finite verb. When it is implicit, the predicate is expressed by a non-finite form. Up to this point, our concept differed little from the traditional one. But we had also proposed that the notion of predicate can be extended to the prepositions *on* and *for* as they appear in sentences like

(6) *The book is on the table*
(7) *This ticket is for Peter.*

We concluded that the concept of predicate had been considerably modified in our model with respect to traditional grammar. For us, the predicate has become something more general and abstract than the traditional predicate, in that the traditional predicate is a subtype of **predicate** used in the wider sense of an attribute or relationship posited of arguments. **Predicate** must be understood as a component in a thought structure, not yet tied to its linguistic expression as a verb, as a preposition, or as any other grammatical category. **Predicate** is anything which is attributed to something else (if the predicate has only one argument) or any relationship instituted between two or more things (if the predicate has more than one argument). If we accept this broad definition, it then becomes evident that the words *on* and *for*, when they appear in sentences like (6) and (7), express relations and therefore are predicates.

Notwithstanding these extensions, there was still a point of contact in the preceding chapter between our concept of predicate and the traditional one, that is, the fact that in all predicates one finds a superficial element of "verbness." In *sleeps* the end of the verb places it in the finite mode, in *to sleep* (as the predicate of an implicit subordinate) the particle *to* makes the predicate an infinitive verb. In *is similar to* or *is for* the copula gives the sense of "verbness." Within representations like (5), however, even this point of contact with traditional grammar disappears. Our concept of predicate is made still more abstract. Now the element of "verbness" can also be absent, and yet we continue to speak of a predicate. This is possible only with our

Adverbials

radical definition of predicate. In sentence (2), *in* expresses a relation between *Mary knit the sweater* and *the living room*, and hence is a predicate.

This expanded notion of a predicate permits us to represent all the elements which appear in a sentence and yet are outside the nucleus. For example the sentences

(8)   *Frank gave Peter a book on Tuesday.*
(9)   *John solved the problem with ease.*
(10)   *Clare went to the store for her mother.*

are given these representations:

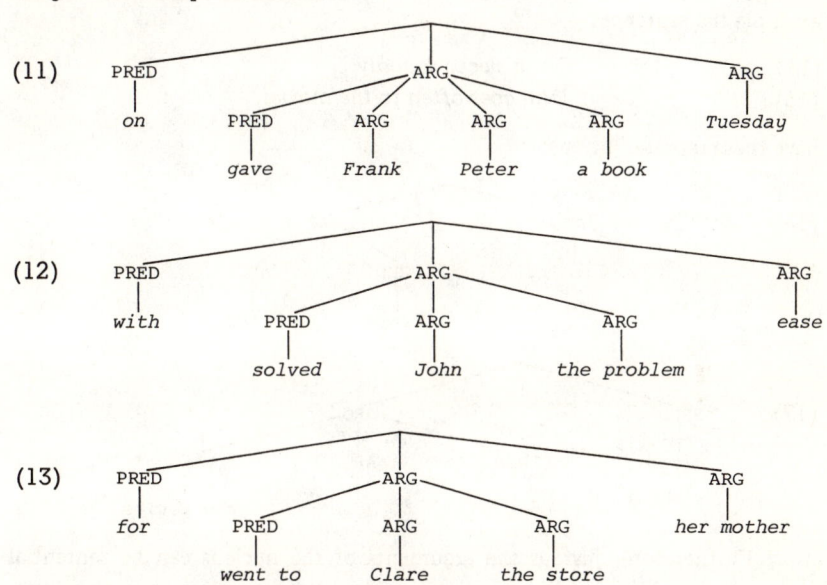

(11)
```
PRED         ────ARG────                    ARG
 │          ╱    │    ╲                      │
 on       PRED  ARG  ARG  ARG            Tuesday
           │    │    │    │
          gave Frank Peter a book
```

(12)
```
PRED         ────ARG────                    ARG
 │          ╱    │    ╲                      │
with       PRED  ARG       ARG              ease
            │    │          │
          solved John   the problem
```

(13)
```
PRED         ────ARG────                    ARG
 │          ╱    │    ╲                      │
for        PRED  ARG       ARG           her mother
            │    │          │
          went to Clare   the store
```

These representations express the fact that *on Tuesday, with ease,* and *for her mother* are outside the nucleus of their respective sentences, in that they are not elements which the meanings of *gave, solved* and *went* intrinsically require. Furthermore, these representations indicate the nature of the relation between these elements and the rest of the sentence. In sentences (8), (9), and (10) three events are expressed—the three nuclei *Frank gave a book to Peter, John solved the problem,* and *Clare went to the store*. The prepositions *on, with* and *for* place these three events in their respective relationships to *Tuesday, ease* and *her mother*. Thus we know that *Frank gave a book to Peter* coincided temporally with Tuesday, that *John solved the problem* was accompanied by a show of facility on John's part, and finally *Clare went to the store* was determined in some way by her mother. We will give the name adverbials to these adjunctive predicate–argument structures which have the nucleus as one of their arguments. Thus *in the living room* in sentence (2), and *on Tuesday, with ease,* and *for her mother* all function as adverbials. In this way we can also distinguish between **nuclear predicates** and **adverbial predicates**. That which in the preceding chapter was the predicate in an absolute sense has now become a particular type of predicate, a nuclear predicate, which must be distinguished from other types of predicates.

Up to this point we have seen adverbials which contain a predicate with two arguments. But there are also adverbials made up of a predicate with only one argument, in which by definition that single argument is the nucleus. For example the sentences

(14)   *Frank sleeps soundly.*
(15)   *John goes often to the movies.*

have these representations:

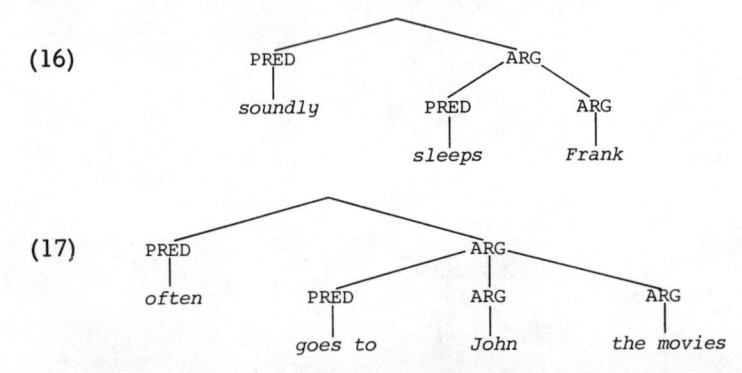

(16)
```
              PRED         ARG
               |            |
            soundly      PRED   ARG
                          |      |
                        sleeps  Frank
```

(17)
```
        PRED              ARG
         |                 |
        often       PRED   ARG    ARG
                     |      |      |
                   goes to John  the movies
```

Furthermore, just as the arguments of the nucleus can be sentential structures (that is, predicate–argument structures) serving as nuclear subordinates, it is also true that the arguments of the adverbial can be sentential structures serving as adverbial subordinates. The sentences

(18)   *When Frank entered the room, his colleagues stood up.*
(19)   *We stayed home because John was tired.*
(20)   *I read that book although the critics hated it.*

have the following representations:

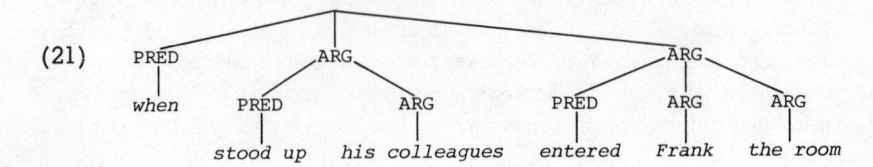

(21)
```
   PRED        ARG                         ARG
    |           |                           |
   when    PRED      ARG           PRED    ARG    ARG
            |         |             |       |      |
         stood up  his colleagues entered Frank  the room
```

Adverbials

(22)
```
PRED        ARG                    ARG
 |         /   \                  /   \
because  PRED  ARG  ARG         PRED   ARG
          |    |    |            |     |
        stayed we  home       was tired John
```

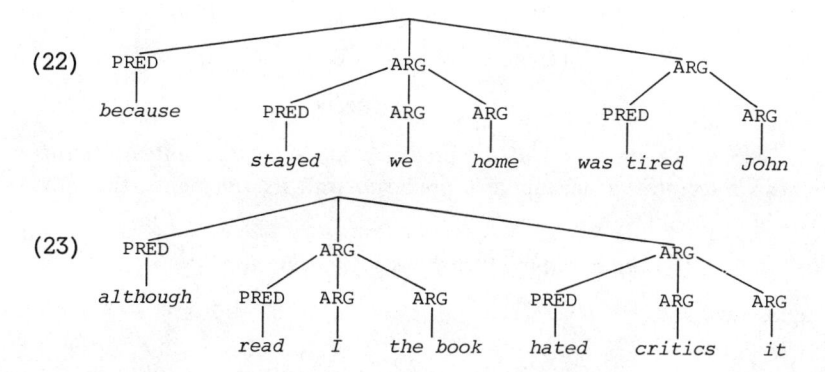

(23)
```
PRED         ARG                    ARG
 |         / | \                  / | \
although PRED ARG ARG           PRED ARG ARG
          |   |   |              |    |   |
        read  I the book       hated critics it
```

As in the case of nuclear subordinates, adverbial subordinates can be explicit, like those of sentences (18), (19), and (20), or implicit as those in sentences

(24)   *We went to Florida in order to see some friends.*
(25)   *On hearing those words, Mark shuddered.*

which have the representations

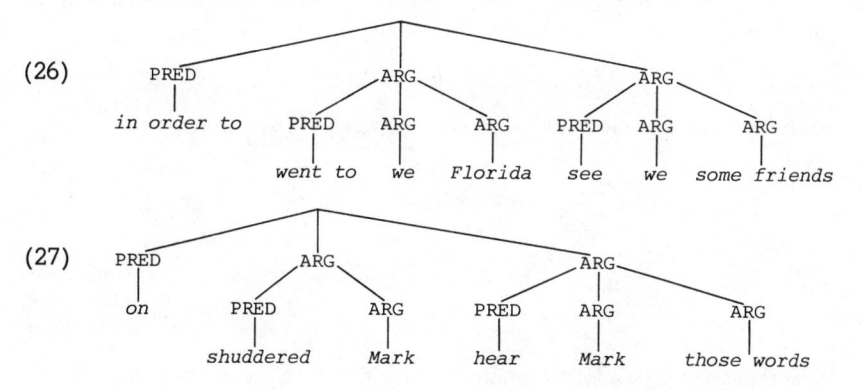

(26)
```
PRED           ARG                   ARG
 |           /  |  \                /  |  \
in order to PRED ARG ARG         PRED ARG  ARG
             |   |   |            |   |    |
           went to we Florida    see  we some friends
```

(27)
```
PRED         ARG                 ARG
 |          / | \               / | \
 on       PRED ARG           PRED ARG  ARG
           |   |              |   |    |
       shuddered Mark        hear Mark those words
```

At this point we have introduced the concepts that we need to be able to represent some essential aspects of the semantic structure of a sentence. With these concepts, keeping in mind the mechanism of recursion (that is, the construction of structures as parts of other, analogous structures), we can represent very complex sentences. First, we know that the fundamental mechanism underlying sentences is that of a predicate with one or more arguments. Thus the sentence

(28)   *Frank left.*

is represented as

(29)
```
        PRED      ARG
         |         |
        left     Frank
```

Second, the arguments of the predicate can in turn be sentential structures, in themselves made up of a predicate with its arguments. thus, the sentence

(30) *Louise told me that she is going to Boston.*

is represented as

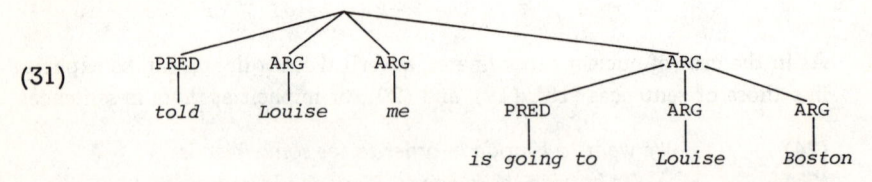

(31)
```
   PRED    ARG    ARG              ARG
    |       |      |        PRED   ARG    ARG
   told  Louise   me         |      |      |
                         is going to Louise Boston
```

Sentences (28) and (30) consist only of a nucleus, the essential element in every sentence. But the nucleus can in turn be the argument of a higher predicate. We have called this latter structure the adverbial, which may or may not be present in a sentence. Thus in the sentence

(32) *Frank left early.*

Frank left is the nucleus and *early* is the adverbial. The representation of (32) is:

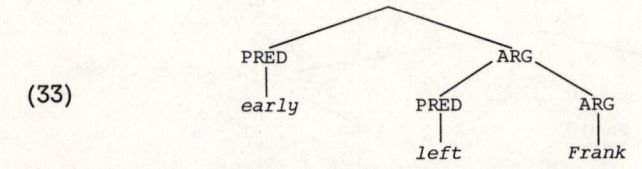

(33)
```
     PRED         ARG
      |       PRED    ARG
    early      |       |
              left   Frank
```

Adverbials can have another argument, in addition to the one occupied by the nucleus, and this second argument can be another sentential structure. Hence, the sentence

(34) *Frank left before the fight broke out.*

has the representation

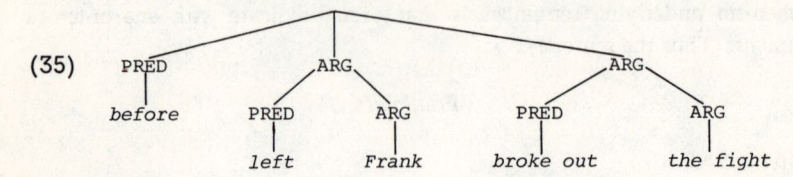

(35)
```
  PRED      ARG              ARG
   |    PRED   ARG      PRED     ARG
 before  |     |         |        |
        left  Frank   broke out  the fight
```

Adverbials 39

So, in addition to the nuclear subordinate exemplified by *Louise is going to Boston* in (30), we have adverbial subordinates exemplified by *the fight broke out* in (34).

Finally, we can apply the mechanism of recursion to all of the mechanisms introduced so far. An adverbial—a predicate which takes a nucleus as one of its arguments—can be present in subordinate clauses as well, both nuclear and adverbial, as in the sentences

(36)   *John told me that tomorrow he will go to Toledo.*
(37)   *Frank left before a fight unexpectedly broke out.*

which have the representations

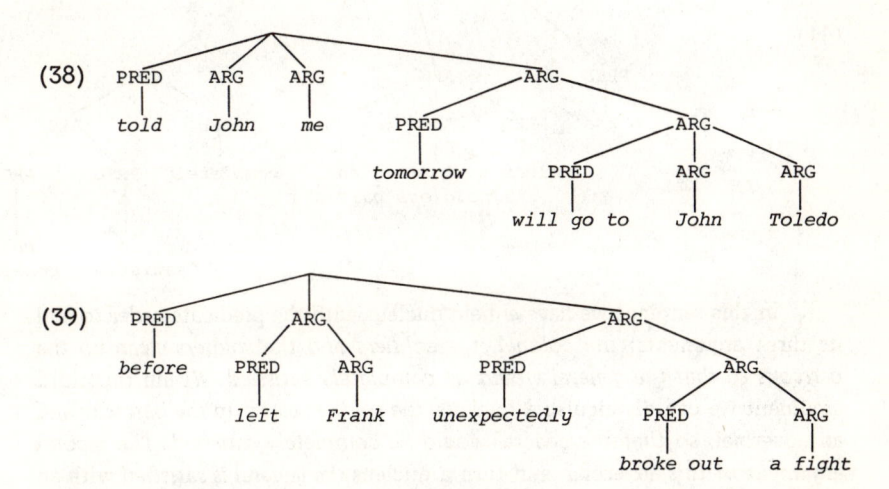

(38)   [tree diagram: PRED *told*, ARG *John*, ARG *me*, ARG → PRED *tomorrow*, ARG → PRED *will go to*, ARG *John*, ARG *Toledo*]

(39)   [tree diagram: PRED *before*, ARG → PRED *left*, ARG *Frank*, ARG → PRED *unexpectedly*, ARG → PRED *broke out*, ARG *a fight*]

This demonstrates that the concept of nucleus must be applied within a subordinate clause as well, in order to distinguish the nucleus from an adverbial there as well. Hence, a sentence can be made up of more than one nucleus. We must then speak of the nucleus of the main clause (which will be restricted to only one for each sentence) and the nuclei of whatever subordinate clauses are present in the sentence (at least in principle, a potentially infinite number).

Putting together the various mechanisms that we have introduced so far, we can represent even so complex a sentence as

(40) *On arriving, the colonel immediately ordered the soldiers to clean the barracks up so that the general would be completely satisfied.*

which follows:

(41)

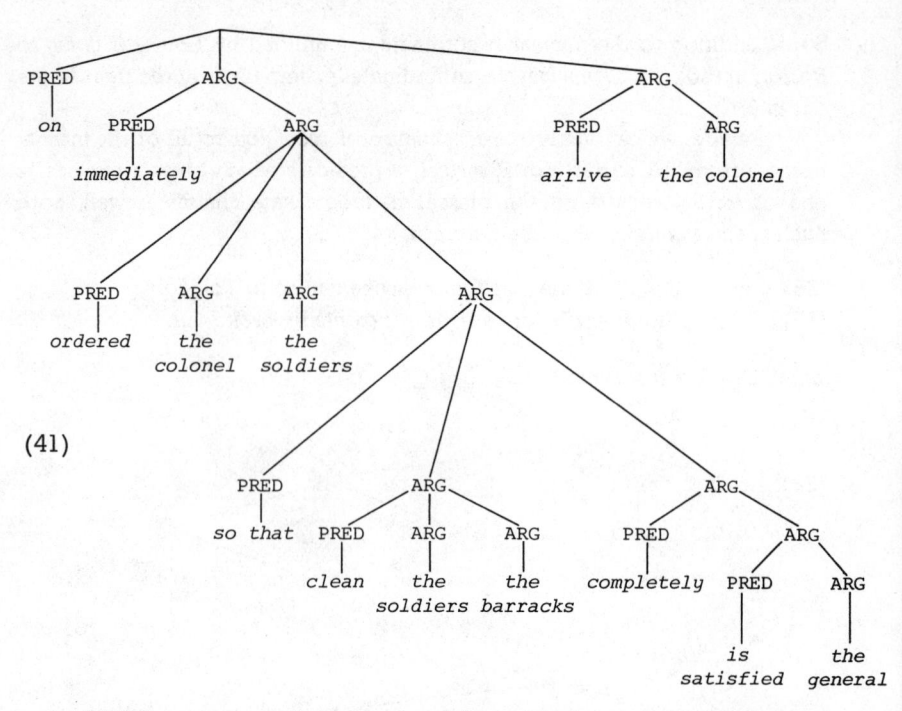

[Tree diagram for sentence (41)]

In this sentence we have a main nucleus with the predicate *order to* and its three arguments: *the colonel, the soldiers* and *the soldiers clean up the barracks so that the general would be completely satisfied*. Within this third argument we can distinguish a nucleus, *the soldiers clean up the barracks* and an adverbial, *so that the general would be completely satisfied*. The second argument of this adverbial is in turn a nucleus *the general is satisfied* with an adverbial *completely*. Returning to the main nucleus, we find that this has a first adverbial *immediately* and a second adverbial *on arriving*. This last adverbial is in turn formed by a nucleus *the colonel arrives* and the adverbial predicate *on*.

Componential Analysis

4

With the concepts introduced in the two preceding chapters—predicate, argument, nucleus, adverbial, and subordinate sentential structure—we can furnish a representation for a good part of the semantic structure of sentences. In Chapter 5, on nominals, we will complete this aspect of representation. All of these concepts are useful in analyzing the meaning of sentences with given word meanings as starting points. Thus for a sentence like

(1) *John gave a bottle to Frank.*

we can furnish a representation like

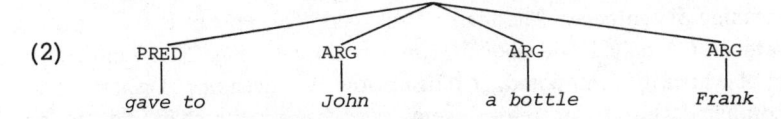

(2)
```
         PRED         ARG         ARG         ARG
          |            |           |           |
       gave to        John      a bottle      Frank
```

But with representations like (2), we cannot pretend to have reached our goal of furnishing a complete analysis of the meaning of sentences. In fact, (2) presents in explicit form only a small part of the meaning of sentence (1), i.e., the fact that the sentence is composed of a predicate *give to*, which establishes a certain semantic relationship among its three arguments, *John, a bottle* and *Frank*. In this chapter, we will take an important step toward a more complete representation of sentence meaning. We will begin to deal with the meanings of words.

Notice the elements that have been placed at the ends of the branches of trees as in (2). All of the elements are words in the English language: *gave, John, a bottle, Frank*. As in the case of sentences, words also consist of two parts: a sound and a meaning. To clarify this difference, every time that we refer only to the meaning of a word, we will use capital letters. We will use minor case letters to refer to either the sound by itself, or as we have done so far, the complete word as a union of sound and meaning. Hence, *dog* will indicate a certain English word or its sound, and DOG will stand for the meaning of that word.

The sound of a word is the product of certain movements of the phono-articulatory organs: lungs, larynx, tongue, teeth, lips, etc. The meaning is the product of a specific type of cerebral activity, and therefore is a concept or a mental operation.

Given this distinction between the sound and meaning of words, we must modify slightly our representation for sentences. Since we seek to represent the meaning of sentences rather than their sounds, the meaning of sentence *John gave a bottle to Frank* will no longer be represented by (2), but rather by the representation

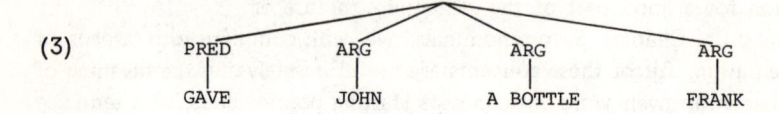

(3)   PRED   ARG   ARG   ARG
        | | | |
        GAVE   JOHN   A BOTTLE FRANK

In other words, instead of placing words at the ends of the branches, we put their meanings.

It is obvious that such a change, however correct and useful, is purely notational and does not carry us much closer to an explicit representation of the meaning of sentences. The reason is evident: (3) represents the meaning of sentence (1) only if we take for granted the meanings of the individual words of which it is composed. It tells us how the meanings of single words are combined, but treats these meanings as basic units that undergo no further analysis—as if it were impossible to enter into the "insides" of these units.

If we include directly among our representations such semantic elements as GIVE, etc., all that we can assert regarding their form is that one element is different from another. Yet we know that every speaker of a language is able to perceive intuitively precise differences and similarities among word meanings. For example, a speaker can, if asked, paraphrase one sentence with another. That is, he can formulate the same semantic content with different words. A speaker can also compare the elements that make up the meanings of two different sentences, and establish whether the sentences are different or equivalent. Furthermore, speakers can also determine in what respect two given sentences are similar or different. The semantic representations we have presented so far do not contain any explicit representation of

Componential Analysis

these various similarities and differences. It is clear that every speaker has available, as part of his linguistic competence, information that is in no way accounted for in our representations. We must now seek some explicit means of representing this additional kind of information.

Consider the following two sentences:

(4)   Her face was red.
(5)   The door was open.

Any speaker can tell us that these two sentences are interrelated, in a very precise way, with the following two sentences:

(6)   Her face reddened.
(7)   The door opened.

There is nothing in our representations that can handle these relations. The four sentences are each composed of a predicate with one argument. Within the model presented thus far, they have these representations:

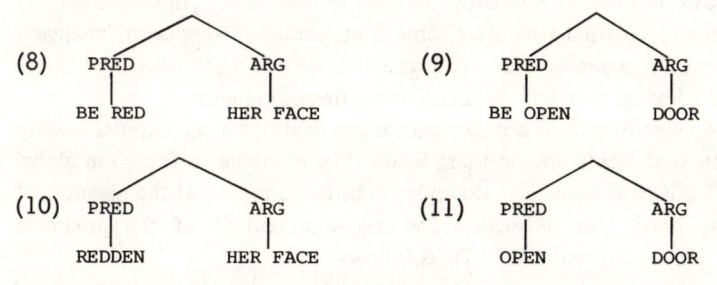

(8) PRED — ARG   (9) PRED — ARG
     BE RED   HER FACE   BE OPEN   DOOR

(10) PRED — ARG   (11) PRED — ARG
     REDDEN   HER FACE   OPEN   DOOR

Since the four predicates are each different from the others, all that we can say about these representations is that the four resulting sentences are different. Beyond this fact, no other relations are captured by the model. Suppose that a speaker is asked to paraphrase sentence (6). In all probability, he will produce a sentence such as

(12)   Her face became red.

If (6) and (12) are paraphrases, they should by definition have the same semantic representation. Since the element *her face* is the same in both sentences, it follows that the semantic representation of the single word *redden* must be equivalent to the representation of the two words *become red*. Returning to the relation between *be red* and *redden*, it is precisely this relation that is expressed by the word *become*. We must find some way to insure that our semantic representations express such facts. The above three examples give us some idea of how to proceed. We can subdivide the global meaning of *redden* into at least two parts, representing the combined meanings of both *be red* and *become*. We suggest that part of the meaning of *redden* consists of the predicate RED and an argument.

(13)
```
        /\
    PRED  ARG
     |     |
    RED    X
```

The second element of the meaning of *redden*, the one which is shared with *become*, is represented with a one-argument predicate that we will call CHANGE:

(14)
```
        /\
    PRED  ARG
     |     |
   CHANGE  X
```

This predicate represents abstractly the idea of something (the argument X) which comes to be what it is after some transformation—hence, a "change". Such elementary semantic elements into which we will break down the global meaning of a lexical item will be called **semantic components**.

By representing these components as predicates, we can express exactly the relation that holds among them when they combine to form the global meaning of a lexical item. For example, in order to represent the meaning of *redden*, we need only substitute for the argument X of the predicate CHANGE the entire predicate RED, as follows:

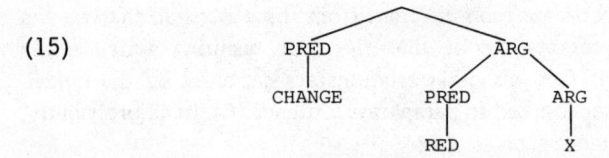

(15)
```
          /\
       PRED  ARG
        |    /\
     CHANGE PRED ARG
             |    |
            RED   X
```

The two semantic components taken separately represent the meanings of *become* and *be red*, respectively. If such components did not take the form of predicates, we would not be able to relate the representations of words such as *be red* to words such as *redden*. RED, the only component of *be red* as it appears in sentences such as (4), must have this form in order to function as the predicate of a sentences. Furthermore, by analyzing such semantic components as predicates, we are also able to represent the exact relationship holding between the two components in making up the meaning of *redden*. The two "ideas" that these represent are not simply juxtaposed in the

Componential Analysis

meaning of *redden*, but are in a precise relation to one another. That is, RED is what the argument X becomes after a change, and not vice versa. Thus, returning to sentence (6), we can derive the representation

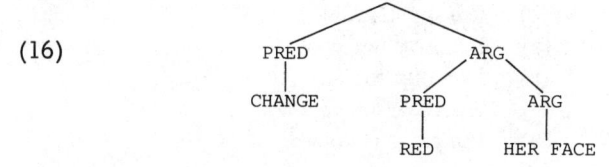

(16)
```
              PRED         ARG
               |          /    \
             CHANGE     PRED    ARG
                         |        |
                        RED    HER FACE
```

The first component represents something like "X comes to be." The X argument in (16) is in turn composed of another predicate, RED, with its single argument HER FACE.

The procedure of substituting the arguments of a predicate with further predicate–argument structures can be extended as far as we care to take it. This procedure permits us to construct complex groups of predicates that represent the meaning of all possible lexical items in a language. We will call such a structured group of predicates a **predicate configuration** or **semantic configuration**. Note, however, that the word **predicate** has now become an ambiguous term. It originally designed a single lexical item, one of the elements of the semantic representation of a sentence considered as a whole. Now we have discovered that such an element can and must be broken down into units called **semantic components,** and that these semantic components have the same form as predicates with one or more arguments. From now on we will use the term **predicate** to refer only to such lower units. On the other hand, the old predicates are now **predicate configurations.** But the term **predicate configuration** is too wide and general in that it designates any structured group of semantic components, whether or not they correspond to a lexical item in a particular language. To distinguish among these various types of semantic configurations, we will use the term **predication** to describe the semantic configuration underlying those elements that we earlier called the predicate of a sentence. Hence, in (16), the representation of *Her face reddened*, CHANGE, and RED are predicates that make up the predication which is the meaning of *redden*.

We have now reached our goal. The simple comparison between the semantic representations (8) and (16) permits us to determine precisely the relationship between their two corresponding sentences, (4) and (6). We have explicitly represented both the similarities and differences. And once we have assigned the same representation to two such sentences, we have automatically accounted for the fact that speakers will accept the two sentences as paraphrases.

The same relation just observed holds within a large number of sentence pairs, e.g.,

(17) (a) *The sky was black.*
      (b) *The sky blackened.*
(18) (a) *The soup was cool.*
      (b) *The soup cooled.*
(19) (a) *The pages are yellow.*
      (b) *The pages yellowed.*

For each sentence (b), we also have the paraphrases

(17) (c) *The sky became black.*
(18) (c) *The soup became cool.*
(19) (c) *The pages became yellow.*

All these relations can be represented using our component CHANGE:

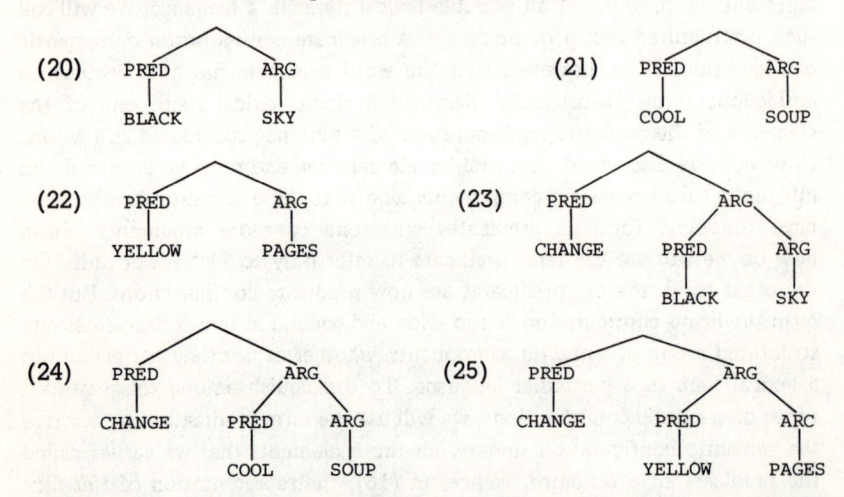

(20) PRED   ARG
      | |
      BLACK SKY

(21) PRED ARG
      | |
      COOL SOUP

(22) PRED   ARG
      | |
      YELLOW PAGES

(23) PRED   ARG
      | / \
      CHANGE PRED ARG
             | |
             BLACK SKY

(24) PRED   ARG
      | / \
      CHANGE PRED ARG
             | |
             COOL SOUP

(25) PRED   ARG
      | / \
      CHANGE PRED   ARG
             | |
             YELLOW PAGES

Furthermore, the same semantic relation also holds between (5) and (7), despite the fact that the English language in this case does not permit paraphrases with the word *become*, as in

(26)   **The door became open.*

The fact that in cases like (26) there is no paraphrase lexicalizing the component CHANGE into a single word is entirely independent of the possibility that such a component exists. In fact, even if we had absolutely no single lexical item corresponding to a single semantic component, this would

Componential Analysis

not in itself mean that the semantic component did not exist. CHANGE exists as a semantic component insofar as it explicitly represents the relation existing between sentences (4), (5), (18a), (19a), and (20a) and their corresponding sentences (6), (7), (18b), (19b), and (20b). Thus, (5) and (7) will be represented respectively as

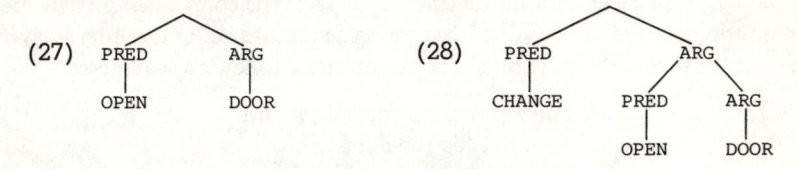

```
(27)    PRED    ARG              (28)    PRED    ARG
         |       |                        |       \
        OPEN   DOOR                     CHANGE   PRED    ARG
                                                  |       |
                                                 OPEN   DOOR
```

An analogous relation exists among the sentence pairs

(29)   (a)   *The stick is broken.*
            (b)   *The stick broke.*
(30)   (a)   *The window was closed.*
            (b)   *The window closed.*

despite the fact that in this case there is no relation between a verb and an adjective, but rather between a verb and its participle. Semantically the relation is the same, and hence we will assign to such sentence pairs representations that are analogous to (27) and (28).

It should also be clear at this point that our representations pertain solely to the level of meaning, and are entirely independent of the similarity or dissimilarity in phonetic material used to express those meanings. Although in the cases examined so far there was always a certain phonetic similarity between the pairs of predications, there are also cases in which two predications have the same semantic relation even though there is no phonetic similarity between them. A case of this kind is represented, for example, by the following two sentences:

(31)   *John was at school.*
(32)   *John arrived at school.*

The meaning of *arrive* entails a change after which something comes to be in a certain place. (31) and (32) can be represented as:

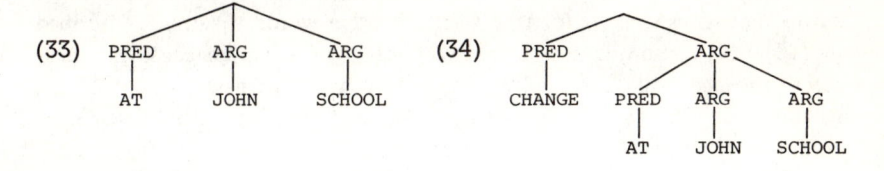

```
(33)  PRED  ARG   ARG       (34)   PRED    ARG
       |     |     |                 |       \
       AT  JOHN  SCHOOL           CHANGE   PRED    ARG    ARG
                                            |       |      |
                                            AT    JOHN   SCHOOL
```

The only difference between this and the preceding cases is that one of the two semantic components (BE AT) has two arguments.

We have so far examined only one type of systematic relationship between the meanings of various predications and the sentences in which they occur. We have described this particular relation by breaking down the global meaning of a lexical item into elements, or semantic components. There are, of course, many other relations that the same mechanism of meaning analysis permits us to describe. Consider, for example, the following sentences:

(35)   The egg-yolk blackened the silver.
(36)   John opened the door.
(37)   Mary cooled the soup.
(38)   Somebody broke the stick.
(39)   He closed the window.

According to the analyses presented in the preceding chapters, these sentences would all be represented as predications with two arguments each. Again, however, in this kind of representation there is nothing that would permit us to capture the clear semantic relation existing between these sentences and sentences like the following:

(40)   The silver blackened.
(41)   The door opened.
(42)   The soup cooled.
(43)   The stick broke.
(44)   The window closed.

The predications contained in each pair of sentences would not be related, even though they have the same phonetic form. This is true because the predications of (35) through (39) have two arguments while the corresponding sentences (40) through (44) have only one argument. Once again we must go "inside" the meaning of (35) through (39) if we want to describe this relation. In very general terms, we can say that each of the sentences (35) through (39) "contains" as part of its meaning the meaning of sentences (40)–(44). In hearing (35)–(39) we know that there is some silver becoming black, a door opening, some soup cooling, etc. But (35) through (39) add something further with respect to (40) through (44)–the idea of another entity that is responsible for that event. In other words, the events described in (40)–(44) come about as a result or effect of a certain cause (in these cases: *the egg yolk, John, Mary,* etc.). How will this new element of the meanings of (35)–(39) be represented? We will introduce another semantic component, called CAUSE, with two arguments:

Componential Analysis

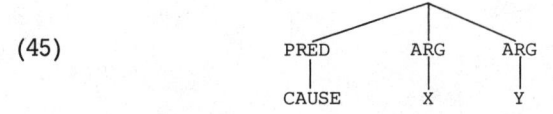

(45)
```
        PRED    ARG    ARG
         |       |      |
        CAUSE    X      Y
```

This component formalizes the relation existing between two elements X and Y such that X is the cause of Y. Since in (45), Y represents the effect, it will be sufficient to substitute this argument with the semantic representations of sentences (40) through (44). We can then represent the systematic relation existing between (35)–(39) on the one hand and (40)–(44) on the other by substituting for the X argument of CAUSE the arguments which appear as the subjects of sentences (35)–(39). The representations of (35)–(39) will then become

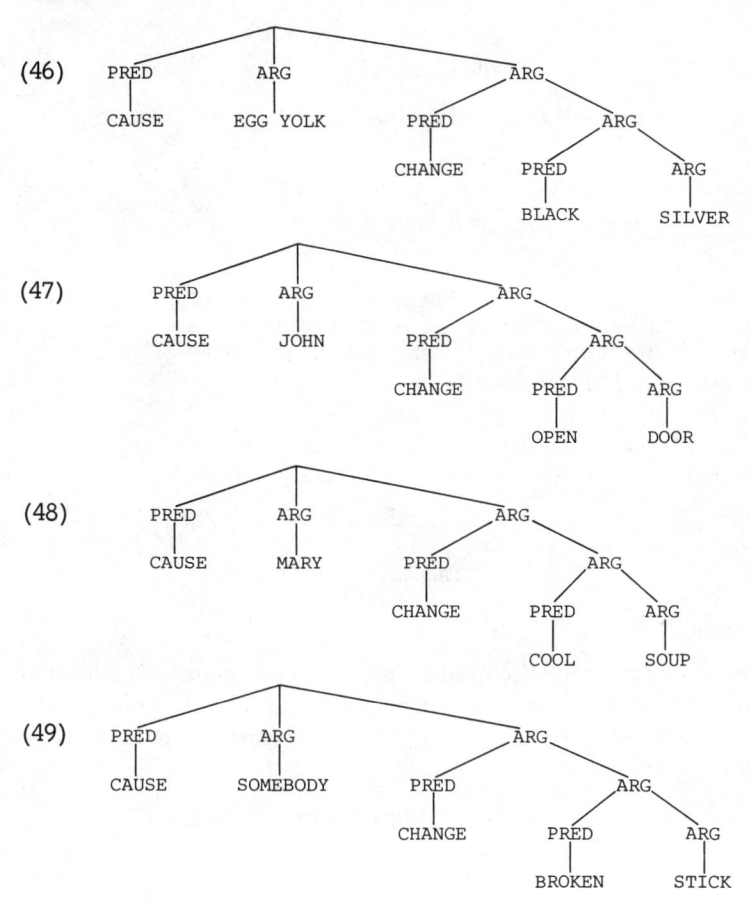

(46)
```
  PRED      ARG              ARG
   |         |
  CAUSE   EGG YOLK    PRED            ARG
                       |
                      CHANGE    PRED         ARG
                                 |            |
                                BLACK       SILVER
```

(47)
```
  PRED      ARG              ARG
   |         |
  CAUSE    JOHN       PRED            ARG
                       |
                      CHANGE    PRED         ARG
                                 |            |
                                OPEN        DOOR
```

(48)
```
  PRED      ARG              ARG
   |         |
  CAUSE    MARY       PRED            ARG
                       |
                      CHANGE    PRED         ARG
                                 |            |
                                COOL        SOUP
```

(49)
```
  PRED      ARG              ARG
   |         |
  CAUSE  SOMEBODY    PRED            ARG
                      |
                     CHANGE    PRED         ARG
                                |            |
                              BROKEN       STICK
```

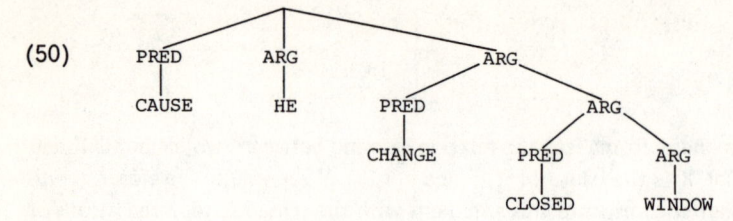

(50)
```
        PRED    ARG           ARG
         |       |         ___/  \___
        CAUSE   HE        PRED       ARG
                           |      ___/  \___
                         CHANGE  PRED      ARG
                                  |         |
                                CLOSED    WINDOW
```

As in the previous case, there need not be any phonetic resemblance between the verb and its corresponding causative. We have so far examined only cases in which the two verbs have had the same acoustic form. Sentences like the following demonstrate instead that two verbs can share the same semantic relation even though they take a totally different phonetic form:

(51)　　　　　　　　*John died.*
(52)　　　　　　　　*Bill killed John.*

(51) describes a change of state, and can consequently be analyzed as

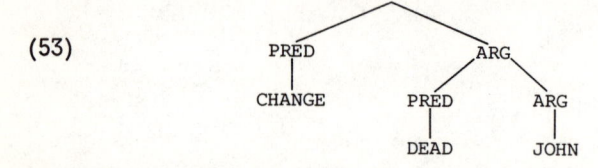

(53)
```
           PRED           ARG
            |         ___/  \___
          CHANGE    PRED      ARG
                    |          |
                   DEAD       JOHN
```

(53) describes the same event, adding Bill as the cause of that event. Consequently it will be represented as

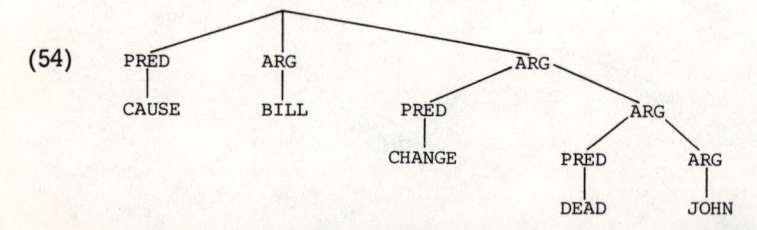

(54)
```
       PRED   ARG                ARG
        |      |           _____/  \_____
       CAUSE  BILL       PRED           ARG
                          |         ___/  \___
                        CHANGE    PRED      ARG
                                   |          |
                                  DEAD       JOHN
```

In other cases, the causative predication, the predication indicating the change of state, and the predication indicating the state itself, are expressed through three different verbs. This is the case in the predications of the three sentences

(55)　　　　　　　　*Bill taught John Chinese.*
(56)　　　　　　　　*John learned Chinese.*
(57)　　　　　　　　*John knows Chinese.*

Componential Analysis   51

The semantic relations holding among sentences (55)–(57) are the same ones that we have seen, for example, in (5), (7), and (36). Thus, we can assign to (55)–(57) the same type of semantic representations used for (5), (7), and (36):

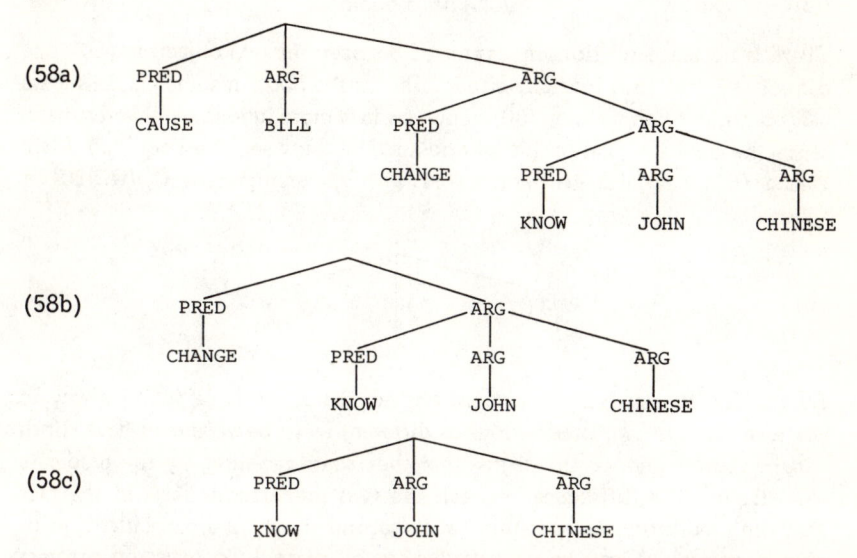

(58a)
```
         PRED    ARG         ARG
          |       |
        CAUSE   BILL    PRED          ARG
                         |
                       CHANGE    PRED   ARG    ARG
                                  |      |      |
                                KNOW   JOHN  CHINESE
```

(58b)
```
       PRED              ARG
        |
      CHANGE     PRED    ARG    ARG
                  |       |      |
                KNOW    JOHN  CHINESE
```

(58c)
```
         PRED    ARG    ARG
          |       |      |
        KNOW    JOHN  CHINESE
```

We have still considered only two systematic relations existing among various lexical items in a language, relations that can be formalized using the semantic components CHANGE and CAUSE. This type of semantic analysis can, however, be pushed further, permitting us to capture other interesting similarities among lexical items. Consider again sentence (31) and its semantic representation (33). Let us examine what is meant be the idea of *being at a place*, which we represented with the semantic component AT. If we abstract from this relation the specific idea of place, we can also say that, in its broadest sense, AT expresses a relationship between an object and another object (in this case, the two objects *John* and *school*). To be exact, an object coincides with another object. We suggest that this general relation consists in conceiving of two objects as coinciding, in the most abstract sense possible. We therefore propose a semantic component that we will call COINCIDE, which represents such a relation. (31) will thus be represented as

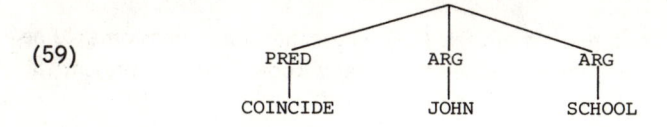

(59)
```
         PRED       ARG      ARG
          |          |        |
       COINCIDE    JOHN    SCHOOL
```

It may seem that we have simply reformulated in different words the same idea underlying representation (33), a step which may appear unjustified and unnecessary. Consider, however, the following sentence:

(60)   *John has a book.*

There is no place relationship expressed between the two objects in (60); one cannot say that (60) localizes either *John* or the *book* in some place. But we can continue to think that (60) expresses in a most fundamental and general sense the abstract relationship of "coinciding" between the *book* and *John*. Hence (60) can also be represented with the component COINCIDE as follows:

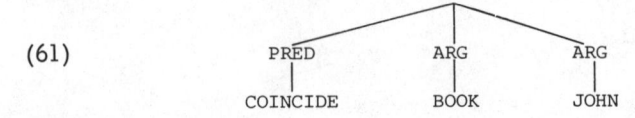

(61)
```
              ┌──────────┼──────────┐
            PRED        ARG        ARG
             │           │          │
          COINCIDE      BOOK       JOHN
```

By pushing the analysis to a more abstract level, we have found a way to place in relation two predications as different as *to be at* and *to have*. Both can be represented, to the degree that they share meaning, by the predicate COINCIDE. The difference between the two predications rests in the fact that the predication *be at* requires as its second argument a particular type of object, one which can be conceived of as a "place." *To have*, by contrast requires no such condition on its second argument.[1] Having found this more general resemblance, we can understand why pairs of sentences like the following are paraphrases:

(62)   (a)   *The book is on the table.*
               (b)   *The table has a book on it.*
(63)   (a)   *Two apples were on the tree.*
               (b)   *The tree had two apples.*

It is because of the shared component COINCIDE that these two sentences can be expressed alternatively with the predications *is on* and *have*. Another advantage of our analysis is that it permits us to explain why in the two sentences

(64)   *John got to Chicago.*
(65)   *John got a book.*

the same predication *get* can appear. (64) means that something *comes to be at*, while (65) means *come to have*. We already know how to represent the

---

[1] In Chapter 7 we will see how to represent explicitly this additional information distinguishing *have* and *be at*.

Componential Analysis

idea of change of state contained in *get*, through the use of the component CHANGE. If we did not also have the preceding analysis of COINCIDE, we would have to represent the meaning of *get* in the two sentences in two different ways, so that (64) would be

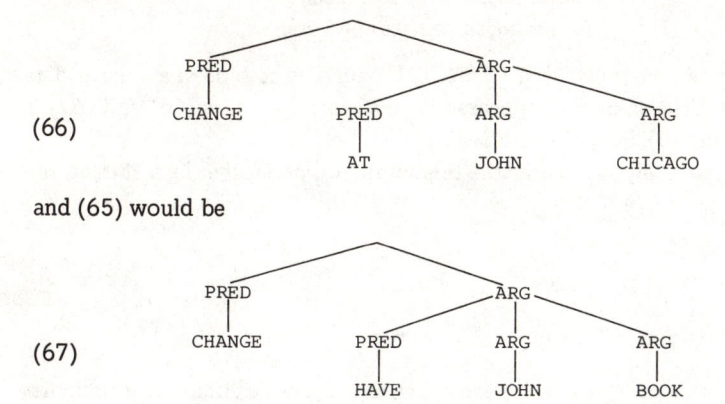

(66)
```
          PRED         ARG
           |         /  |  \
         CHANGE   PRED ARG  ARG
                   |    |    |
                   AT  JOHN CHICAGO
```

and (65) would be

(67)
```
          PRED         ARG
           |         /  |  \
         CHANGE   PRED ARG  ARG
                   |    |    |
                  HAVE JOHN BOOK
```

This would leave us unable to explain why two different structures like (66) and (67) can be lexicalized with the same verb *get*. If, however, we provide *get* with the following representation:

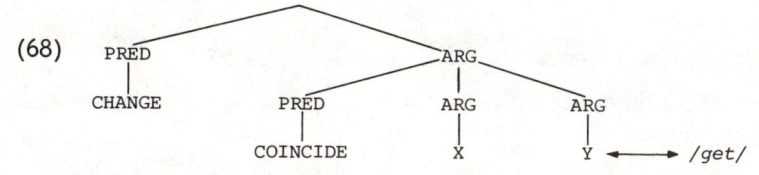

(68)
```
       PRED              ARG
        |            /    |    \
      CHANGE      PRED   ARG   ARG
                   |      |     |
               COINCIDE   X     Y  ⟶  /get/
```

then it can function in both cases as a single underlying meaning for the verb *get* in both the two sentences.

This last example also demonstrates the usefulness of separating within the predication *to be at* the abstract idea of coincidence versus the requisite that the second argument be constructed as a place. *Get*, which contains the component COINCIDE, is not sensitive to the condition that the second argument be a place, and hence can be used to express both *get to Chicago* and *get a book*. But there is another verb which has the same meaning as *get* in (64), and does require such a place condition. We are speaking now of the verb *arrive*, as it appears in (32) and (34). We will represent this verb as

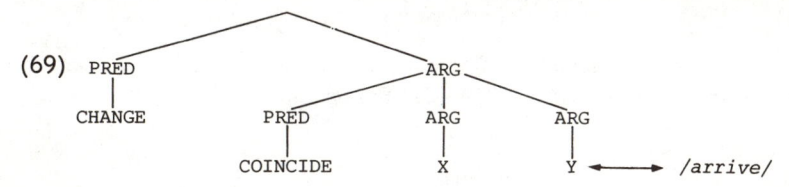

(69)
```
       PRED              ARG
        |            /    |    \
      CHANGE      PRED   ARG   ARG
                   |      |     |
               COINCIDE   X     Y  ⟶  /arrive/
```

This representation also must contain the condition that the second argument Y must be a place. Consider further that (64) and (65) can be paraphrased (though not optimally) with

(70)   John began to be in Chicago.
(71)   John began to have the book.

We already demonstrated that COINCIDE underlies both *be in* and *have*. The component CHANGE that appeared in the representations (66) and (67) is lexicalized in (70) and (71) with *begin*.

This last analysis suggests the representation of another lexical item, the verb *begin*, as

(72)
```
        ╱──────╲
      PRED     ARG
       │        │
     CHANGE     X  ◄──────► /begin/
```

On the other hand as we have seen above that the same component underlies the verb *become*, which appears in (17)–(19)c. Therefore, *become* will also be represented as

(73)
```
        ╱──────╲
      PRED     ARG
       │        │
     CHANGE     X  ◄──────► /become/
```

There is also a third verb which shares the same core meaning—the verb *start*. Sentences such as

(74)   John started to smoke.

mean that there has been a change such that first John did not smoke, and now he smokes. Therefore, we can represent *start* as

(75)
```
        ╱──────╲
      PRED     ARG
       │        │
     CHANGE     X  ◄──────► /start/
```

This equivalence between (72) and (75) explains why (74) can be paraphrased with

(76)   John began to smoke.

In this case, as well, there are differences among the three verbs that share the basic meaning represented by CHANGE. For example, we have

Componential Analysis

(77)   *The door began to be closed.*
(78)   *The door became closed.*

but not

(79)   **The door began closed.*
(80)   **The door became to be closed.*

This fact suggests that if we have a representation like

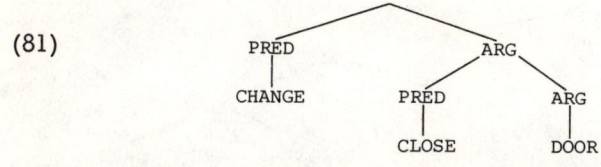

(81)
```
            ┌─────────┴─────────┐
          PRED                 ARG
           │          ┌─────────┴─────────┐
         CHANGE      PRED                ARG
                      │                   │
                    CLOSE                DOOR
```

we can lexicalize CHANGE with *begin,* but we must then express the component CLOSE with a verb. But, if we choose to lexicalize CHANGE with *become,* then the component CLOSE must be lexicalized with an adjective or participle. Other conditions that we cannot consider here also exist for the verb *start.* Some of these problems regard the mechanisms that map meaning into sound, to be considered in Chapter 8. The essential point for this chapter is that by representing meaning in terms of semantic components, we can capture similarities existing among varied lexical items.

Another consequence of introducing the component COINCIDE is the ability to represent the relationship between the two sentences

(82)   *Bill put a book on the table.*
(83)   *Bill gave a book to John.*

(82) means something like "Bill does something such that a book comes to be on the table"; (83) means "Bill does something such that John comes to have a book." We now have all the elements we need to represent such sentences. Using the component CAUSE introduced earlier, we can give the representations

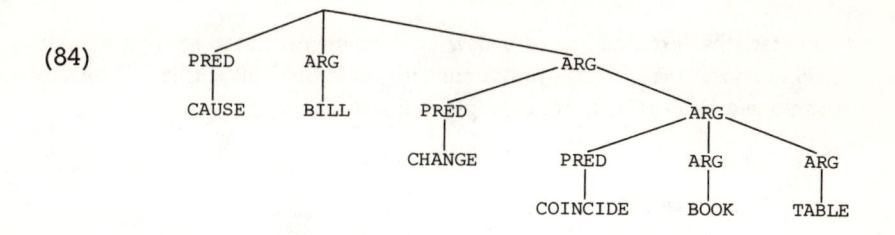

(84)
```
        PRED    ARG            ARG
         │       │       ┌──────┴──────┐
       CAUSE   BILL    PRED           ARG
                        │        ┌─────┴─────┐
                      CHANGE   PRED   ARG   ARG
                                │      │     │
                            COINCIDE  BOOK  TABLE
```

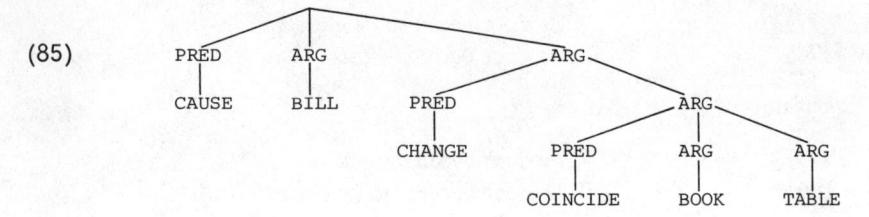

(85)
```
        PRED    ARG              ARG
         |       |                |
        CAUSE   BILL     PRED    ARG
                          |       |
                        CHANGE  PRED   ARG   ARG
                                 |      |     |
                              COINCIDE BOOK  TABLE
```

Both *give* and *put* have meanings that can be represented as

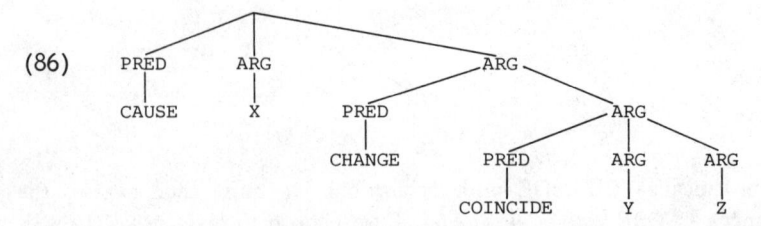

(86)
```
        PRED    ARG              ARG
         |       |                |
        CAUSE    X       PRED    ARG
                          |       |
                        CHANGE  PRED   ARG  ARG
                                 |      |    |
                              COINCIDE  Y    Z
```

The difference between *give* and *put* is, once again, the same difference noted earlier between *be at* and *have*. *Put* requires that its argument Z be a place.

If, as we have seen, *arrive* or *get to* can be analyzed as something like *change to be in a place*, what can we say about the predication appearing in:

(87)   John left Chicago.

(87) means that, after a change takes place, John is no longer in Chicago. Introducing a further semantic component NEGATION (NEG), we can represent the meaning of this last predication so that it appears in its proper relationship to *arrive*. *Leave* is represented as

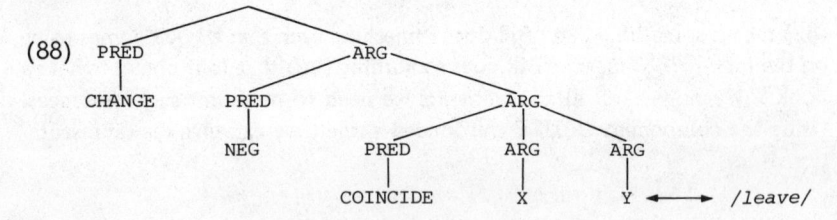

(88)
```
        PRED            ARG
         |               |
        CHANGE   PRED   ARG
                  |      |
                 NEG   PRED   ARG  ARG
                        |      |    |
                     COINCIDE  X    Y  ⟷  /leave/
```

Thus far, the introduction of a new component permitted us to systematically analyze other relationships among lexical items. This is true for the new component NEG as well. For example, the verb *lack*, in

(89)   John lacks courage.

would be represented as

Componential Analysis

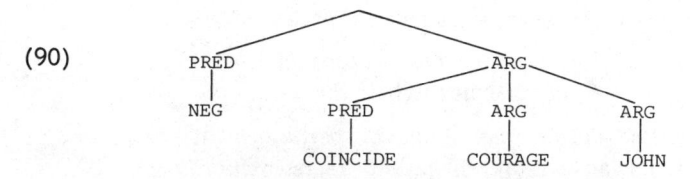

(90)
```
          PRED          ARG
           |           /   \
          NEG      PRED    ARG    ARG
                    |       |      |
                 COINCIDE COURAGE JOHN
```

The same representation could be given to the paraphrase

(91)   *John doesn't have any courage.*

in which, as we already know, *have* lexicalizes the predicate COINCIDE, and *not* is the lexicalization of NEG.

It is apparent that *lack* is identical in representation to the lower portion of the representation of *leave* in (88). One might ask if there exists a word that lexicalizes only the upper portion of (88), which would be

(92)
```
         PRED          ARG
          |           /   \
        CHANGE     PRED   ARG
                    |      |
                   NEG     X
```

The predication suggested by this representation would be *stop*. This would, in fact, correspond to the meaning of *stop* in a sentence such as

(93)   *John stopped smoking.*

Hence, *start* means "change to" and *stop* means "change to not." It might also be asked, what is the meaning of the word *continue*? To represent this kind of verb, we need to use the component NEG not once but twice:

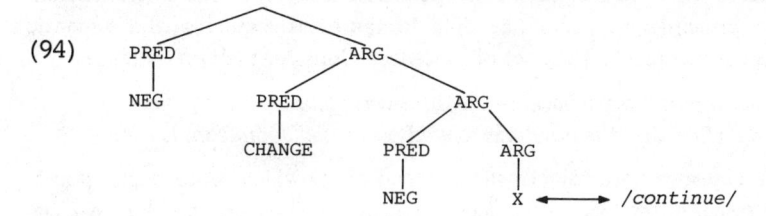

(94)
```
    PRED              ARG
     |               /   \
    NEG          PRED     ARG
                  |      /   \
               CHANGE  PRED   ARG
                        |      |
                       NEG     X  ⟵⟶ /continue/
```

Therefore, *continue* is the same thing as "not to change to not." If this analysis is correct, then we can also represent two similar verbs, appearing in the sentences

(95)   *John stayed at school.*
(96)   *John kept the book.*

In fact, these two sentences can be paraphrased with

(97) *John continued to be at school.*
(98) *John continued to have the book.*

Once again, we find the familiar alternation between *be at* and *have*. This would suggest that *keep* and *stay* will have the representation

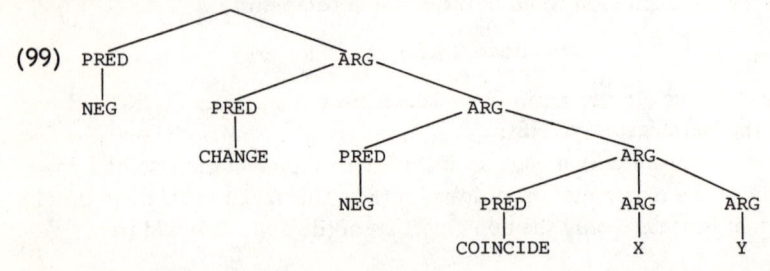

(99)
```
        PRED         ARG
         |
        NEG    PRED          ARG
                |
              CHANGE   PRED          ARG
                        |
                       NEG    PRED    ARG   ARG
                               |       |     |
                           COINCIDE    X     Y
```

The difference between *keep* and *stay* is the same difference that holds between *have* and *be at*, and *give* and *put*. That is, *stay* requires that the second argument Y be conceived as a place.

As should be clear, the mechanism of componential analysis is extremely powerful and has permitted us to analyze with only four semantic components—CAUSE, CHANGE, NEG, COINCIDE—the meaning of at least 15 verbs: *have, be at, get, arrive, begin, become, start, put, give, leave, lack, continue, keep, stay, stop*. It is obvious the kind of advantage in generality and simplicity that is obtained with this approach. But still more important and advantageous is the fact we can explicitly and systematically interrelate the meanings of lexical items. When we can see the internal organization of these verbs, we can explain paraphrase phenomena among sentences using those verbs. If we could extend componential analysis to the entire lexicon, then in principle we should be able to represent explicitly the semantic relations existing among any set of sentences. Consider the two sentences

(100) *John didn't leave because the door was locked.*
(101) *The fact that the door was locked prevented John from leaving.*

In both cases we have something—a locked door—which causes a situation in which some event does not occur, i.e., John does not go out. We can represent the meaning of both sentences as

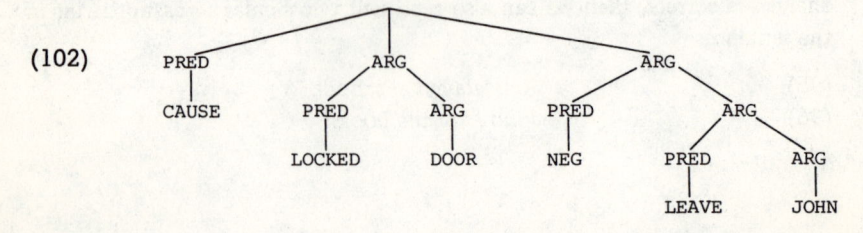

(102)
```
          PRED            ARG                  ARG
           |
         CAUSE     PRED         ARG      PRED          ARG
                    |            |        |
                  LOCKED        DOOR     NEG    PRED    ARG
                                                 |       |
                                               LEAVE   JOHN
```

Componential Analysis 59

The difference between (100) and (101) has to do with the way in which (102) is divided up. In sentence (100) we have a nucleus *John did not go out* and an adverbial *because the door was locked*. Hence, the second argument of CAUSE in (102) becomes the main clause, CAUSE itself is expressed with the word *because*, and the first argument of CAUSE becomes an adverbial subordinate. By contrast, in (101) we have a nucleus, without adverbials, in which each of the sentential structures *The door was locked* and *John left*[2] serve as the two arguments of the nuclear predicate, lexicalized as *prevented*.

Comparing (100) and (101), it is obvious that the words change from one sentence to the other. Ignoring for the moment words like *the fact* and other details, we will concentrate on the words *not*, *because*, and *prevented from*. To these words we can assign the following meanings:

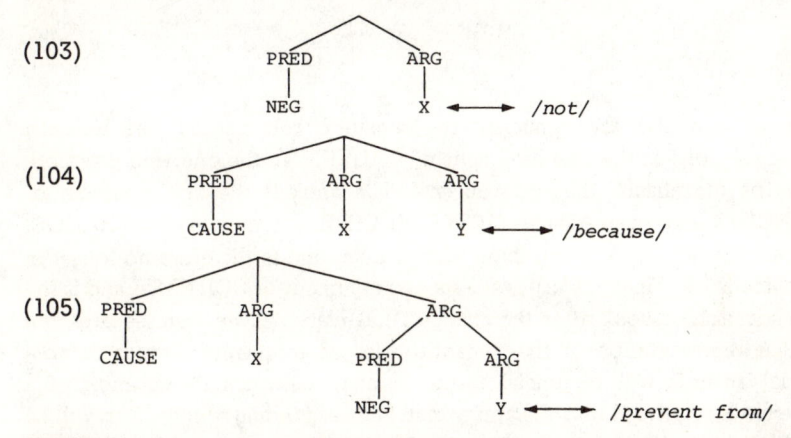

(103)
```
        PRED      ARG
         |         |
        NEG        X  ←→ /not/
```

(104)
```
    PRED     ARG     ARG
     |        |       |
    CAUSE     X       Y  ←→ /because/
```

(105)
```
 PRED    ARG           ARG
  |       |         ╱       ╲
 CAUSE    X       PRED      ARG
                   |         |
                  NEG        Y  ←→ /prevent from/
```

Examining these three meanings closely, one can see why it is possible to substitute *because* and *not* in (100) with *prevented* in (101), while still holding the meaning in (102) constant. Hence, the meaning of *prevented from* is the combination of the meanings of *not* and *because*.

This more complete way of representing the meaning of a sentence also permits us to understand in greater depth the semantic structure of sentences examined in previous chapters. For example, in the representations we gave earlier to

(106)   John gave a book to Mary.

we could only say that *give* is a predication with three arguments: *John*, *a book*, and *Mary*. We know that these three arguments have very different

---

[2] We will ignore here the fact that these two nuclear subordinates have particular characteristics, such that the first is preceded by *the fact that*, and the second, an implicit subordinate, has as its argument *John*, which seems to serve as an argument of *prevent*.

semantic roles with respect to their predication. We know that *John* is the one who gives, the *book* is the thing that is given, and *Mary* is the one who receives the book. But representations like (21) in Chapter 2 do not permit us to represent these roles explicitly. At best, we can only point out that the particular place occupied by each argument in the graphic representation is important (see page 19).

If, instead, we represent the same sentence with a componential analysis such as

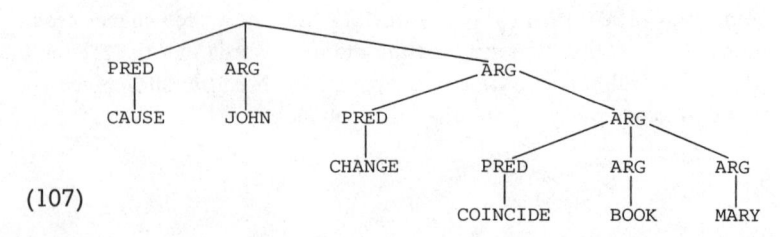

(107)
```
         PRED      ARG            ARG
          |         |             / \
         CAUSE     JOHN        PRED   ARG
                                |    / \
                              CHANGE PRED  ARG
                                      |   / \
                                   COINCIDE BOOK MARY
```

then we can also see explicitly the semantic role carried out by each argument. *John* is the first argument of CAUSE, i.e., the one who is responsible for the change that we call *give*. The *book* is the first argument of COINCIDE and, given that in (107) COINCIDE is dominated by CHANGE, we can say that *book* is the thing that changes and is therefore no longer in the same place. Finally, *Mary* is the second argument of COINCIDE and is the final location of *book* after the change takes place. As we shall see later, the explicit representation of the semantic roles of arguments through componential analysis will be crucial at the moment in which the meaning of a sentence is translated into the appropriate, corresponding sounds. This will be particularly true for the definition of our notion of sentence subject.

For the moment, let us examine some advantages of componential analysis for the solution of some problems that we have already encountered. Remember that sentences such as

(108)   *John is sad.*
(109)   *The film is sad.*

pose problems for traditional analysis. Traditional parsing approaches must furnish the same analysis for both sentences, offering *is sad* as the predicate and *John* or *the film* as subjects. But, as we have seen, this sort of analysis would not permit us to explain why *John is sad* can be paraphrased by *John feels sad*, while the same paraphrase cannot be extended to the second sentence, i.e., *The film feels sad*. The problem is that *John* and *the film* have different semantic roles with respect to the predicate *is sad*, even though the

Componential Analysis

traditional grammar calls them both subjects. *John* is the one who feels sadness, while *the film* is something which makes someone feel sad. Componential analysis will permit us to capture this difference. (108) and (109) have different semantic representations. (108) is represented as

(110)
```
        PRED    ARG
         |       |
        SAD    JOHN
```

(109) is represented, instead, with

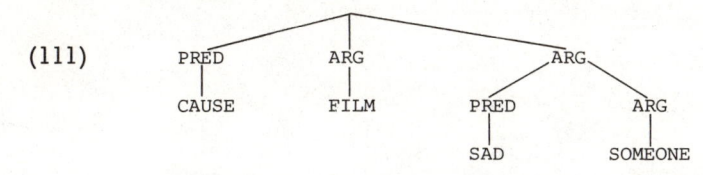

(111)
```
     PRED      ARG              ARG
      |         |          PRED      ARG
    CAUSE     FILM          |         |
                           SAD     SOMEONE
```

In other words, in sentence (108), *is sad* is a predication with only one argument, which (in lieu of a more profound analysis) we indicate with the component SAD, attributing a sentiment of sadness to someone. Instead, in (109) *is sad* is a predication combining two arguments, containing a predicate CAUSE and the predicate SAD. The two arguments are, respectively, that which causes the sentiment of sadness, and someone who feels that sentiment. Notice that *is sad* requires that there be someone, however unspecified or imprecise, who feels that sentiment. There is another word in English which would permit us to express the same structure (111), for cases in which the argument of SAD is no longer unspecified. This would be the verb *sadden*. Hence, the sentence

(112)   *The film saddens Julia.*

has the representation

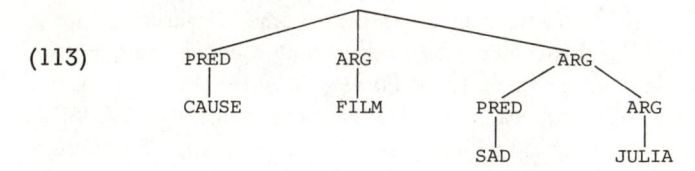

(113)
```
     PRED      ARG              ARG
      |         |          PRED      ARG
    CAUSE     FILM          |         |
                           SAD      JULIA
```

Another problem encountered in Chapter 2 was posed by the sentences

(114)   *The house is burning.*
(115)   *John is burning the house.*

In these two sentences *the house* always has the same semantic role with respect to the predication *is burning*, i.e., the role of that which undergoes the physical process we call "burning." Nevertheless, within traditional grammar, *house* is the subject of (114) and the object complement in (115). We can now furnish for these two sentences an analysis which will capture the identical semantic role of *the house* in the two sentences. The semantic representation of (114) would now become

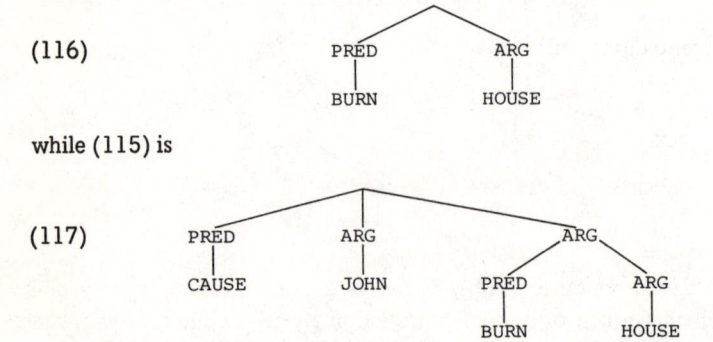

(116)
```
        PRED        ARG
         |           |
        BURN       HOUSE
```

while (115) is

(117)
```
     PRED    ARG         ARG
      |       |        /      \
    CAUSE   JOHN    PRED      ARG
                     |         |
                    BURN     HOUSE
```

BURN is the single semantic component[3] expressed by the word *is burning* in (114). In (115), both BURN and CAUSE are combined into the predication *is burning*. But, in both cases, *the house* always has the same role with respect to the semantic component BURN.

The two predications *is sad* and *is burning* pose an interesting problem that will require us to modify somewhat what we have said so far about the meaning of words. Until now we have seen that a word expresses a structure determined by semantic components, with a fixed number of arguments. Now we see that *is sad* and *is burning* express only one component in one sentence, and two components in another sentence. This suggests that some word meanings consist of a group of semantic components, expressed by that word in all the sentences in which it appears, plus one or more optional components that the same word may express in some sentences but not in others. If the word expresses an optional component, then a new argument is occasionally created, as occurred for *is burning* in (115). In other cases, a lexical item may represent one of its optional components, e.g., CAUSE in the use of *is sad* in (109), and still express only one argument. Therefore, if we want to represent the lexical items *sad* and *to burn*, including both optional and obligatory components, we will have

---

[3] As in the case of SAD, BURN is a predicate that could undergo further analysis. As represented here, it is the attribution of a certain physical process to something.

Componential Analysis

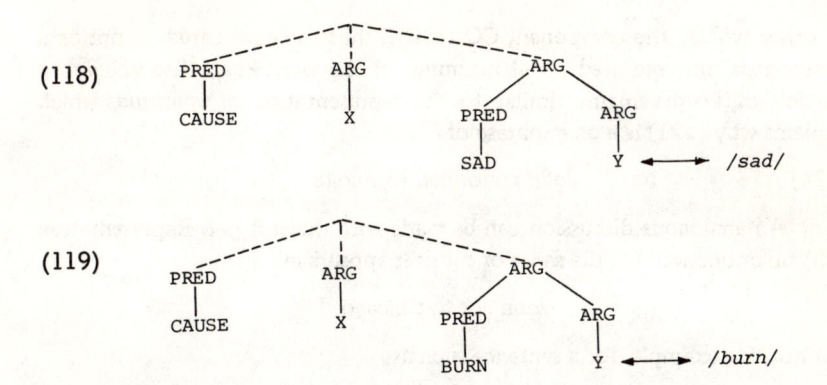

(118)
```
        PRED    ARG         ARG
         |       |         /    \
       CAUSE    X       PRED    ARG
                         |       |
                        SAD      Y  ⟵⟶ /sad/
```

(119)
```
        PRED    ARG         ARG
         |       |         /    \
       CAUSE    X       PRED    ARG
                         |       |
                       BURN      Y  ⟵⟶ /burn/
```

in which the components marked by the dotted line are optional.

This phenomenon of optional components is not rare. For example, the meaning that we assigned to *keep* earlier works well for the use of *keep* in

(120)   John kept the book.

but not for the use of *keep* in the sentence

(121)   John kept smoking.

The structure of (120) is obviously

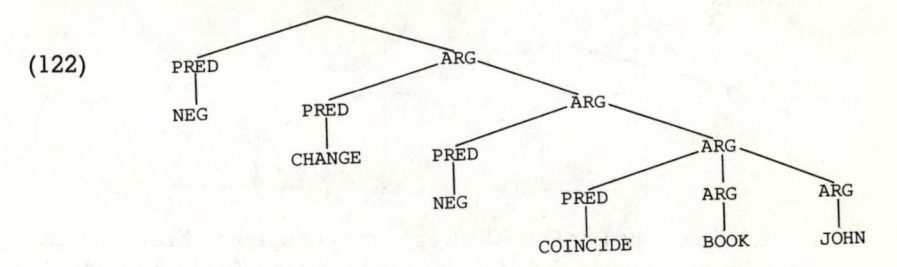

(122)
```
     PRED           ARG
      |           /     \
     NEG      PRED       ARG
              |        /      \
           CHANGE   PRED       ARG
                    |        /     \
                   NEG    PRED    ARG    ARG
                           |       |      |
                       COINCIDE  BOOK   JOHN
```

while the structure underlying (121) is

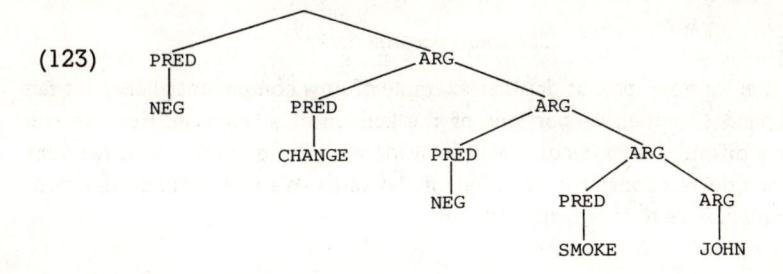

(123)
```
     PRED           ARG
      |           /     \
     NEG      PRED       ARG
              |        /     \
           CHANGE   PRED      ARG
                    |       /     \
                   NEG   PRED     ARG
                          |        |
                        SMOKE    JOHN
```

In other words, the component COINCIDE must be considered an optional component, not required in all meanings of the word *keep*. The obligatory portion of *keep* remains similar to the representation of *continue*, which explains why (121) is a pharaphrase of

(124)   *John continued to smoke.*

An analogous discussion can be made with the verb *get*. Representation (68) functions well for the sense of *get* as it appears in

(64)   *John got to Chicago.*

but not, for example, for a sentence such as

(125)   *The room got dark.*

This sentence can be represented as

(126)
```
            PRED         ARG
             |          /   \
          CHANGE      PRED   ARG
                       |      |
                      DARK   ROOM
```

This means that a more correct representation for the verb *get* is the following:

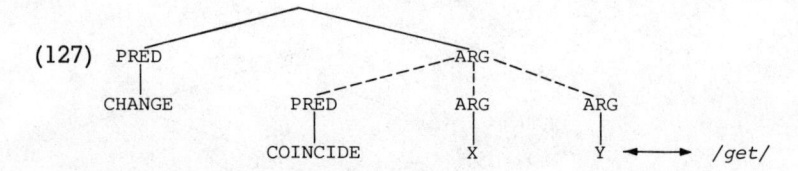

(127)
```
       PRED                  ARG
        |          _____/ | _____
      CHANGE     PRED         ARG    ARG
                  |            |      |
              COINCIDE         X      Y  ←→  /get/
```

in which the component COINCIDE appears to be optional. Even in this case, note that the representation of the meaning of *get* in (126) becomes identical to the representation assigned to *become* (73). This would explain the possibility of paraphrasing (125) with

(128)   *The room became dark.*

Let us now look at another example of how componential analysis can be applied to extensive portions of the lexicon of a language. Here we will select a different area, traditionally considered quite complex in its network of semantic relations: the so-called **modal verbs**. We will examine the verbs *must, may, have to, can, will,* and *shall*.

Componential Analysis

First let us consider sentences with the verb *must:*

(129) *Frank must go out.*
(130) *John must stop.*
(131) *I must go to the office every day.*

Compare these with the following three sentences, without the verb *must:*

(132) *Frank goes out.*
(133) *John stops.*
(134) *I go to the office every day.*

The difference between these sentences gives us some initial ideas about the meaning of *must*. It is sufficient to consider what the first sentences add with respect to the second set. Intuitively, the answer is simple enough: A sentence containing *must* adds the idea of the existence of an obligation to carry out the action expressed by the corresponding sentence without the verb *must*. To represent this difference, we offer the hypothesis that the meaning of *must* consists of a semantic component (a predicate) with only one argument—the component BIND. In essence, the general idea that this component formalizes can be expressed as "X is bound," where X will represent the corresponding action. Therefore, at this point, the lexical structure of the verb *must* will be

(135)
```
        PRED       ARG
         |          |
        BIND        X
```

Hence, *It is bound that Frank go out, It is bound that I go to the office everyday,* etc. This corresponds fairly well to the intuitive difference among the groups of sentences. But this is not sufficient. The verb *must* in sentences (129)–(131) is not limited to communicating that there is something binding on the actions described by the sentences. These sentences also imply the existence of some other event (which is unexpressed in the three sentences) that brought the bind-state into existence. This becomes clearer if we consider a sentence such as

(136) *Frank must go out to buy cigarettes.*

This sentence, at least in its written form, is ambiguous.[4] In one reading *to*

---

[4] In its spoken form, the first interpretation is expressed by making a small pause after *go out.*

buy cigarettes tells us what causes the existence of the obligation on Frank to go out. In the second reading *to buy cigarettes* only tells us the reason why Frank goes out, but there is no mention of what causes the existence of the obligation. The first reading has the following non-ambiguous paraphrase:

(137)   *To buy cigarettes, Frank must go out.*

whereas the second reading cannot be paraphrased as (137). Now this second reading still implies an unspecified causing event, while this is not true of the first reading. In fact we can add a second *to*-clause to the second reading in order to make clear what causes the existence of the obligation, as in

(138)   *Frank must go out to buy cigarettes to please me.*

which would become ungrammatical if interpreted according to the first reading.

This would permit us to conclude that the meaning of *must* always carries the implication of an event that binds the realization of the action expressed by the sentence. At this point, we already know how to represent this part of the meaning of *must*, using the same semantic component CAUSE introduced earlier to represent the meaning of other verbs. The lexical structure of the verb *must* will be

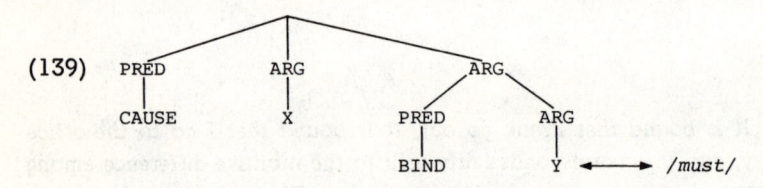

(139)
```
         PRED      ARG           ARG
          |         |           /    \
        CAUSE       X         PRED    ARG
                              |        |
                             BIND      Y  ←→ /must/
```

The representation of the first interpretation of (134) will be

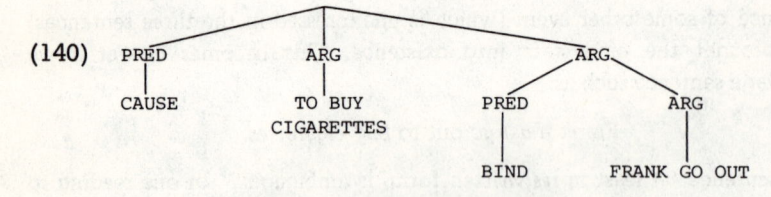

(140)
```
         PRED         ARG              ARG
          |            |             /     \
        CAUSE      TO BUY         PRED      ARG
                  CIGARETTES       |         |
                                 BIND    FRANK GO OUT
```

The same sentence, with the second interpretation, will have the representation

Componential Analysis

(141)
```
        PRED         ARG              ARG
         |            |               / \
       CAUSE    TO PLEASE ME      PRED   ARG
                                   |      |
                                 BIND  FRANK GO OUT
                                       TO BUY CIGARETTES
```

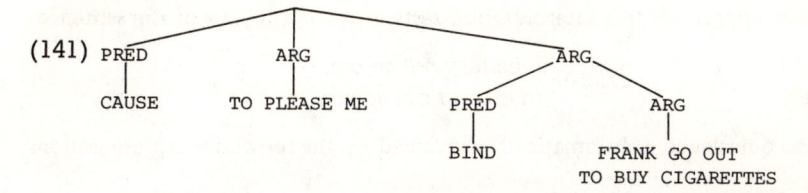

It is important to note some characteristics of the way in which the semantic configuration containing *must* is mapped. The X argument of CAUSE—i.e., the event that causes the bind-state—is never expressed in the same simple sentence containing *must*. This is why one can have complete sentences, like (129)–(131), in which the thing causing the existence of the bind-state is never mentioned. This causal event could be expressed with another sentential structure, subordinate to the one containing the verb *must*. This is true in sentence (136), as represented in (140). The subject of the sentential structure that is the Y argument of CAUSE becomes the subject of *must*, which in turn becomes the main verb of the whole sentence.

This analysis of *must* is still inadequate. However, before improving on it, it would be helpful to consider the verb *may*, to which the semantic material introduced so far can be immediately extended. Let us consider a few such sentences:

(142)   *Frank may go out.*
(143)   *You may go to the movies.*

It is clear what the word *may* contributes to the meaning of these sentences—just as *must* carried the idea of obligation, *may* adds the idea of "permission." It is interesting that this elementary idea of permission can be expressed in terms of an idea of obligation accompanied by a double negation. Therefore, to say that *X may do Y* is equivalent to saying that *X does not have not to do Y*. Since we know how to represent *must*, we also know how to represent the meaning of *may*:

(144)
```
     PRED    ARG           ARG
      |       |           /   \
    CAUSE     X        PRED    ARG
                        |     /   \
                       NEG  PRED   ARG
                             |    /   \
                           BIND PRED   ARG
                                 |      |
                                NEG     Y  ⟵⟶ /may/
```

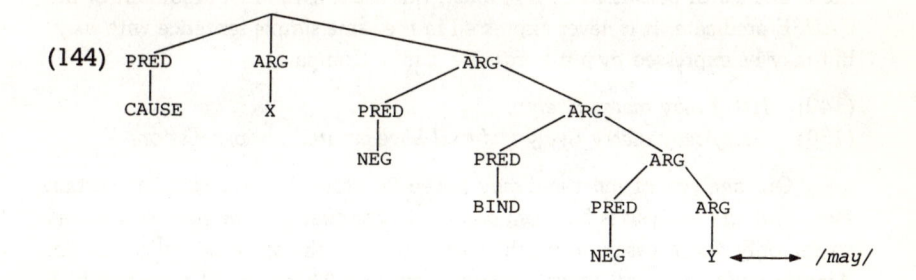

Some support for this interpretation rests in the synonymy of the sentences

(145)   *John may not go out.*
(146)   *John must not go out.*

This equivalence is automatically explained by the respective representations

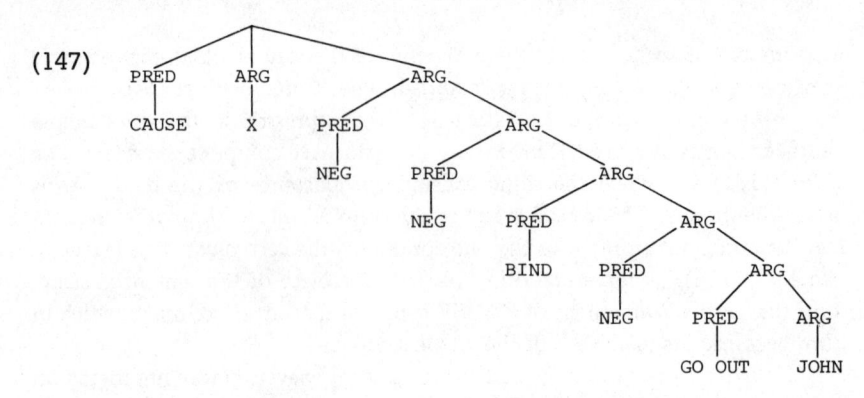

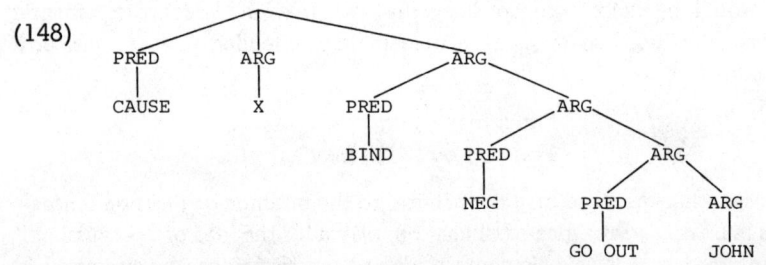

(147)

```
PRED   ARG           ARG
 |      |       _____|_____
CAUSE   X    PRED           ARG
              |        _____|_____
             NEG    PRED           ARG
                     |        _____|_____
                    NEG    PRED           ARG
                            |        _____|_____
                           BIND    PRED           ARG
                                    |        _____|_____
                                   NEG    PRED           ARG
                                           |              |
                                          GO OUT        JOHN
```

(148)

```
PRED   ARG           ARG
 |      |       _____|_____
CAUSE   X    PRED           ARG
              |        _____|_____
             BIND   PRED           ARG
                     |        _____|_____
                    NEG    PRED           ARG
                            |              |
                           GO OUT        JOHN
```

(147), which is the representation of *John may not go out*, reduces to (148), the representation of *John must not go out*, by cancelling out the two NEG components that dominate the BIND predicate in (147).

May also always implies the presence of another event X which causes the existence of permission. As in *must*, this event is the first argument of the CAUSE predicate. It is never expressed in the same simple sentence with *may*, but may be expressed by a subordinate clause. Compare

(149)   *Harry may marry Evelyn.*
(150)   *Harry may marry Evelyn, since I have granted my permission.*

Our analysis of *must* and *may* has so far permitted us to explain certain facts. But the analysis is far from complete. For example, we have considered so far only those cases in which *must* is used in the sense of obligation (or **deontic must,** as it will be called from now on). These are all cases in which *must* can be paraphrased by *it is necessary that.* Thus instead of (129)–(131), we could have

Componential Analysis

(151)   It is necessary that Frank go out.
(152)   It is necessary that John stop.
(153)   It is necessary that I go into the office every day.

But sentences containing *must* can also have a completely different sort of meaning, not paraphrasable by *it is necessary that*. Consider, for example, the sentences

(154)   It must be five o'clock.
(155)   Frank must have left.

These uses of *must* are best paraphrased with

(156)   I believe that it is five o'clock.
(157)   I believe that Frank left.

and thus would be anomalous if we substituted *it is necessary that* for *must*, as in

(158)   *It is necessary that it be five o'clock.
(159)   *It is necessary that Frank has left.

The speaker uses the verb *must* in these contexts to express uncertainty regarding the state of affairs described by the sentence. It is as if he had said *It is probable that it is five o'clock* or *it is probable that Frank has left*. Given the semantic representation provided above, one should ask how it is possible to use *must* to express this meaning.

Recall the analysis presented earlier concerning obligatory versus optional components in the meaning of a given lexical item. It seems intuitively plausible that the two uses of the verb *must* may be explainable by the presence or absence of some kind of optional component in one of those two uses. In order to account for the belief, or **epistemic**, use of the verb *must*, we introduce a two-place predicate BELIEVE, which expresses a relation between a person and a state of affairs. What is actually happening with the epistemic use of the verb *must* is that the speaker is bound to believe some state of affairs, and that this bind-state is brought about by some other event or fact that is the first argument of the predicate CAUSE underlying *must*. Hence, sentences (154) and (155) will be given the representations

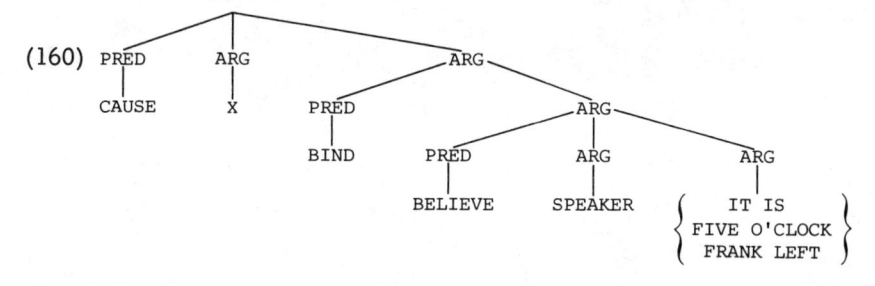

(160)
```
         PRED    ARG        ARG
          |       |          |
        CAUSE     X        PRED    ARG
                            |       |
                          BIND    PRED    ARG
                                   |       |
                                BELIEVE  SPEAKER    ARG
                                                     |
                                                  { IT IS
                                                   FIVE O'CLOCK
                                                   FRANK LEFT }
```

This would mean that the lexical representation for *must* should now be modified to include the optional predicate BELIEVE, as follows:

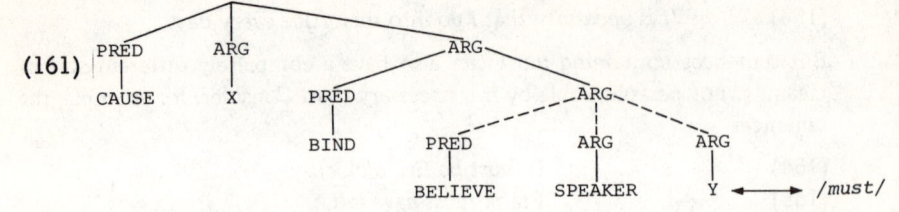

(161)
```
        PRED    ARG         ARG
         │       │           │
       CAUSE     X     PRED      ARG
                        │         │
                      BIND   PRED    ARG    ARG
                              │       │      │
                           BELIEVE  SPEAKER   Y  ⟷  /must/
```

in which the dotted lines indicate the optional components of that lexical item. This analysis means that a sentence containing *must* is often ambiguous, unless the nature and cause of the obligation is in some way made explicit in the sentence, or unless that obligation is implicit in the context. For example, the ambiguous sentence

(162)   They must be married.

can be rendered explicit by either of the two sentences

(163)   They must be married, to join the club.
(164)   They must be married, since they look so cheerful.

In both cases, the conditions governing the presence or absence of BELIEVE rest in the semantic nature of the first argument of CAUSE, i.e., whether that argument is a reason for believing in the state of affairs Y, or whether the X argument directly imposes a bind state on the event described in the main clause.

A similar epistemic analysis can be extended to the verb *may*, which as we have seen, is the double-negative of *must*. For example, the sentences

(165)   It may be five o'clock.
(166)   John may have left.

do not mean that someone has granted permission that it be five o'clock, nor that John left because he had permission. Instead, this is an epistemic use of *may*, in which the semantic structure described in (142) is expanded to become

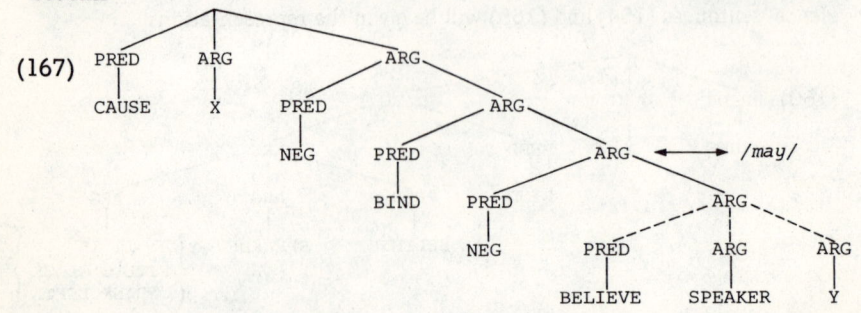

(167)
```
       PRED    ARG         ARG
        │       │           │
      CAUSE     X     PRED       ARG
                       │          │
                      NEG   PRED      ARG  ⟷  /may/
                             │         │
                           BIND   PRED     ARG
                                   │        │
                                  NEG   PRED   ARG   ARG
                                         │      │     │
                                      BELIEVE SPEAKER  Y
```

Componential Analysis 71

Here, as with **epistemic** *must*, the last argument is expanded to the predicate-argument structure BELIEVE (SPEAKER, Y). Therefore, sentences (165) and (166) can be represented as

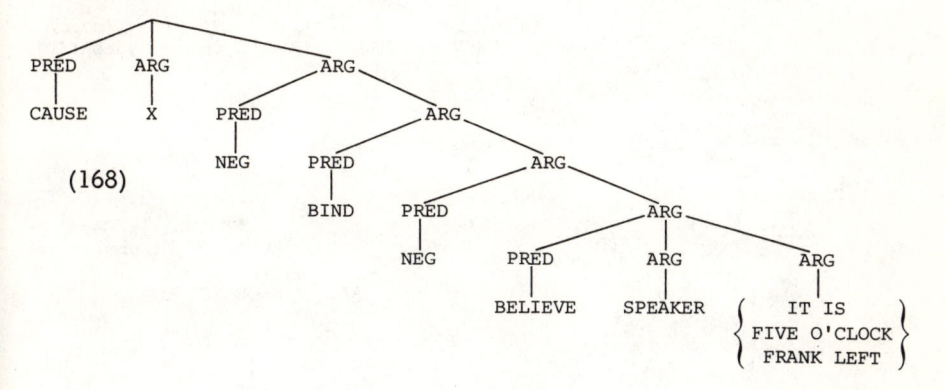

(168)
```
PRED   ARG        ARG
 |      |          |
CAUSE   X      PRED      ARG
               |          |
              NEG    PRED       ARG
                     |           |
                    BIND   PRED       ARG
                           |           |
                          NEG    PRED      ARG         ARG
                                 |          |           |
                              BELIEVE    SPEAKER    { IT IS
                                                     FIVE O'CLOCK
                                                     FRANK LEFT }
```

in which the "permission" structure of *may* applies to the speaker's feeling that he is "permitted" to believe that it is five o'clock, or that Frank has left.

Let us now go back to deontic *must* and permissive *may*. Consider the sentences

(169)   *John must be a young man.*
(170)   *John may be a young man.*
(171)   *The sun must rise from behind those hills.*
(172)   *The sun may rise from behind those hills.*
(173)   *It must be five o'clock.*
(174)   *It may be five o'clock.*

(169–174) can have only an epistemic interpretation, and they become deviant if read in a deontic or permissive sense. This means that the deontic or permissive interpretation imposes some restriction on the semantic nature of the sentence which takes the place of Y in (139) and (144). Consider some characteristics of sentences (169–174). In (169–170) we have a human subject, but a stative predication. In (171–172) the predication is nonstative, but the subject is nonhuman. In (173–174) we have both a stative predication and a nonhuman subject. From this small set of examples it follows that a sentence containing *must* can have a deontic interpretation (and a sentence containing *may* a permissive interpretation) only if the subject of the sentence is human (or human-like) and the predication expresses some kind of activity and not a state. We will represent these features by means of a new semantic component: DO. DO is a two-place predicate, whose first argument is always a person and the second a sentential structure. Our analysis of deontic *must* and permissive *may* will be accordingly modified as follows:

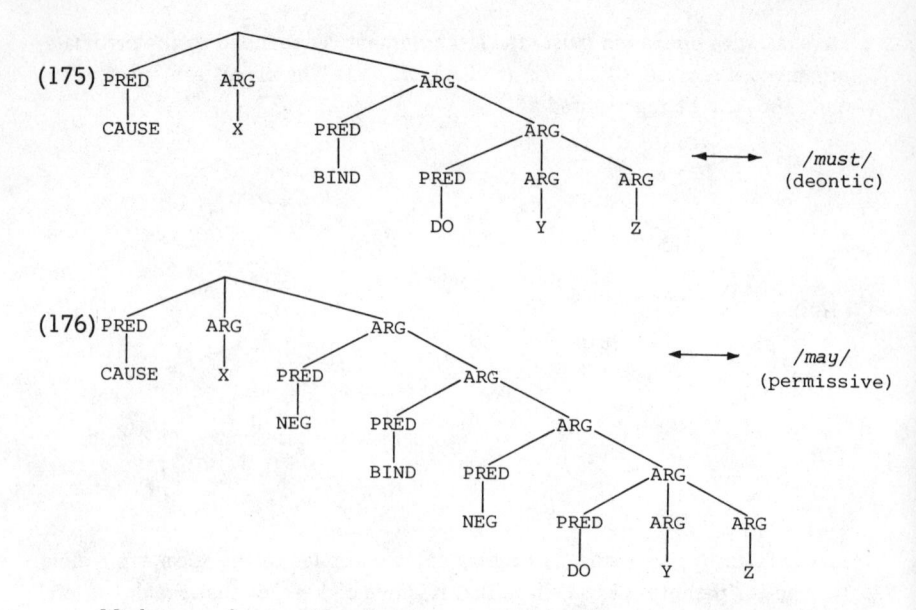

(175)
```
PRED      ARG           ARG
 |         |           /    \
CAUSE      X         PRED    ARG
                      |     /    \
                     BIND  PRED  ARG  ARG
                            |     |    |
                            DO    Y    Z
```
⟷ /must/ (deontic)

(176)
```
PRED      ARG           ARG
 |         |           /    \
CAUSE      X         PRED    ARG
                      |     /    \
                     NEG  PRED    ARG
                           |     /    \
                          BIND  PRED   ARG
                                 |    /    \
                                NEG  PRED  ARG  ARG
                                      |     |    |
                                      DO    Y    Z
```
⟷ /may/ (permissive)

We have so far considered only two modal verbs, *must* and *may*. Now we are in a position to say something about *have to* and *can*. In sentences such as

(177)   John has to go out.

have to can be assigned the same representation as deontic *must*, i.e., (137). For most speakers of English, *have to* seems to be confined to the deontic sense. Even if deontic *must* and *have to* have the predicational structure, there are at least two differences between them that have to be considered. *Must* and *have to* behave differently in negative sentences. If the sentences

(178)   John must go out.
(179)   John has to go out.

are negated, different results are obtained:

(180)   John must not go out.
(181)   John does not have to go out.

While (180) means that John is obliged not to go out, (181) means that John is *not* obliged to go out. (178) and (179) have the same representations, whereas (180) and (181) do not. The difference is that the position of one of the NEG predicates is different in (180) versus (181), as follows:

Componential Analysis

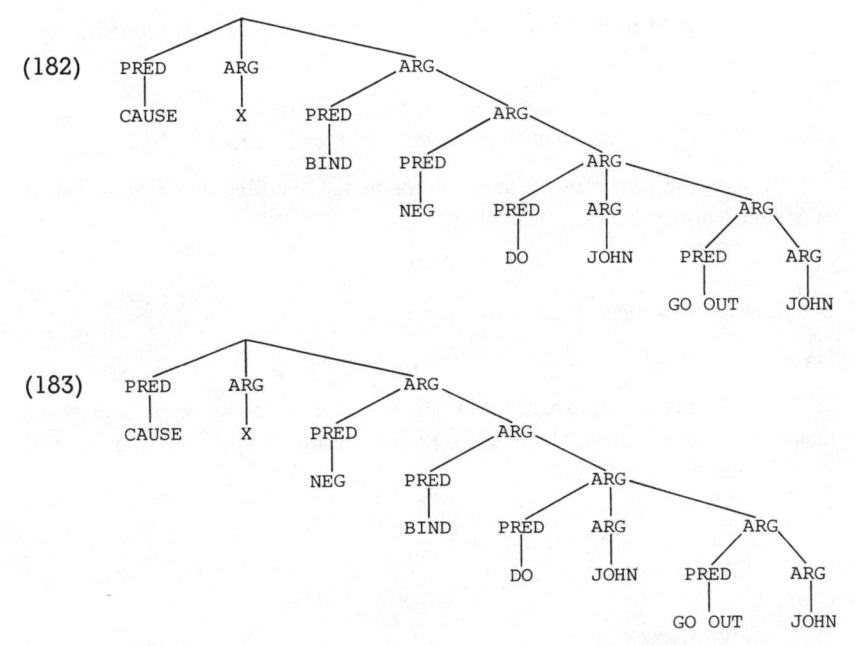

(182) PRED   ARG   ARG
       │   │
       CAUSE X   PRED   ARG
                   │
                   BIND PRED   ARG
                         │
                         NEG PRED ARG   ARG
                              │   │
                              DO   JOHN   PRED   ARG
                                          │   │
                                          GO OUT JOHN

(183) PRED   ARG   ARG
       │   │
       CAUSE X   PRED   ARG
                   │
                   NEG   PRED   ARG
                         │
                         BIND PRED ARG   ARG
                               │   │
                               DO   JOHN   PRED   ARG
                                           │   │
                                           GO OUT JOHN

In addition, there may be a difference in the conditions imposed on the semantic material which is substituted for X in the structures for *must* versus *have to*. *Must* seems to imply that the speaker puts his own authority into the causing event, while this is not the case for *have to*. Compare the sentences

(184)   *You must be in camp by ten.*
(185)   *You have to be in camp by ten.*

As Leech (1969) has observed, (184) "would probably be spoken by an officer giving orders, while (185) could well be spoken by an ordinary soldier informing his comrades of orders issued by someone else."

Can, in its permissive sense, has a predicational structure which is identical to permissive *may*, i.e., (144). As with *must* and *have to*, differences arise in the nature of the causing event. *May* implies that it is the speaker who is granting permission, while *can* has no such implication. Compare

(186)   *You may smoke here.*
(187)   *You can smoke here.*

In (186), the speaker is the subject of the sentence which constitutes the first argument of CAUSE, thus becoming what causes the permission to exist. In (187), the speaker is merely reporting that there is something which causes the permission to exist. This seems to be the reason why (188) sounds more acceptable than (189):

(188) You can smoke here, as far as I know.
(189) ?You may smoke here, as far as I know.

Epistemic *can* offers a more complicated picture. In straightforward epistemic sentences it cannot be used:

(190) *It can be five o'clock.[5]

But in negative sentences *can* is used:

(191) It can't be five o'clock.

It is interesting to observe that negative epistemic *can* is used in place of negative epistemic *must* which, as Boyd and Thorne (1969) have pointed out, sounds "stilted." Instead of

(192) ?They must not be married.

we usually hear

(193) They can't be married.

Our analysis is able to account for this fact. (193) has the following semantic representation:

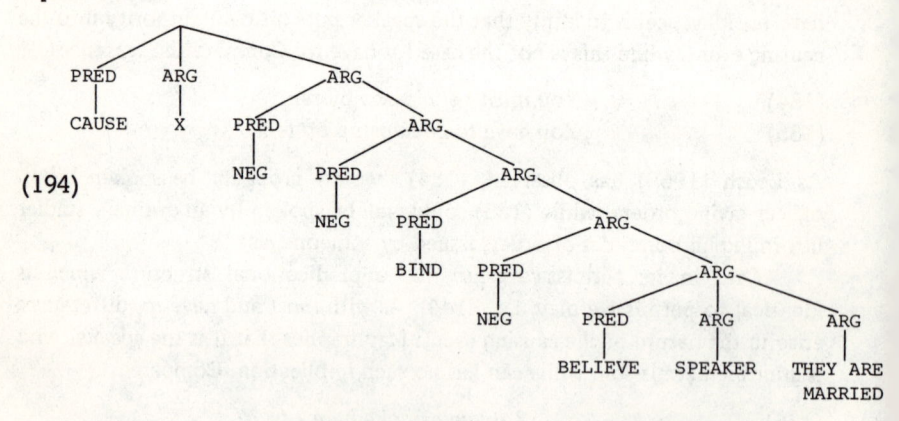

(194) [tree diagram: PRED CAUSE, ARG X, ARG [PRED NEG, ARG [PRED NEG, ARG [PRED BIND, ARG [PRED NEG, ARG [PRED BELIEVE, ARG SPEAKER, ARG THEY ARE MARRIED]]]]]]

---

[5] There are, however, at least two uses of *can* in affirmative sentences which cannot be considered as instances of permissive *can*. These are the so-called "ability sense," as in *John can swim*, and another use, which Boyd and Thorne (1968) consider as marking only the "sporadic" aspect of the sentence, as in *Welshmen can be tall*. We would tentatively suggest that these are instances of epistemic *can*, with the special condition that the first argument of CAUSE be the "intrinsic nature" of the surface subject of the sentence. In other words, what "causes the speaker not to be bound not to believe that

Componential Analysis   75

On the other hand, (192) would have the following representation:

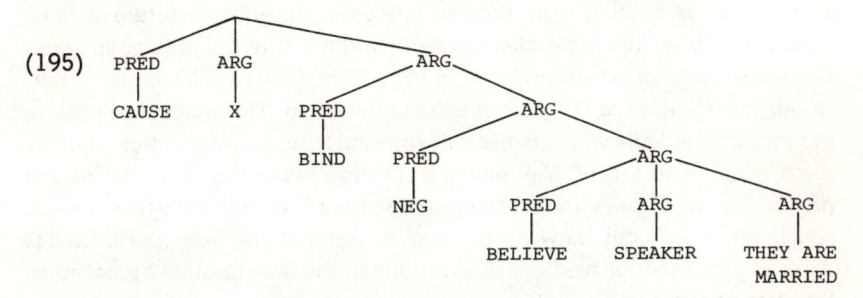

(195)
```
        PRED    ARG         ARG
         |       |           
       CAUSE    X    PRED         ARG
                      |            
                    BIND   PRED        ARG
                            |           
                           NEG   PRED      ARG        ARG
                                  |         |          |
                               BELIEVE   SPEAKER   THEY ARE
                                                    MARRIED
```

It is easy to see that (194) is equivalent to (195), since the two NEGs cancel out.

Let us now consider the modal verb *will*. A number of different meanings have been traditionally associated with it. Let us begin by considering one of them, namely its epistemic sense. It is commonly asserted that the use of *will* in this sense serves to express the future tense of the accompanying verb, as the following sentences seem to show:

(196)   *He will go to London tomorrow.*
(197)   *Next year John will live in Moscow.*

However, this is not quite exact. There are a lot of cases in which the use of epistemic *will* does not really express the future tense of the accompanying verb. Consider

(198)   *She will be waiting outside now.*
(199)   *John will know the answer to this problem. Let's ask him.*
(200)   *In this moment, he will be reading my letter.*

The time location of (198)–(200) is the present. Note, further, that sentences (198)–(200) are also similar to the same sentences containing epistemic *must*:

(201)   *She must be waiting outside now.*
(202)   *John must know the answer. Let's ask him.*
(203)   *In this moment, he must be reading my letter.*

We could, therefore, characterize sentences (198)–(200) as inferences by the speaker concerning the state of affairs referred to by the sentences. On the

---

Z" is not some external event, but is something which is internal to the subject, its intrinsic properties. This would explain the subtle difference between *That building may be 30 stories high* and *That building can be 30 stories high* said of a building under construction. Note, however, that this second sentence cannot take the "sporadic" use suggested by Boyd and Thorne, i.e., cannot take the adverbial "sometimes."

other hand, sentences (196) and (197) are commonly called **predictions**. But a prediction is nothing more than an inference concerning a future state of affairs. We claim, therefore, that epistemic *will* has only this inferential sense. What distinguishes sentences (196)–(197) from (198)–(200) is the understood time location of the state of affairs referred to. This is not conveyed by the meaning of *will* (which is neutral with respect to this distinction), but by some other element of the sentence (a time adverbial, the use of the progressive form, etc.). In fact, there are sentences containing epistemic *will* which are ambiguous between the two senses, and the hearer understands them as inferences or predictions according to the time location he assigns to the state of affairs:

(204)   He will know the answer (a) try and ask him.
                                    (b) by the time he finishes the book.
(205)   She will be singing (a) now.
                         (b) when her mother arrives.

We will formalize the meaning of epistemic *will* as follows:

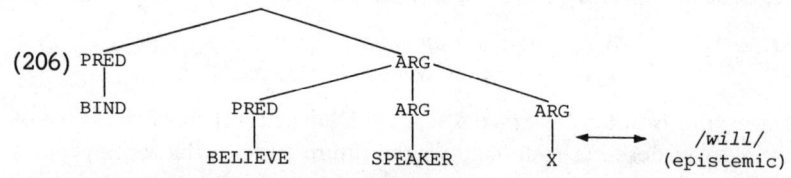

(206)
```
        PRED              ARG
         |              /     \
        BIND        PRED   ARG    ARG
                     |      |      |       ⟵⟶  /will/
                  BELIEVE SPEAKER   X         (epistemic)
```

This explains the already noted similarity between epistemic *will* and *must*, the only difference between them being the presence of an additional CAUSE predicate in the lexical representation of *must*.[6] Here below are the semantic representations underlying (204) and (205):

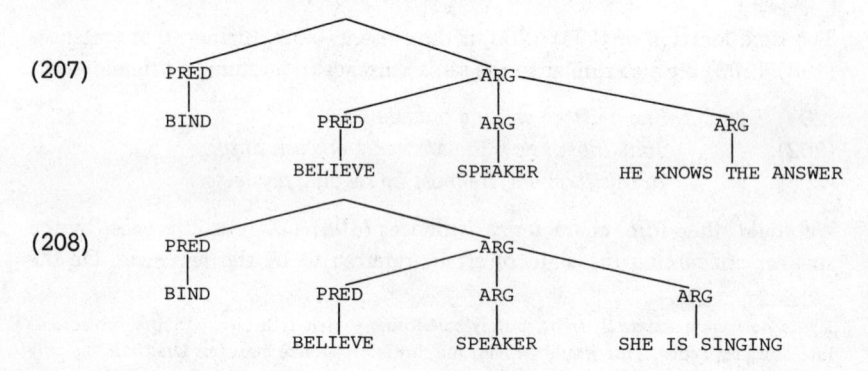

(207)
```
        PRED              ARG
         |              /     \
        BIND        PRED   ARG       ARG
                     |      |         |
                  BELIEVE SPEAKER   HE KNOWS THE ANSWER
```

(208)
```
        PRED              ARG
         |              /     \
        BIND        PRED   ARG       ARG
                     |      |         |
                  BELIEVE SPEAKER   SHE IS SINGING
```

[6] It seems to us that the difference between the use of *must* and the use of *will* in sentences (198)–(203) rests precisely in the suggestion that *must* always requires refer-

Besides its epistemic sense, *will* also has another sense, appearing in

(209)   You will go in the first car and John in the next one.

that are interpreted as requests or commands. Note that, under the request interpretation, (209) is closely related to (210), where deontic *must* appears:

(210)   You must go in the first car and John in the next one.

In both cases the modal verb expresses the existence of an obligation on the two subjects of the conjoined sentence. The difference between (209) and (210) is that the use of *will* uniquely identifies the speaker as the source of the obligation. As evidence for this, notice that a sentence such as

(211)   You must go in this car, but it is not me who is asking you to.

is perfectly acceptable, but

(212)   ?You will go in this car, but it is not me who is asking you to.

sounds somewhat strange and contradictory, if *will* is interpreted in its deontic sense. Therefore, for this reason, we will represent this particular sense of *will* as follows:

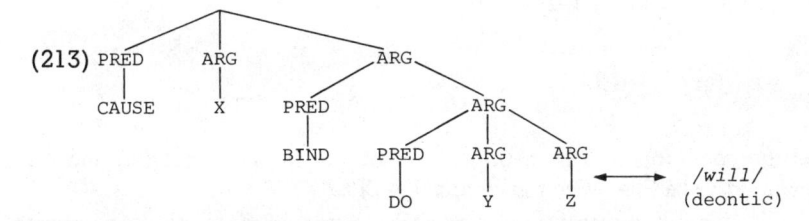

(213) PRED   ARG   ARG
        | |
       CAUSE X   PRED   ARG
                    |
                   BIND   PRED   ARG   ARG
                          | | | ⟶ /will/
                          DO   Y   Z   (deontic)

In addition, we will require that the subject of the sentence representing the causing event (the X variable) will always be the speaker himself. On the other hand, when the Y variable also is the speaker, as in

(214)   I will marry her.

we have what has been traditionally called the expression of an **intention**. That is the imposition of an obligation on the speaker by the speaker himself.

Our last topic is the modal verb *shall*. This verb has been traditionally associated with *will*, but it is quite difficult to work out a precise analysis of it, since most native speakers of English do not use it anymore. Consider sentences

---

ence to some causal event, while this is not true of simple sentences containing epistemic *will*. However, we have not succeeded in finding convincing evidence for this point.

(215)   *You shall have the answer right now.*
(216)   *He shall go.*

It is commonly asserted that *shall* in such a context is a "promissory emphatic." Boyd and Thorne (1969) explain its meaning by means of the following paraphrases: "I guarantee his going; I make myself responsible to bring about his going; I commit myself to bring about his going." It is clear that *shall*, like the deontic *will*, identifies the speaker as the source of the obligation. But while in sentences with deontic *will* the obligation is understood as being on the surface subject of the sentence, here it seems that, regardless of the surface subject of the sentence, the obligation is undertaken by the speaker himself. That is, we would say that *shall* communicates that the speaker is binding himself to do something whose result is the state of affairs described by the sentence. Once again, we can formalize this idea conveyed by the meaning of *shall* in terms of the semantic representation we set up for deontic *will*:

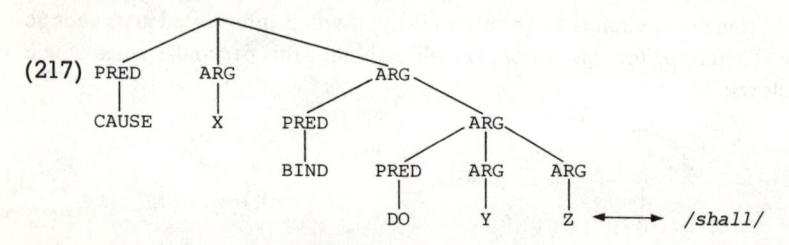

(217)
```
         PRED   ARG           ARG
          |      |              |
        CAUSE    X     PRED    ARG
                       |        |
                     BIND    PRED  ARG  ARG
                              |     |    |
                             DO     Y    Z  ⟷ /shall/
```

plus the condition that both the subject of the causing event (X) and the argument (Y) be filled with the component SPEAKER.

So far our semantic analyses have been applied primarily to those English lexical items which are verbs. But, as we have stated several times, the way in which we analyze the meanings of words should always be the same, regardless of the traditional grammatical category to which those words belong. We have already furnished representations for words such as *because*, which is classed as a conjunction, and to words like *not*. Now we would like to attempt an analysis of the meanings of other kinds of words, defined by the traditional grammar as prepositions, conjunctions, adverbs, etc. Consider, for example, the preposition *at* in the sentences

(218)   *Frank sleeps at the Regency Hotel.*
(219)   *Frank fainted at five o'clock.*

Sentence (218) tells us that the place where the event *Frank sleeps* occurs is *the Regency Hotel*, while (219) tells us that the time at which the event

Componential Analysis

Frank fainted took place was *five o'clock*. To represent the relation that *at* establishes between *Frank sleeps* and *the Regency Hotel*, and between *Frank fainted* and *five o'clock*, we can use a semantic component that was introduced earlier and used several times: COINCIDE. The preposition *at* expresses the simple predicate COINCIDE; whether that coincidence is **spatial**, as in (218), or **temporal**, as in (219), depends on the nature of the lexical items that are connected by *at*. Thus, the lexical representation for *at* will be

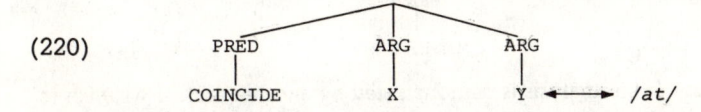

(220)
```
           PRED        ARG         ARG
            |                       
         COINCIDE       X           Y  ←→  /at/
```

and sentences (218) and (219) will have the respective representations

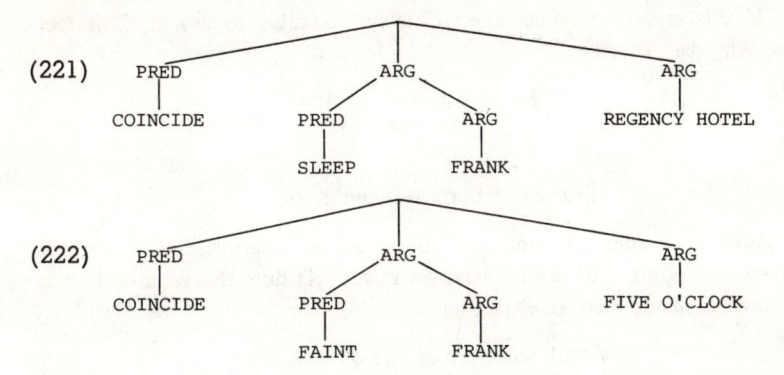

(221)
```
        PRED              ARG                    ARG
         |                                        |
      COINCIDE      PRED        ARG         REGENCY HOTEL
                    |            |
                  SLEEP        FRANK
```

(222)
```
        PRED              ARG                    ARG
         |                                        |
      COINCIDE      PRED        ARG          FIVE O'CLOCK
                    |            |
                  FAINT        FRANK
```

Another preposition with a meaning as abstract as *at* is *in*. Consider these two sentences:

(223)   *Frank sleeps in the living room.*
(224)   *Frank was born in April.*

In these sentences *in* carries out the same function as *at*, telling us the place in which the event *Frank sleeps* occurs (223), and the time at which the event *Frank was born* took place (224). Therefore, we can assign to *in* the same component assigned to *at*, the component COINCIDE. But how can we distinguish *at* from *in*? Consider these two sentences:

(225)   *Frank is at the airport.*
(226)   *Frank is in the airport.*

Both *at the airport* and *in the airport* tell us the place where Frank can be found. But the first sentence is indifferent with respect to the particular point of the airport where Frank is (for example, he could be in the parking lot near the terminal, or on the highway nearby), while the second sentence tells us that Frank is necessarily inside the place. Hence, we will give to *in* the following representation:

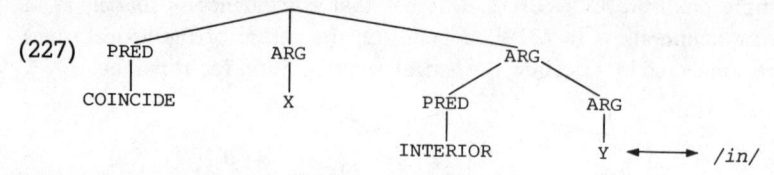

(227)
```
        PRED         ARG              ARG
         |            |               / \
       COINCIDE       X            PRED  ARG
                                    |     |
                                 INTERIOR Y ←→ /in/
```

The correctness of this analysis is demonstrated by another fact. If we wish to establish a coincidence between one object and the inside of another, it is evident that the second object must be one that can be conceived as having an inside. If this is not possible, then it is not possible to use *in*. This fact explains why we can have

(228)   *Frank was born in April.*

but not

(229)   **Frank was born in five o'clock.*

While *April* is a span of time, and thus has an interior, five o'clock is conceived as a point, and cannot have an inside. *At* does not require that an object have an inside, and so we can have

(230)   *Frank was born at five o'clock.*

There are other words that provide similar limits to the kinds of objects that can take a given relation. We have seen how *in* requires that the object Y have an inside. The same can be said of *during*, given that sentence (228) can be paraphrased with

(231)   *Frank was born during April.*

while the sentence

(232)   **Frank was born during five o'clock.*

is as unacceptable as (229). And so to *during* we can assign the following lexical representation:

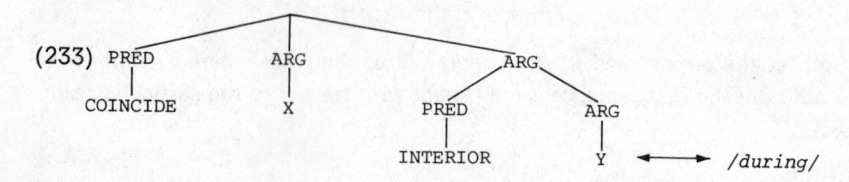

(233)
```
        PRED         ARG              ARG
         |            |               / \
       COINCIDE       X            PRED  ARG
                                    |     |
                                 INTERIOR Y ←→ /during/
```

Componential Analysis 81

However *during*, in contrast with *in*, can only be used to express a time relation. We cannot have, to correspond with (223), the sentence

(234) **Frank sleeps during the living room.*

Thus there is a constraint that the semantic material which occupies the argument Y in (233) must contain the semantic component TIME.

In traditional grammar *during*, *at*, and *in* are prepositions. In our model, this means that the second argument is either a noun or a nominalization,[7] but not an explicit subordinate. If the nominal is an explicit subordinate, *during* cannot be used. For example, we cannot say

(235) **Frank slept during John played.*

In such instances, we must instead say

(236) *Frank slept while John played.*

During and *while* seem, then, to have the same meaning, and so the same lexical representation (233), with the single difference that *during* is selected when the second argument Y is a noun or a nominalization, whereas *while* is selected when the second argument Y is an explicit subordinate clause.

Another word which seems to have the same meaning as *during* and *while*, differing only with regard to the nature of the second argument Y, is *meanwhile*. Consider the sentence

(237) *Meanwhile, Frank was sleeping.*

This sentence cannot be fully interpreted outside of some linguistic context. Consider instead the following unit of discourse:

(238) *John was playing, and meanwhile Frank slept.*

In this case the second sentence is fully interpretable and has more or less the same meaning as (236). We suggest that *meanwhile* has the same meaning as *while* and *during*, and so the same lexical representation, except that the listener, in order to find the second argument of *meanwhile*, must go outside the sentence containing *meanwhile* and seek the argument Y in some preceding bit of discourse. Such use of the context to communicate meanings is common in language and will be examined further in Chapter 8.

We have seen a case in which three different words, classified by the traditional grammar as a preposition, a conjunction, and an adverb, respectively, share the same meaning. They differ only with respect to the type of nominal contained in the second argument. An analogous case is the word *before*, which has the same meaning in these three sentences:

---

[7] For the concepts **noun** and **nominalization**, see the following chapter.

(239)   Frank arrived *before five o'clock.*
(240)   Frank arrived *before my uncle left.*
(241)   Frank arrived *before.*

Yet traditionally, *before* is a preposition in (239), a conjunction in (240), and an adverb in (241). In fact, *before* has only one lexical representation, which we can represent as

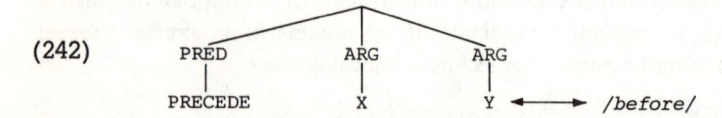

(242)
```
           PRED        ARG        ARG
            |           |          |
          PRECEDE       X          Y  ←——→  /before/
```

with the further condition that X and Y must each contain the component TIME. The difference among the three uses of *before* in (239)–(241) are due to the fact that *before* is followed by a noun in (239) and by an explicit subordinate clause in (240), whereas in (241) the second argument must be sought in the context, as is the case for *meanwhile* in the preceding example.

In this chapter we have presented two hypotheses regarding the meaning of words. The first is that such meanings can be analyzed into components, that is elementary mental operations used recurrently in the meanings of different words. The second is that these components are elementary predicates with one or more arguments, so that the representation of the meaning of sentences is homogeneous with the representation of the meanings of words. We illustrated this approach with the analysis of the meanings of a certain number of words, analyses which, we feel, demonstrate both the overall plausibility of the approach and its ability to capture systematic relations existing among different words, and between the level of words and the level of sentence meaning. Obviously, componential analysis (as illustrated in this chapter) must be expanded and, above all, verified before it can be accepted as a satisfactory model of word meanings. Research must be aimed at identifying what is presumably a finite set of elementary components. These components in turn should prove to have a certain universality—that is, they should be useful for the analysis of lexical material in any human language.

It should also be possible to find the origin and development of these components in the cognitive activity of man. Above all, the approach referred to here as componential analysis should be extendable to all areas of the lexicon. It may seem, with regard to this last point, that the application of componential analysis to the area traditionally called nouns will pose particular problems. Indeed, it is no accident that the illustrations presented

Componential Analysis

in this chapter are primarily componential analyses of verbs, prepositions, adverbs, etc., rather than nouns. Initially, it may well be that the large class of nouns will pose particular problems for analysis. But there is no reason to conclude a priori that such efforts are doomed.

Before closing this chapter dedicated to word meanings, we should mention another aspect of this discussion which, while not yet well defined, may prove to be especially important for any complete and adequate model of language. For each lexical item, we have thus far sought to represent its meaning with a configuration of semantic components. But in addition to this type of meaning, which we will call **lexical meaning,** there is another type of information available for virtually all words. All lexical items are to some extent connected with areas of knowledge in the speaker's mind, knowledge that is related to the meaning of a particular word but does not actually make up part of the lexical meaning of that word. We will call this second aspect of the meaning of lexical items the **encyclopedia.** What is the difference between lexical meaning and encyclopedic knowledge connected with a given lexical item? The lexical meaning is knowledge that is indispensable to the existence of that lexical item, in the absence of which the sound connected with that lexical item becomes a simple sound, without meaning. Thus, lexical meaning is present inherently and necessarily in all uses of that word.[8] The encyclopedia consists instead of bits of knowledge that the speaker adds to a lexical item which is already defined by a sound and a lexical representation. The encyclopedia may be called into play in some uses and not in others, and only parts of it may be called up in other instances. The lexical meaning of words tends to be the same between any two native speakers, while the encyclopedia may vary greatly. If the lexical meaning of a word is not substantially the same, communication quickly misfires, whereas if the encyclopedia varies there is still an ample margin of communication.

Let us look at a few examples. To know that the automobile is a means of transportation is to know the lexical meaning of the word *automobile*. But to know that automobiles also run on gasoline is part of the encyclopedia connected with the word *automobile*. It is for this reason that the sentence

(243) **This is an automobile, but it is not a means of transportation.*

has very little sense (except as a humorous remark). But the sentence

---

[8] This assertion does not contradict the existence, within the lexical meaning of a word, of optional components (see text). In fact, such optional components become obligatory in certain contexts, a condition which never holds on the knowledge that makes up the encyclopedia connected with the lexicon.

(244)   *This is an automobile, but it does not run on gasoline.*

may be quite acceptable.

On the other hand, the encyclopedia can have a systematic role in the interpretation of sentences. Take the example

(245) *The City Council refused a parade permit to the student organization because they are radicals.*

Most American speakers of English have no trouble interpreting the antecedent of *they* in (245), because of encyclopedic information that students are more likely to be radical than city council members. Similarly, in the sentence

(246)   *John is writing a book on an old typewriter.*

there are two possible interpretations. One is that John is writing a book using an old typewriter as a writing instrument. The other interpretation—far less likely—is that John is writing a book about an old typewriter. Encyclopedic knowledge tells us immediately that the second interpretation is far less probable than the first. As a further illustration, take the example

(247)   *John goes to New York for a conference some time in 1980.*

Although the verb *goes* is expressed in the present tense, it is interpreted for encyclopedic reasons as a prediction about the future (given, of course, that the sentence is uttered some time prior to 1980). However, in the sentence

(248)   *Columbus goes to see Queen Isabella some time in 1488.*

the verb *goes* is interpreted as a narrative use of the present tense, a way of talking about events that have clearly occurred in the past. The information that permits these two different interpretations of *goes* is not in the sentence itself, but rather in the speaker's knowledge about the time of utterance versus the time mentioned in the sentence. For the same reasons, the sentence

(249)   *Columbus goes to see Queen Isabella some time in 1974.*

would be unacceptable to most listeners with any knowledge of Western history.

We have seen, then, that lexical items, in addition to their lexical meaning, have an encyclopedia that enters systematically into the use of language, in both speaking and understanding. Indeed, one might say that communication takes place on the basis of this store of knowledge, which we call an encyclopedia, and that often the understanding of a sentence consists in successfully inserting that sentence into our encyclopedia. With regard to the formal representation that we would suggest for the encyclopedia—in other words, the proper means for inserting the encyclopedia into our semantic model—we feel that the units of knowledge that make up the encyclopedia might also be represented as configurations of semantic components. Such an organization would, if it proves to fit the data, provide for smooth integration between lexical and encyclopedic knowledge in the production and understanding of sentences. Nevertheless, there are a great many problems that remain regarding both the formal representation of encyclopedic knowledge, and the function of the encyclopedia in linguistic communication. Such problems will clearly require much more research.

Nominals 5

In the preceding chapter we have, in a sense, placed the semantic representations of sentences under a microscope, to see their finer structure. In fact, we defined componential analysis as the break down of sentence meaning into its smallest elements. In this chapter, we will return again to the more macroscopic level of nucleus and adverbial, without examining the semantic components within these larger units. This means that we are returning to the level of predication, the level at which elementary predicates have already been grouped into configurations that correspond to lexical items.

Like the chapters on the nucleus and the adverbial, this chapter pursues an analysis of the mechanisms of sentence formation. As we know, all sentences consist of an obligatory nucleus, made up of a predication with its arguments, and possibly one or more optional adverbials, i.e., added predications that take the nucleus as one of their arguments. Up to this point we have looked primarily at predications, either nuclear or adverbial, without considering the proper representation for arguments. We have managed to avoid that problem by using proper names and other simple expressions as arguments, giving the impression that these present few problems for representation. This approach is consistent with our strategy of proceeding from simple to more complex sentences. But at this point we must stress that both nuclear and adverbial arguments can also be extremely complex. In addition to such sentences as

(1)   Mary put the sweater in the living room.
(2)   Mary knit the sweater in the living room.

represented as

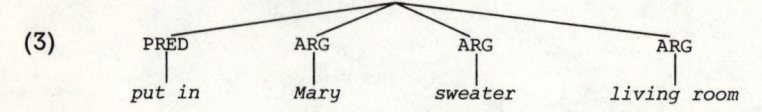

(3)
```
        PRED      ARG      ARG        ARG
         |         |        |          |
       put in    Mary    sweater   living room
```

Nominals

(4) 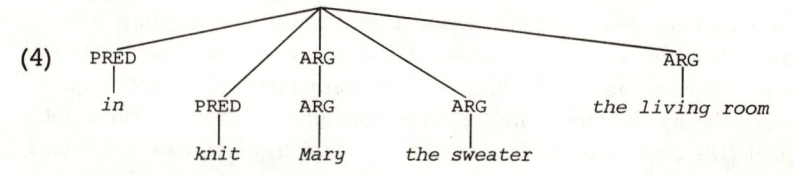
```
     PRED ——————— ARG ——————————————— ARG
      |         /  |  \                |
      in    PRED  ARG  ARG      the living room
             |    |    |
            knit Mary the sweater
```

we also find sentences such as

(5) *I read that fantastic book that my brother gave me.*
(6) *Frank's insistence on the proposal to hold the meeting immediately surprised everyone.*

To these last sentences, we can provisionally offer the following representations:

(7)
```
   PRED    ARG         ARG
    |       |          /△\
   read     I      that fantastic book which
                    my brother gave me
```

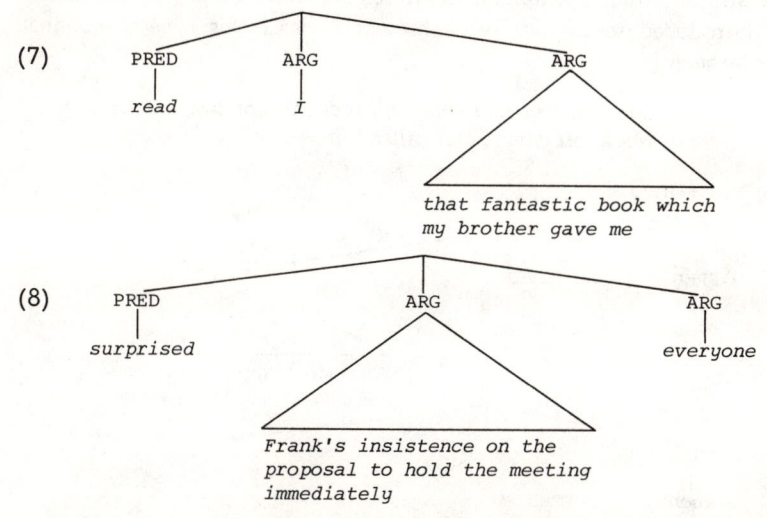

(8)
```
   PRED ——————————— ARG ———————————— ARG
    |               /△\               |
 surprised  Frank's insistence on the everyone
            proposal to hold the meeting
            immediately
```

It is obvious that *that fantastic book that my brother gave me* and *Frank's insistence on the proposal to hold the meeting immediately* are arguments of their respective predications, *read* and *surprised*. However, it is equally obvious that with the mechanisms introduced so far, we cannot analyze the internal structure of these more complex arguments. In the provisional representations (7) and (8), we placed triangles over complex arguments, a convention indicating that these are arguments with an internal articulation (represented by the triangle) which has not yet been analyzed. This chapter is devoted to a representation of the internal structure of such arguments.

Before continuing, we want to introduce a new term. As we shall see, this term does not designate a new construct, but instead sanctions an already existing analysis. We noted that the adverbial is a predication which takes the nucleus as one of its arguments. So, for any complex argument which is also a nucleus, we know what sort of representation to give. To all arguments in the representation of a sentence **except** the nucleus, we will give the name **nominals**. The nucleus itself will have a set of arguments which are nominals. An adverbial by definition must have at least one argument which is not a nominal (the nucleus). But if an adverbial has other, nonnuclear arguments, then those arguments are also nominals. In this chapter, then, our problem is how to represent nominals.

We just stated that the mechanisms available to us so far do not permit us to represent nominals, particularly the more complex ones such as those in (7) and (8). Actually, this is not completely true. Recall that in the chapters on both the nucleus and the adverbial, we did provide analyses for nuclear and adverbial subordinate clauses. Subordinates were treated simply as arguments with an internal sentential structure. This means that with the mechanisms introduced so far, we can represent at least this type of nominal. Sentences such as

(9)   *Frank hopes that John will speak tomorrow.*
(10) *Mark left when Peter called him.*

can be represented as

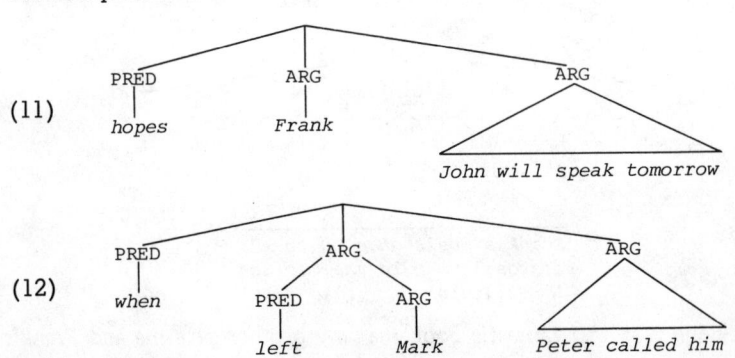

(11)
```
     PRED         ARG         ARG
      |            |
     hopes       Frank    John will speak tomorrow
```

(12)
```
     PRED              ARG                    ARG
      |              /     \
     when         PRED     ARG         Peter called him
                   |        |
                  left     Mark
```

Both *Frank* and *John will speak tomorrow* are nominals in (9); both *Mark* and *Peter called him* are nominals in (10). Of these four nominals, *John will speak tomorrow* and *Peter called him* are complex, in the sense that they have an internal structure, like the nominals in (7) and (8). Nevertheless, we do know how to represent all the nominals in (9) and (10), as follows:

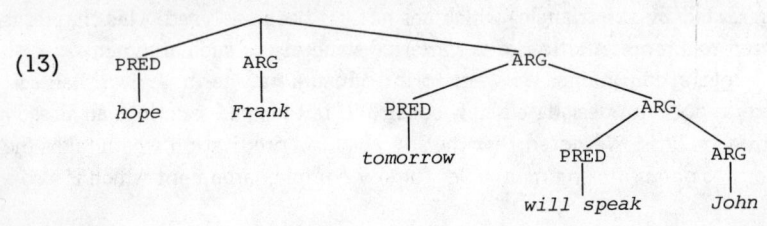

(13)
```
      PRED    ARG          ARG
       |      |
      hope  Frank     PRED        ARG
                      |          / \
                    tomorrow   PRED  ARG
                                |     |
                            will speak John
```

Nominals 89

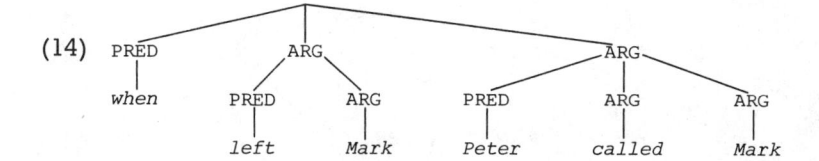

(14)
```
        PRED ─── ARG ──────────── ARG
         │       │                 │
        when  PRED─ARG      PRED─ARG─ARG
              │    │         │    │   │
             left Mark     Peter called Mark
```

All the complex nominals in (9) and (10) are explicit subordinates, in that the predicate is expressed as a verb in the finite mood. Analogously, we know how to treat those nominals which are implicit subordinates, in which the predicate is expressed with an infinitive verb. Thus for sentences such as:

(15) *George was afraid to arrive late.*
(16) *Roger returned to Toledo in order to meet Clare in the afternoon.*

we are not restricted to the representations

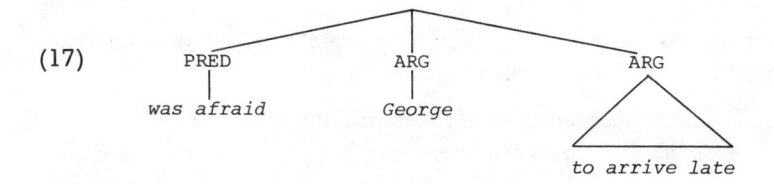

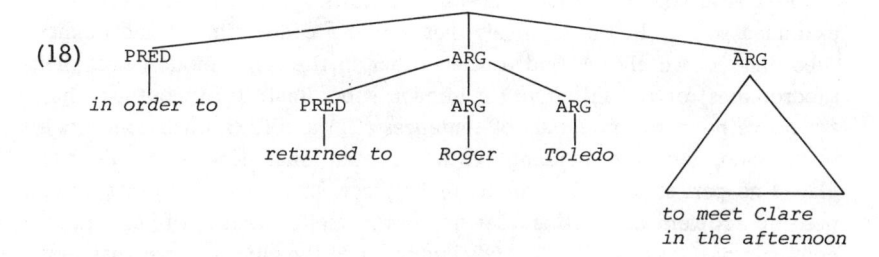

(17)
```
      PRED        ARG          ARG
       │           │            △
   was afraid   George     to arrive late
```

(18)
```
      PRED              ARG                ARG
       │         ┌───────┼───────┐          △
   in order to  PRED    ARG     ARG    to meet Clare
                 │       │       │     in the afternoon
            returned to Roger  Toledo
```

Instead, we can offer the more detailed representations

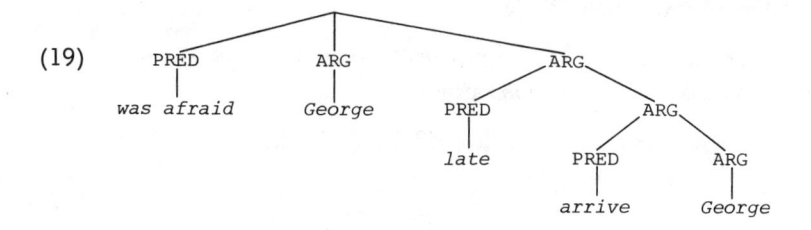

(19)
```
      PRED       ARG          ARG
       │          │     ┌──────┴──────┐
   was afraid  George  PRED          ARG
                        │       ┌─────┴─────┐
                       late    PRED        ARG
                                │           │
                              arrive      George
```

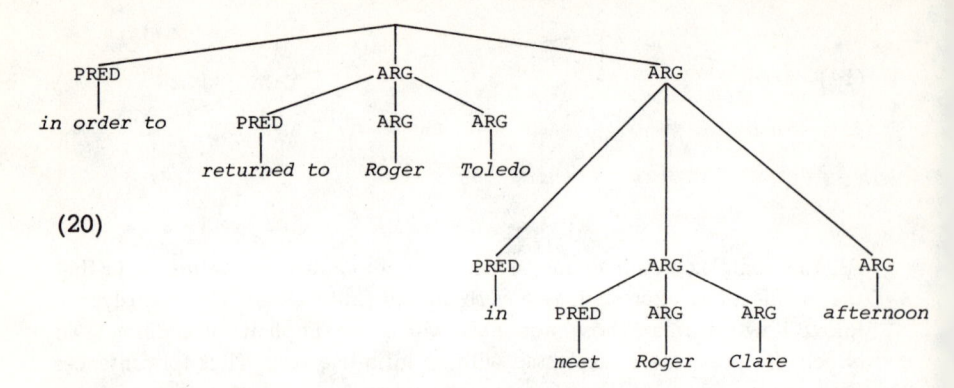

```
                    PRED          ARG                    ARG
                 in order to   PRED    ARG   ARG
                              returned to Roger Toledo
(20)
                                        PRED      ARG           ARG
                                         in    PRED  ARG  ARG  afternoon
                                              meet Roger Clare
```

We can, then, with the concepts already available, represent a few very complex nominals. In particular, we can represent nominals consisting of a sentential structure, i.e., a nucleus and optional adverbials, which is used within a sentence as an argument of either a nucleus or an adverbial. This includes both explicit and implicit nuclear and adverbial subordinates. Therefore, this entire class of nominals presents no problems of representation for us.

Let us now see if the same kind of representation can be extended to other nominals. Consider the following sentences:

(21)   *The engineer announced the completion of the bridge.*
(22)   *John's arrival surprised me.*

In these sentences we have two nominals, *the completion of the bridge* and *John's arrival* which, at first glance, appear to be quite different from those examined so far. In the nominals that we have called explicit and implicit subordinates, we always find a verb—either in the finite mode (in explicit subordinates) or the infinitive (in implicit subordinates). By contrast, there are no verbs in the nominals of sentences (21) and (22). Such concepts as verb, noun, etc.—the building blocks of traditional parsing models—have played no part so far in our model of language. Thus these categories should pose no problem here either. Let us see if, despite the lack of verbs in the nominals of (21) and (22), it is possible to apply the same analyses that work for other nominals in (9), (10), (15), and (16). Some support for this extension rests in the fact that sentences (21) and (22) can be paraphrased by the following two sentences:

(23)   *The engineer announced that the bridge had been completed.*
(24)   *It surprised me that John arrived.*

In these paraphrases, the nominals of (21) and (22) take on the same form as

Nominals

the nominals analyzed previously as nuclear subordinates. Therefore, to sentences (21) and (22) as well we will give the following representations:

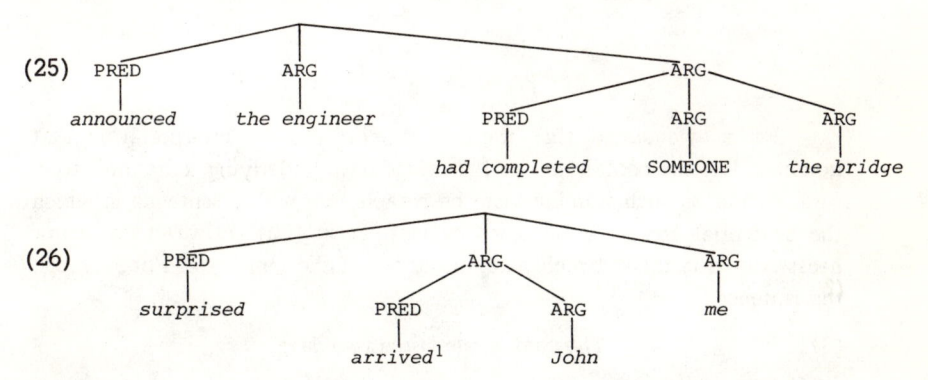

(25)
```
         PRED        ARG                    ARG
          |           |              _____|_____
       announced  the engineer      PRED   ARG      ARG
                                     |      |        |
                                 had completed SOMEONE the bridge
```

(26)
```
         PRED              ARG            ARG
          |          _____|_____        |
       surprised   PRED         ARG        me
                    |            |
                 arrived¹       John
```

In (25) we represent the first argument of *completed* with the component SOMEONE, which is simply a way of saying that this argument is unspecified and hence cannot be expressed. Contrast (20) with the sentence

(27)   *The engineer announced the completion of the bridge by the workers.*

which has a representation identical to (25), with one single difference: The first argument of *completed* is now *the workers*.

In any case, it frequently happens that with this type of nominal one or more of the arguments is unspecified and therefore is not expressed. Such expressions often create a certain ambiguity, resolvable only by referring to the context. For example, the sentence

(28)   *John's pardon surprised everyone.*

is ambiguous, because it can mean that John pardoned someone (which surprised everyone) or that John had been pardoned by someone (which surprised everyone). In the first case (28) is represented as

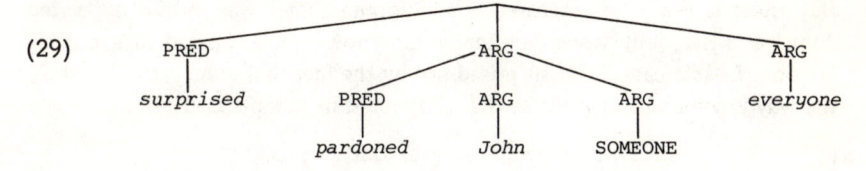

(29)
```
        PRED                 ARG                   ARG
         |           _____|_____            |
      surprised    PRED    ARG      ARG         everyone
                    |       |        |
                 pardoned  John   SOMEONE
```

In the second interpretation, (28) is represented as

---

[1] Actually, as we noted in Chapter 4, *arrived* is a two-place predicate, in which the second argument is the place to which the first argument arrived.

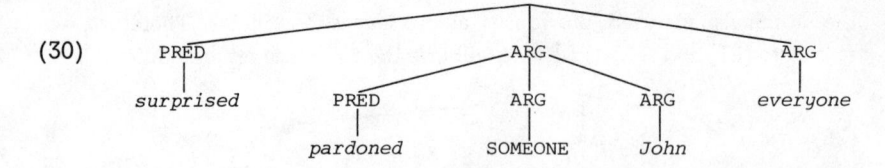

(30)
```
          PRED              ARG                          ARG
           |        ┌────────┼────────┐                   |
       surprised  PRED      ARG      ARG               everyone
                   |         |        |
                pardoned  SOMEONE    John
```

Earlier we stated that there is support for the interpretation that nominals like *the completion of the bridge* have underlying sentential structure, insofar as such nominals can be paraphrased with a sentence in which the sentential structure becomes evident, as in (23). However, it is not necessarily true that all such paraphrases are of the same type. For example, the sentence

(31)   *The cookie sale lasted two days.*

cannot be paraphrased as

(32)   *That someone sold the cookies lasted two days.*

A better paraphrase would be

(33)   *The activity of selling the cookies lasted two days.*

It is also possible for the same nominal to have more than one paraphrase, each with a different meaning. Hence the sentence

(34)   *John's arrival surprised me.*

is ambiguous. In one interpretation, I was surprised by the fact that John arrived, i.e.,

(35)   *It surprised me that John arrived.*

or

(36)   *The fact that John arrived surprised me.*

But there is a second interpretation. Suppose that I was indeed expecting John to arrive, but when he finally did show up, he landed in a hot air balloon. In this case, I am surprised not by the fact that John arrived, but by the way in which he arrived. So that (34) could be paraphrased by

(37)   *The way in which John arrived surprised me.*

Finally, there can be other nominals, of the type we have been considering here, for which it is difficult to find any paraphrase that would make the underlying sentential structure explicit. But it should be clear by now

Nominals

that the availability of a sentential paraphrase is not a necessary condition for attributing an underlying sentential representation to such nominals. An acceptable paraphrase may not exist for a variety of reasons, yet it may still be true that the nominal is made up of pieces that can be analyzed as a predicate with arguments and optional adverbials.

We have seen some nominals with an underlying predicate that can be expressed as a verb. There are also nominals, similar to those considered so far, whose underlying predicate can be expressed as an adjective. For example,

(38)   *Charlie's illness worries me.*
(39)   *Everyone notices Clyde's homeliness.*

have these representations:

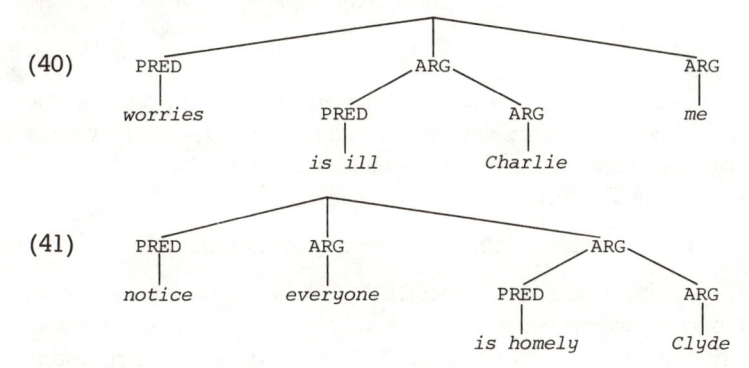

(40)
```
        PRED              ARG                ARG
         |              /      \              |
       worries       PRED      ARG           me
                     |          |
                   is ill    Charlie
```

(41)
```
      PRED      ARG              ARG
       |         |             /     \
     notice   everyone       PRED    ARG
                              |       |
                          is homely  Clyde
```

With this type of nominal as well, the mechanism of recursion which we have seen at work in the chapters on nuclei and adverbials, permits us to construct nominals of increasing complexity. Consider the two sentences

(42)   *A soldier repeated the announcement that Caesar had won.*
(43)   *John accepted the proposal to hold the meeting immediately.*

and in particular, the two nominals *the announcement that Caesar had won* and *the proposal to hold the meeting immediately*. In (42) we have a sentential structure *Caesar had won* inserted as an argument of another sentential structure *someone announced that Caesar had won*, which is in turn inserted as an argument of a third sentential structure, i.e., the whole of sentence (42). In (43) we have the same situation, with the single difference that the first sentential structure *someone holds the meeting immediately* appears on the surface with an infinitive verb, like an implicit subordinate. Hence, (42) and (43) can be represented as

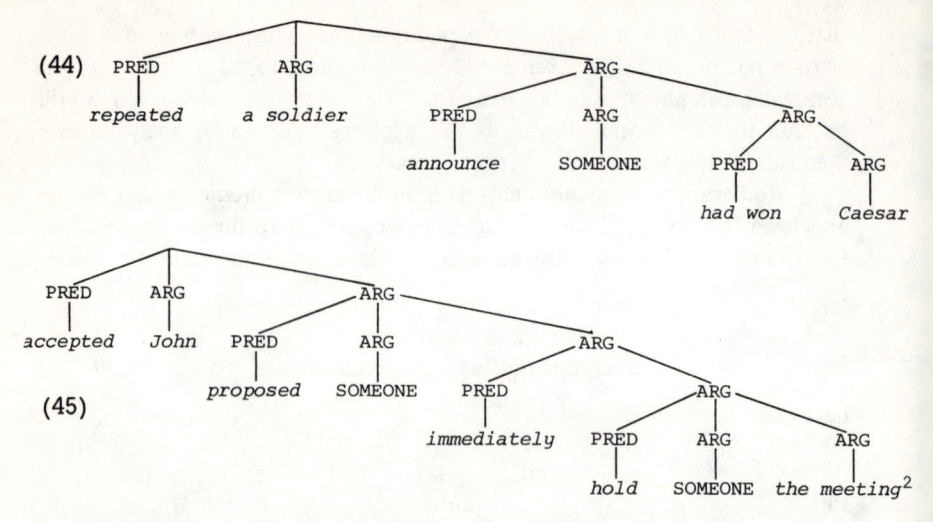

(44)
```
         PRED        ARG              ARG
          |           |                
       repeated   a soldier      PRED    ARG         ARG
                                  |       |
                               announce SOMEONE  PRED    ARG
                                                  |       |
                                               had won  Caesar
```

(45)
```
    PRED     ARG          ARG
     |        |
  accepted  John      PRED   ARG      ARG
                       |      |
                    proposed SOMEONE PRED        ARG
                                       |
                                   immediately  PRED   ARG     ARG
                                                 |      |
                                                hold SOMEONE the meeting²
```

In sentences (42) and (43), the lowest sentential structure appears on the surface as a subordinate object of *announce* and *propose* respectively. We can also find complex nominals in which the underlying sentential structure is a subject subordinate. For example, in the sentence

(46)   *The team exploited the advantage of playing at home.*

we have a sentential structure SOMEONE *plays at home* inserted as an argument of a second sentential structure, *to play at home is an advantage*. This last structure is in turn an argument of the sentential structure consisting of the whole sentence, (46). Sentence (46) has, then, the representation

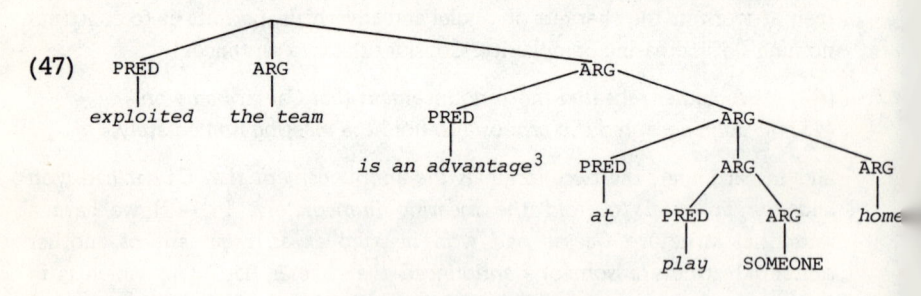

(47)
```
      PRED      ARG              ARG
       |         |
   exploited  the team    PRED             ARG
                           |
                      is an advantage³  PRED    ARG        ARG
                                         |
                                        at   PRED   ARG   home
                                              |      |
                                             play SOMEONE
```

---

[2] *Meeting* might also be analyzed as a nominal, with the underlying sentential structure SOMEONE *meets*.

[3] As with the nominal *meeting*, *advantage* could be analyzed as a nominal with the underlying predication *to advantage*.

Nominals 95

At this point it is useful to stop a moment, to see how far we have come in filling the objective prescribed for this chapter. We wanted to furnish representations for nominals, i.e., to all arguments of either the nucleus or the adverbial, except for that argument of the adverbial which is itself the nucleus of a sentence. We stated that the concepts introduced so far were sufficient to represent a good many of these nominals. In fact, all of the nominals examined so far have an underlying sentential structure, that is, a nucleus (a predication with its arguments) and optional adverbials (other predications that take the nucleus as one of their arguments). To all these nominals that share the feature of apparent derivation from sentential structures, we will apply the term **nominalization**.

But it is possible to have nominals that are not nominalizations, i.e., that are not derived from underlying sentential structures. Consider the sentence

(48) John's dog is running.

Until now we would have given (48) the representation

(49)
```
          PRED           ARG
           |              |
       is running      John's dog
```

We cannot find the same sort of sentential structure underneath *John's dog* that underlies the preceding nominals. There is no underlying structure of which *John* is an argument and *dog* is the predicate, nor could we suggest that *John* is the predicate and *dog* an argument. Our problem at this point is to devise a representation for nominals which are not nominalizations. To distinguish these from the preceding nominalizations, we will call them **pure nominals**.

Take the sentence

(50) I read the book that Mark gave me.

In (50) we have a predication *read* with two arguments, *I* and *the book that Mark gave me*. So that (50) will at least have the following representation:

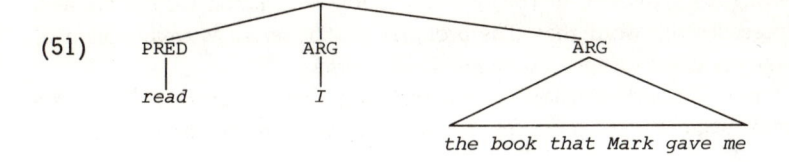

(51)
```
    PRED      ARG              ARG
     |         |                |
    read       I       the book that Mark gave me
```

Our problem is to represent in a more analytic way the nominal

(52) the book that Mark gave me

At first this nominal appears similar to

(53) the announcement that Caesar had won

i.e., to a nominalization. But a brief reflection should convince us that *the book that Mark gave me* is not a nominalization, and cannot be represented in the same way as (53). While *that Caesar had won* is an argument of the underlying predicate *announce*, it is not possible to find under *book* a predication of which *that Mark gave me* is an argument. This is the first difference between nominalizations like (53) and a pure nominal like (52). There is a second difference. Let us return to the two expressions that follow the word *that: Caesar had won* and *Mark gave me*. In the first expression, we have a predication *had won* with its single argument *Caesar*. In the second we have a predication *gave* which requires three arguments: a giver, a receiver, and something given. In *Mark gave me* only the first argument *Mark* and the second argument *me* are expressed, while the third argument is not expressed. Looking closely, however, we still know what the third argument of *gave* is. It is *the book*, the noun preceding the word *that*. This is a fixed rule for the nominals that we are now considering: The expression following *that* is a sentential structure in which one of the arguments is not expressed, but is identical with the noun preceding *that*. This sort of relationship doesn't occur with nominalizations like (53), even though they do externally resemble nominals like (52).

The difference between these two types of nominals becomes clearer in the following two sentences:

(54) *The proposal that we go to Toledo was accepted by everyone.*
(55) *The proposal that we overheard was accepted by everyone.*

In (54), the phrase following *that* is clearly an argument of the predication underlying *the proposal*. In fact, it expresses the content of that proposal, i.e., that which someone proposed. Things are quite different for the phrase following *the proposal* in (55). The expression *that we overheard* is not an argument of *proposal* (in fact, the content of the proposal is unspecified in sentence (55)). Instead, in (55) we find a double function for the nominal that precedes the word *that*. *The proposal* in (55) serves as an argument of both the predicate *accept* and the predicate *overhear*.

The relationship between *proposal* and *that we overheard* is quite different from the relationships presented so far. The sentential structure

Nominals

following the word *that* is not an argument of the predicate underlying the nominalized expression *proposal*. But even though it is clear that some kind of systematic relationship exists in (55), how is it possible to tie the expressions *proposal* and *that we overheard* together? The simple predicate-argument structures that have sufficed so far are no longer adequate. To represent the complex relationship present in (55), we need a new kind of mechanism, one that, in essence, goes outside the sentence configuration. Our proposal for representing a sentence like (55) is the following:

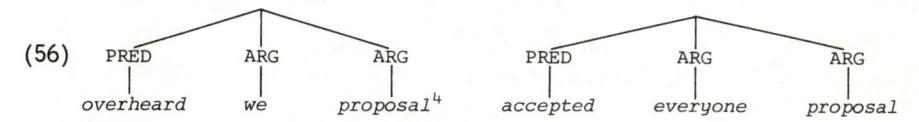

(56)
```
        PRED      ARG      ARG           PRED       ARG       ARG
         |         |        |             |          |         |
      overheard   we    proposal⁴      accepted   everyone  proposal
```

In other words, the representation of the meaning of sentence (55) consists of two configurations: a main configuration (on the right in (56)) and an associated configuration (on the left in (56)). The second configuration is associated in the sense that it is part of the nominal of the first configuration. The relationship between the portion of the nominal that remains within the main configuration (*proposal*) and the portion that is represented outside, in the associated configuration (*we overheard proposal*) consists in the fact that one of the arguments of the associated configuration is identical to an argument remaining within the main configuration—in this case, *proposal*.

The part of the nominal which is "outside," in the associated configuration, is an optional part of the meaning of that nominal. In other words, it can be entirely absent, but the main sentence will nevertheless be complete. But the other part of the nominal, the part remaining within the main configuration, is obligatory. If it were missing, the sentence would be incomplete. In contrast to these nominals, the matter is quite different for nominalizations. In a nominalization, the expression following the word *that* is never optional. It is, instead, an argument of the nominalized predication, and is indispensable for the completion of the sentence—even though it can remain unspecified and therefore unexpressed in sounds.

The notion of associated configuration proves to be very powerful. Consider these two sentences:

(57)   *We crossed a corridor that was narrow.*
(58)   *We crossed a narrow corridor.*

To the first sentence, we can give the representation

---

[4] For reasons that will become clear shortly, we will begin to omit the articles from the representation of nominals.

(59)

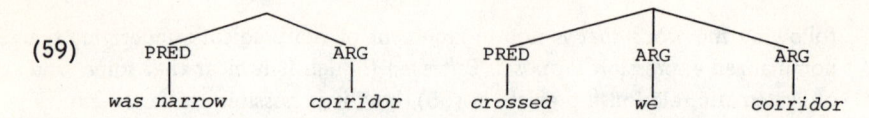

```
     PRED        ARG           PRED        ARG      ARG
      |           |              |          |        |
  was narrow   corridor       crossed      we    corridor
```

But given the fact that (58) is a paraphrase of (57), we could give it the same representation, (59). The difference is that in (58), there is no expression *that*, and the finite verb indicator (in this case, the copula *was*) has disappeared.

With the mechanism of associated configurations, the sentences

(60)   I saw a man identical to Mark.
(61)   I was looking at the book on the table.
(62)   The ticket for Claude is ready.

can be represented as

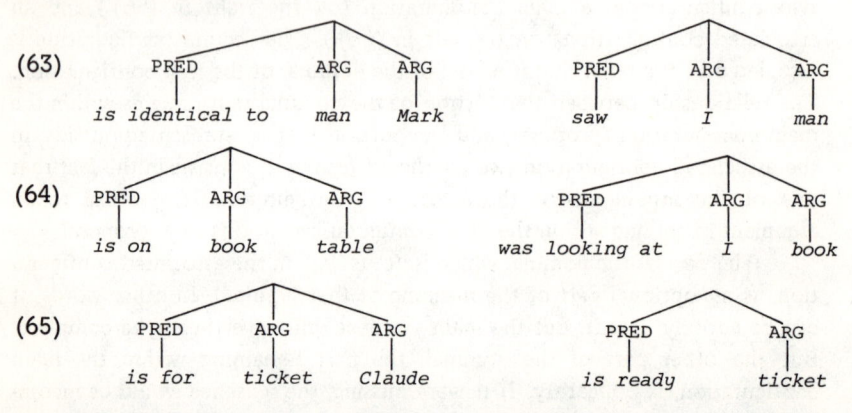

(63)
```
     PRED          ARG    ARG        PRED      ARG    ARG
       |            |      |           |        |      |
  is identical to  man   Mark         saw       I     man
```

(64)
```
     PRED     ARG    ARG         PRED          ARG    ARG
       |       |      |            |            |      |
     is on   book   table    was looking at     I     book
```

(65)
```
     PRED    ARG     ARG           PRED          ARG
       |      |       |              |            |
    is for  ticket  Claude        is ready      ticket
```

This new concept of associated configuration permits us to make a further advance in the representation of nominals. As we have seen, pure nominals consist of an obligatory part and an optional part. Sentences (50), (57), (58), and (60) through (62) contain the following pure nominals, within which we distinguish the obligatory part from the optional part:

	Obligatory	Optional
(50)	book	that Mark gave me
(57)	corridor	that was narrow
(58)	corridor	narrow
(60)	man	identical to Mark
(61)	book	on the table
(62)	ticket	for Claude

Nominals

We will call the obligatory part of a nominal **noun,** and the optional part **noun modifier.** We represent the noun modifier as a sentential structure associated with the main configuration of the sentence. So that with the notion of associated configuration, we can represent all types of noun modifiers without introducing further mechanisms. At this point, all that remains is to give a representation to the noun, i.e., to the obligatory portion of pure nominals remaining inside the main configuration. When we have done this, we will have completed the representation of the entire nominal.

Consider the following two sentences:

(66)   *Frank is vice president of the company.*
(67)   *The vice president is resting.*

In the first, we have a predication *is vice president,* with two arguments *Frank* and *the company.* Thus its representation will be

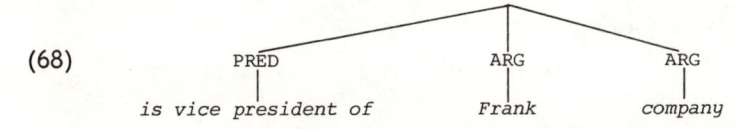

(68)
```
          PRED              ARG         ARG
           |                 |           |
   is vice president of    Frank       company
```

In the second sentence, we have a predication *is resting,* which has only one argument, *the vice president.* Hence (67) will be represented as

(69)
```
         PRED           ARG
          |              |
      is resting    vice president
```

It is interesting to compare the representation of *vice president* in these two sentences. In (66), as we said, there is a predication relating Frank to the company. In (67) there is instead a pure nominal, consisting only of an obligatory portion, the part we have called *noun.* How is the noun represented? If in (66) *vice president* is a predication, would it not be an advantage to be able to represent the noun *vice president* as a predication as well, in (67)? If we reflect on this possibility, we realize that when we call someone *vice president,* as we do in (66), we do nothing other than to attribute to this person some predicate or group of predicates that make up the meaning underlying the English word *vice president.* This would mean that nouns are, in essence, predications. But what, then, is the difference between *vice president* in (66) and *vice president* in (67), i.e., between predications in the strict sense and nouns? The difference apparently consists in this. In (66), *vice president* is a predicate of another element identified independently as *Frank.* In (67), on the other hand, *vice president* is predicated of some entity that is identifiable only because it has been attributed the predication *vice president*. We know nothing further about that entity. In other words, we might say that in (66) we are primarily interested in linguistically identifying something by calling it *Frank* and we then predicate *vice president* of that thing. Instead, in (67) we predicate *vice president* of something in order to linguistically identify it, so that after having identified it we can predicate something further, in this case *is resting*.

So nouns are predicates which are used with the goal of identifying something in order that it can be an argument of higher predicates. We will represent with *x* the arguments of predicates having this function, i.e., the arguments of nouns. The new representation of (67) will, then, be

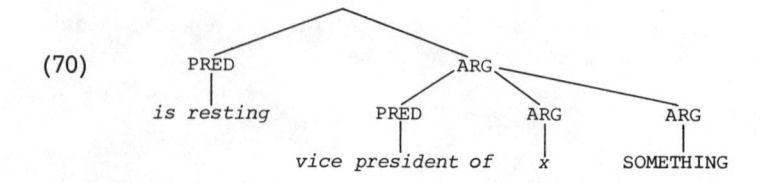

(70)
```
         ┌──────────────┴──────────────┐
        PRED                          ARG
         │              ┌──────────────┼──────────────┐
      is resting       PRED           ARG            ARG
                        │              │              │
                 vice president of     x          SOMETHING
```

Essentially, this sort of predication is used to construct an argument linguistically. It is as if we said "take those *x*'s which have the property VICE PRESIDENT OF." Thus nouns are represented in the lexicon as predicates, like all other lexical items, and in this sense are indistinguishable from verbs, adjectives, prepositions, etc. But what characterizes them is that within a sentence they serve as predications with a unique goal. Predications per se (i.e., predications in the strict sense) serve to place arguments in relation to one another. Predications used as nouns serve instead to construct those arguments linguistically, i.e., to take a segment of reality as one which presents the properties specified by the semantic components of that predication.

Let us look at an additional example. The sentence

(71)   *John's sister has arrived.*

with have the representation

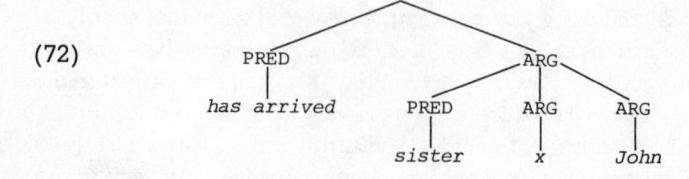

(72)
```
         ┌──────────────┴──────────────┐
        PRED                          ARG
         │              ┌──────────────┼──────────────┐
     has arrived       PRED           ARG            ARG
                        │              │              │
                      sister           x            John
```

A unique type of noun-predicate is the proper name, as in the sentence

(73) Frank runs.

If we ask ourselves what properties of an *x* are expressed by the proper name *Frank*, we find that the only property is that of being called *Frank*. If we say

(74) The dog runs.

i.e., if we use a common noun, we attribute to *x*-that-runs all the complex properties which correspond to the predicate *dog:* being an animal, domestic, mammal, with four feet, etc. Instead, if we use a proper name, as in (73), we do not attribute to *x* any other properties except that it is called in a certain way. Thus a sentence like (74) can be represented as

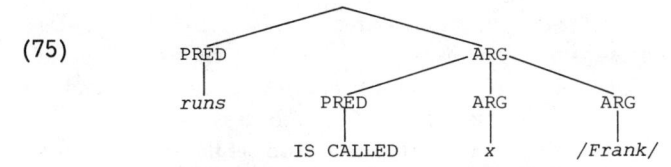

(75)
```
        PRED          ARG
         |           /   \
        runs      PRED  ARG  ARG
                   |      |    |
                IS CALLED x  /Frank/
```

So that a proper name is represented as a relation IS CALLED established between a segment of reality otherwise unidentified (an *x*), and a certain sequence of sounds, such as the sound /Frank/ in (73). (We will represent a sound sequence with the customary linguistic convention, closing it between two slanted bars.)

Our assertion that proper names attribute to an *x* only the property of being called in a certain way might seem contradicted by the fact that, on hearing a sentence like (73), the listener not only knows that *x* is named Frank, but also that he is a person, of the male sex, possibly of a certain national origin, etc. This is all undeniable, but it does not obligate us to modify our analysis of proper names. In fact, one generally does, on hearing a sentence such as (73), deduce that the person being discussed is in fact a person, probably male, etc. But such properties are not an intrinsic part of the meaning of the word *Frank*. Rather, these properties form part of the listener's **encyclopedic** knowledge, whereas the qualities of being a domestic animal, a mammal, etc. are part of the **lexical** meaning of the word *dog*.[5] An *x* can be a person, masculine, of a specified national origin, and still not be called *Frank*, while if the *x* is a quadruped, a domestic animal, a mammal, etc. it will necessarily be a dog. In fact, it is also possible to call an animal

---

[5] This is one reason why such properties of proper names are generally not found in dictionaries.

Frank, just as one can call a woman *Frank*, or a person of any national origin, etc. It is not possible, however, to call anything that is not an animal, domestic, mammal, quadruped, etc. a dog (an exception would be a metaphoric use of the word *dog*, although this is also based on a predication of "dog-like" properties). For this reason, to deduce certain properties from a proper name is always a risk (unless, of course, one already knows the *x* from some other source of information). But the deduction of certain properties from a common noun is precisely the goal for which all common nouns have been invented.

Consider now the two sentences

(76)   *I read the book that Mark gave me.*
(77)   *I met the janitor, who gave me the keys.*

and in particular, consider the two nominals that these contain, *the book that Mark gave me* and *the janitor who gave me the keys*. As we know, these are both pure nominals, consisting of the nouns *the book* and *the janitor*, and the modifiers *that Mark gave me* and *who gave me the keys*, respectively. We know how to represent these nominals: the nouns are predications attributed to otherwise unidentified x's, and the modifiers are sentential structures represented as associated configurations to the main configuration of the respective sentences.

Up to this point the two nominals of sentences (76) and (77) are identical. But there is in fact a difference between the two nominals. More precisely, this difference has to do with the function of the two modifiers with respect to the nouns they modify. In sentence (76), the modifier *that Mark gave me* serves the function of identifying for the listener which book is at issue. In fact, we could ask the speaker "Which book?" and receive the answer "the one that Mark gave me". The situation is different in sentence (77). Here the listener already knows which janitor is being discussed, and the modifier *who gave me the keys* does not, then, have the function of identifying for the listener which janitor is at issue. One could say that in (76) the modifier of the noun is essential; without it the listener wouldn't know which book the speaker is referring to. Instead, in (77) the modifier is not essential; it is as if there were two sentences, both of which are complete and independent. We can name these two separate functions that modifiers can have. When the modifier indicates to the listener which particular x the speaker has in mind, the modifier has a **restrictive** function. When, on the other hand, the modifier simply has the function of giving extra information about x, without identifying the x for the listener, we say that the modifier has a **nonrestrictive** function.

Nominals 103

How is the difference between restrictive and nonrestrictive modifiers represented? As we have noted, restrictive modifiers are in some way presupposed by the sentence in which they are embedded, in the sense that the linguistic act which the speaker intends to carry out using this sentence requires that the listener, in order to understand the sentence, keep in mind the information contained in the modifier. By contrast, nonrestrictive modifiers are not presupposed by the sentences in which they appear, but instead are simply added to a sentence which by itself is a completed linguistic act. So that the difference lies in the relationship between the associated configuration representing the modifier, and the main configuration representing the sentence. For the moment we will limit ourselves to representing this difference as follows, reserving the right to furnish a clearer and more analytic representation in later chapters when we will have introduced some new mechanisms. For now, (76) is represented as

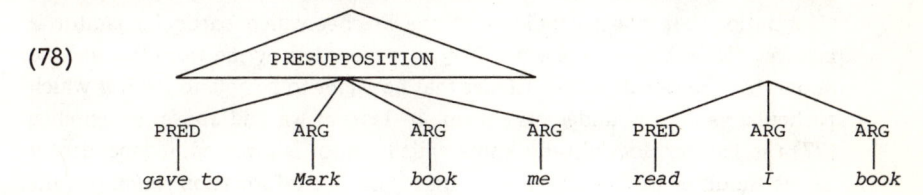

(78)
```
           PRESUPPOSITION
    PRED   ARG    ARG    ARG     PRED   ARG   ARG
    gave to Mark  book   me      read   I     book
```

Sentence (77) receives the representation

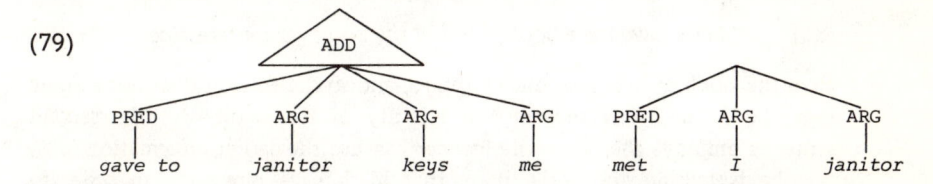

(79)
```
              ADD
    PRED   ARG     ARG   ARG     PRED   ARG   ARG
    gave to janitor keys me      met    I     janitor
```

Let us examine (76) and (77) further. It is evident that in both sentences the listener knows which particular x is being discussed. The only difference is that in (76) he finds this out from the information contained in the noun modifier, while in (77) he already knew the identity of x through some previous means. This does not mean that every time speech occurs the listener must necessarily know which particular x is being discussed. There are times when the speaker is not interested in arriving at such a degree of specificity. It may be enough for him that the listener know something about an x—for example, that that x has the properties expressed by the noun—without knowing which particular x is being referred to. So that, if instead of sentence (76), the speaker used the sentence

(80)   *I read a book.*

what happens is this: the listener finds out that the thing which the speaker read is a book, but he does not know which specific book.

As is evident from (76) and (80), in English there are two words which signal to the listener whether the speaker wants to arrive at a degree of specificity in discussing a particular *x*, or whether he is content to speak of an *x* without indicating which particular *x* is involved. These words are *the* and *a*. If we say *the book*, the listener knows that we are discussing a book, and that the speaker assumes that the listener should already know which book is being discussed. Instead, if we say *a book*, the listener knows that we are talking about a book, and in addition knows that the speaker does not intend to specify which particular book.

Let us return for a moment to sentence (77). We said that in this sentence the noun modifier is of the nonrestrictive type, i.e., it serves to add information but not to indicate to the listener which particular janitor is involved. Nevertheless, the word *janitor* is preceded by the word *the*, and we know that *the* signals to the listener that he ought to be able to recover which particular janitor is under discussion. In fact, as we said above, in sentence (77) the listener does already know which janitor is involved, independently of the modifier which accompanies the noun. The information which permits him to identify which particular *x* the speaker is referring to may have been given earlier by the speaker himself, as in the example

(81)   *Mark gave me a book. I found the book very interesting.*

Here the book is first introduced using *a*, and so the speaker does not assume that the listener can recover the identity of the book. But the second sentence employs *the*, since the listener can use the earlier information (e.g., "...he is talking about the book that Mark gave him...") in order to recognize which book the speaker is referring to now.

In other cases it can be taken for granted that a predetermined *x* is being discussed. For example, in (77) the janitor might be the one who works in the building where the speaker or the listener live. In other cases, the same information, permitting identification of a specific *x*, is furnished to the listener by the physical situation in which the conversation takes place, such as the case in which we say

(82)   *Give me the ashtray.*

when there is only one ashtray on the table.

Common to all these cases is the fact that there is always some kind of information available to which the word *the* refers, so that the listener need

Nominals 105

have no doubts about which x the speaker has in mind. In certain cases such information is not available to the listener, so that the speaker provides that information by using a restrictive modifier, as in (76). In other cases the information is available, so that the speaker can signal the identity of x by using *the* without further modifiers, as in (76), (81), and (82).

In those cases in which such information is lacking, and in which the listener need only know that the referent is an x without knowing which particular x, this state of affairs is signalled by the use of the word *a*. This can occur either in the case in which the speaker does know the identity of the specific x but does not care to signal this to the listener, or in the case in which the speaker himself has no particular x in mind. Hence, the sentence

(83) *I would like a book.*

uttered when entering a bookstore, can be used either when the speaker has to buy a particular book, or when he is about to request the salesman's advice on which book to buy.

Summing up for the moment our analysis of *the* and *a*, we see that these two words must receive a somewhat different representation than is usually given to lexical items. These words do not consist of a set of semantic components, but rather are limited to signalling the presence (*the*) or absence (*a*) of certain presupposed information permitting the listener to recover the identity of an x that is being discussed.

Finally, we should note a particular use of *the* and *a*, illustrated by the two sentences

(84) *The dog is man's best friend.*
(85) *A dog is man's best friend.*

In neither of these sentences do we wish to refer to a particular dog, but rather to dogs in general. What operations do we execute in these two sentences to signal this condition? In (84) we select an individual from the class of dogs, treating that individual not as a specific animal but as the representative of the class. However, since we are talking about a representative or prototypical individual, we use the word *the*. In (85), we select instead the word *a*, to signal directly to the listener that we have no particular dog in mind. The communicative result is the same. In both (84) and (85), the x to which the word *dog* refers is not a specific individual.

Having so analyzed the nominals, we are now able to represent another kind of sentence. We have looked at sentences like *Frank is vice president*, in which *vice president* is used as a predication with Frank as one of its arguments. In addition to this kind of sentence there is a second type, seemingly similar to this one, illustrated by

(86)   Frank is the vice president that I introduced to you.

Our analysis must be different in this second case. Whereas in (66) *vice president* is the predication of the sentence, in (86) the word *vice president* is a noun, as is demonstrated by the fact that it is preceded by the article *the* and followed by a modifier (the relative clause *that I introduced to you*). Thus in (86), the entire expression *the vice president that I introduced to you* is a nominal, whereas *vice president* in (66) is not. In fact, *vice president* in (66) cannot be accompanied by a modifier, as is illustrated in the sentences

(87)   *Frank is good vice president of the company.
(88)   *Frank is vice president that I introduced to you.

How can this difference be accounted for? We said that in (86) *the vice president that I introduced to you* is a nominal. But if it is a nominal, it must be the argument of some predication. What is the predication in this case? Let us reflect for a moment on this sentence. It is composed of two nouns, *Frank* and *vice president*. We explained earlier the function of nouns. They serve to identify linguistically some segment of reality, segments to which one can attribute the properties (the so-called **semantic components**) expressed by a lexical item. In this case, then, the two nouns identify linguistically two individuals: one is identified by the name *Frank;* the other is identified by the attribution of the property *vice president,* further modified by the attribution *the one that I introduced to you.* This kind of operations falls under our concept of *noun.* If this is the case, then the predication that occurs in sentence (86) is clear: (86) asserts an identity relation between two individuals that, as we have seen, have been constructed linguistically in two different ways. We will represent this concept with a semantic component that we will call IDENTITY. The representation of sentence (86) then becomes

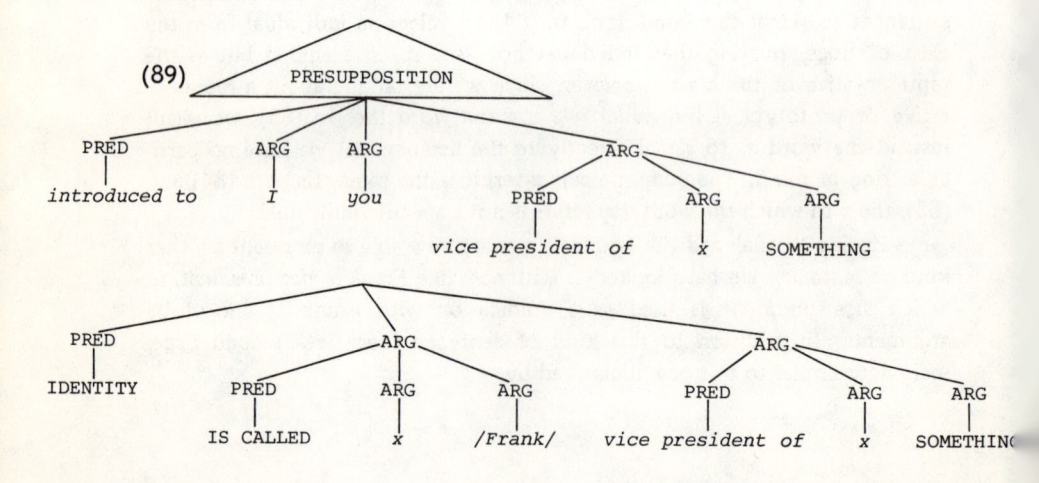

(89)

```
                    PRESUPPOSITION
    PRED        ARG    ARG              ARG
 introduced to   I     you       PRED        ARG    ARG
                                vice president of    x    SOMETHING

  PRED                ARG                    ARG
IDENTITY      PRED     ARG    ARG      PRED        ARG    ARG
           IS CALLED    x    /Frank/  vice president of    x   SOMETHING
```

Nominals

The same holds for a sentence such as

(90) *Frank is a vice president.*

Here too we have two nouns whose referents are placed in an identity relationship. The only difference between (86) and (90) is that, whereas in (86) the speaker intends to communicate to the listener that a particular vice president is involved (and to that purpose uses the article *the* and the presupposed information *that I introduced to you*), in (90) the speaker signals only that there is an *x* who is a vice president, without specifying which particular vice presedent is involved. But this is nothing other than the same difference we just witnessed between *the* and *a*. (90) will, then, be represented in the same way, but without the presupposed portion:

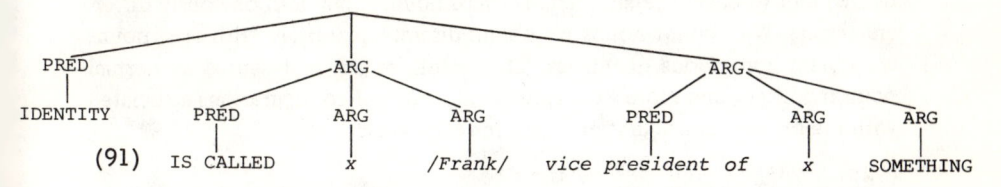

```
              PRED                ARG                           ARG
               |            ___/  |                       ___/  |
            IDENTITY   PRED     ARG    ARG          PRED       ARG    ARG
               |         |       |      |            |          |      |
(91)        IS CALLED    x    /Frank/  vice president of        x   SOMETHING
```

At this point, in order to complete our analysis of nominals, it is necessary to examine an important distinction existing among nouns. As we know, a noun is a predication having as an argument something that is not independently identified, that is an *x*. We will call this *x* the **referent** of the noun.

There are two types of referents, or rather, two different ways to construct *x*. In the first case the referent of the noun is constructed as a multiplicity of individuals. The term *individual* must be taken in its root sense, as something which cannot be further subdivided and still be the same thing that it was before. On the other hand, if two or more individuals are united, they still maintain their individuality, and hence constitute a plurality, which can be counted. To reflect this property, we will call nouns with this first type of referent **count nouns**. An example of a countable referent or count noun is *book*. When I attribute the predication *book* to an *x* not otherwise identified, I create a referent which belongs to a multiplicity or class of individuals, all of which have the properties attributed by *book*. A single book cannot be further subdivided, in the sense that if I divide a book into its subparts, it is no longer a book. And if I unite several books, I have a plurality of things that can be counted.

Now let us examine the second type of referent. This is constructed not as a class of individuals, but as a unified mass, divisible into parts but not into individuals. In other words, if we divide this type of referent, we always obtain something that can be further subdivided. Also, each one of the parts obtained through subdivision presents the same properties as the whole from which it originally came. If I divide a book in two parts, the parts are no longer books. But if I divide water in two parts, the parts continue to be water. With this type of referent, since the parts do not have individuality, when two or more of them are united they do not constitute a plurality and hence cannot be counted. We will call nouns with this second type of referent **mass nouns**. An example of an uncountable referent or mass noun is of course *water*. When I attribute the predication *water* to an *x* not otherwise identified, I obtain a referent that is a single mass. This mass is divisible into parts, but each part of the water is further divisible into smaller parts. And if I unite several parts of water, I never have a plurality, but only a larger portion of water, and for this reason water cannot be counted.

The idea of quantity is applicable both to numerable referents (count nouns) and to uncountable referents (mass nouns)—but with obviously different results. With count nouns we obtain discrete quantities; with mass nouns we obtain continuous quantities. The quantities are represented as normal noun modifiers, and more exactly as predications of configurations associated with the primary configuration. Thus the sentences:

(92)   I saw a book.
(93)   I saw some books.
(94)   I saw four books.
(95)   I saw many books.

will have these representations

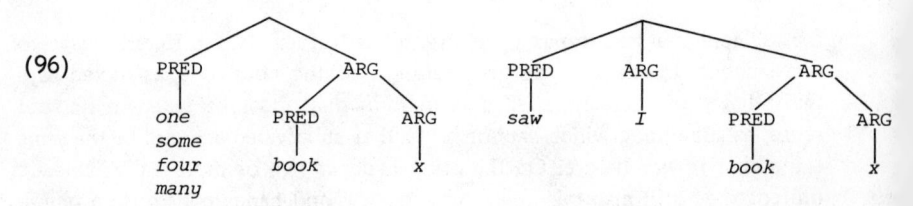

(96)

```
         PRED         ARG                    PRED    ARG              ARG
          |          /   \                    |       |              /   \
         one       PRED   ARG                saw      I            PRED   ARG
         some       |      |                                        |      |
         four      book    x                                       book    x
         many
```

In the previous sentences the speaker leaves undetermined for the listener which **particular** books he has seen. When the listener already knows which book(s), or when he is to be informed in the course of the same sentence, then the above sentences take the following form:

(97)   I saw the book.
(98)   I saw the books..
(99)   I saw the four books.
(100)   I saw the many books.

We know how to represent the difference between these sentences and (92) through (95). The main configuration and the associated configuration are

Nominals

the same as above, but to these we now add a further presupposed, associated configuration, representing precisely that information which permits the listener to identify which particular books are involved.

If we go on now to mass nouns, we find that we can apply quantity modifiers to these as well. But we cannot use those quantities which require that the referent be composed of individuals. We have sentences such as

(101)   I drank some wine.
(102)   I drank a lot of wine.

represented as

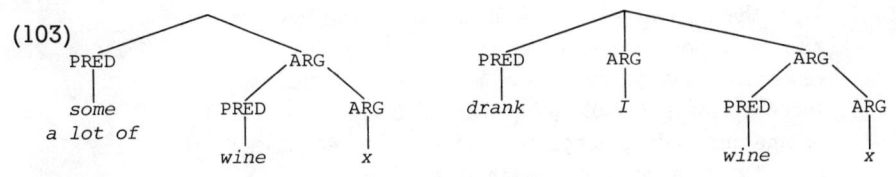

(103)

```
           PRED        ARG                      PRED      ARG              ARG
            |         /    \                     |         |             /     \
           some     PRED   ARG                  drank      I           PRED    ARG
         a lot of    |      |                                           |       |
                    wine    x                                          wine     x
```

But we cannot predicate *one, more than one, four,* etc. of a mass noun. The fact that there exist acceptable sentences such as

(104)   I drank an excellent wine.
(105)   I drank some excellent wines.
(106)   I drank four excellent wines.

does not contradict our assertion, because in these cases the referent to which we apply the quantity *one, more than one, four,* etc. is not *wine* but rather *type of wine* or *quality of wine*, i.e., count nouns. In fact, by introducing something which permits us to differentiate one part from another within a mass noun, we transform those parts into individuals so that we obtain a new referent and a corresponding count noun.

The Performative

6

With the apparatus introduced so far, we can give an explicit representation to much of the meaning of a sentence. However, there is still another aspect of sentence meaning that eludes us. In this chapter, we will extend our model of language to cover this aspect as well.

Consider the following sentences:

(1)   *Frank is going to class.*
(2)   *Is Frank going to class?*
(3)   *Frank, go to class!*

A grammar which gives the same semantic representation to these three sentences would clearly be incomplete. It is obvious that (1), (2), and (3) have something in common, but it is equally obvious that they differ in certain respects. With the mechanisms that we have developed so far, we can represent whatever it is that makes these sentences similar. In all three cases, we have a predicate *go to* with two arguments, *Frank* and *class*. That is, in all three cases we conceive of a relation of "going" that holds between *Frank* and *class*. We can represent this mental activity as follows:

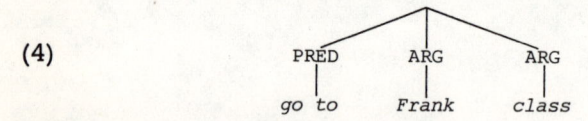

(4)
```
           PRED    ARG    ARG
            |       |      |
           go to  Frank  class
```

or rather, in more detail

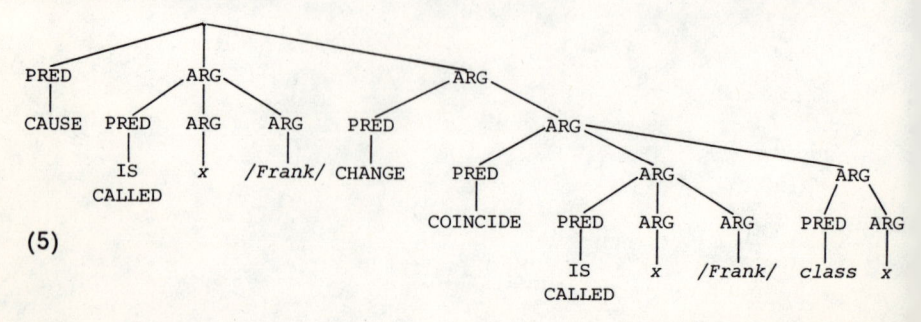

(5)
```
PRED    ARG                    ARG
 |       |                      |
CAUSE  PRED  ARG  ARG  PRED    ARG
        |    |    |     |      
        IS   x /Frank/ CHANGE  PRED    ARG                    ARG
       CALLED                   |       |                      |
                             COINCIDE  PRED  ARG  ARG         PRED  ARG
                                        |    |    |            |    |
                                        IS   x /Frank/        class  x
                                       CALLED
```

The Performative

But we do not know how to go beyond these. The mechanisms that we have introduced so far give no indication of how to represent the differences among the three sentences.

Let us consider, for the moment, some intuitive differences among these three sentences. In saying (1), the speaker is trying to communicate some information; he wants to let the listener know that Frank is going to class. In saying (2), however, the speaker has a different intention. He now wants to receive information; he wants his listener to tell him if Frank is going to class or not. Finally, in the case of (3), the speaker has still another goal. He wants neither to give nor to receive information; instead, he wants Frank to do something, in this case to go to class. If what varies among these three sentences is the particular intention or goal of the speaker in uttering it, then in order to capture these differences we must be able to represent the speaker's intention. Therefore the representation of the meaning of a sentence will consist of two parts: one to tell us the intention of the speaker in using the sentence, and the other to give us the particular content associated with that intention. Thus, in sentences (1), (2), and (3), the intention is different while the content remains the same. In all three sentences the speaker conceives of a relationship of "going" between *Frank* and *class*. But in (1) this relation is the object of an assertion, in (2) it is the object of a question, and in (3) it is the object of a request. We will call the representation of the content of a sentence the **proposition**, because it describes that which is proposed to the mind of the listener without indicating what is to be done with that proposition. We will give the name **performative** to the speaker's intention in using the proposition. This term is derived from the verb "to perform", in the sense of "to bring about" or "to execute".[1] The speaker's intention determines the type of linguistic act which he will carry out in pronouncing a set of words: to inform, to ask for information, to request, etc. The performative tells us what type of linguistic act the speaker wants to execute in using a given sentence. We can thus conclude that sentences (1), (2), and (3) have the same proposition, but different performatives.

How do we represent the performative of a sentence? We have one general hypothesis about how to represent the mental activity which is expressed in language, namely as a configuration of predicates. There is little doubt that the performative is a mental activity of the speaker, just like the proposition. It is sufficient to consider the example of sentence (3), the request performative, to realize that the speaker expects a well-defined result on the part of the listener: that the listener go to class. If the listener, after

---

[1] The use of the term "performative" is taken from the philosopher John L. Austin, who invented this particular use of the word and was the first in recent linguistic theory to study this aspect of language systematically.

hearing (3), limited himself to answering "yes" and then went back to bed, then the speaker would have to repeat the sentence. Therefore, in pronouncing a sentence, the speaker carries out two types of mental activity, one which we represent as the proposition, and another which we represent as the performative.

If we accept that the performative must be represented as a configuration of semantic components, there is another problem. How do we connect the configuration that represents the performative with the one that represents the proposition? In intuitive terms, we might say that the proposition is the object of the performative. Thus the relationship between *going*, *Frank*, and *class* is the object of an assertion in (1), a question in (2), and a request in (3). It seems fairly obvious, then, that the proposition should be represented as an argument of the performative. Later on we will see why this is the correct choice.

The representation of the meaning of a sentence is, then, a configuration of semantic predicates among which we can distinguish a dominant configuration, the performative, and a dominated configuration, the proposition. The performative represents the type of linguistic act which the speaker wants to carry out in uttering the sentence, and the proposition represents the particular content of this linguistic act. Schematically the representation of a sentence should be the following:

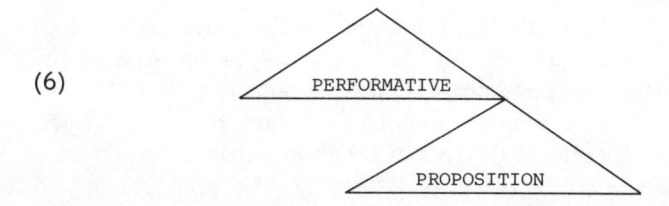

(6)

```
      PERFORMATIVE
       PROPOSITION
```

Do all sentences have a representation like (6)? That is, do they all include a performative and a proposition? The answer is clearly yes. This is part of the definition of a sentence. A sentence, in its actual usage, is not simply a sound that strikes the listener's ear, but it is also a sound produced by a speaker with a specific communicative intention. On the one hand, a sentence is a "sign", a relation between a signifier and a signified, in the same way that clouds can be a sign of rain. But it is also a communicative and linguistic sign, a signifier (a sound) produced intentionally by a speaker so that a listener will react in a specific way to the signified, the content of the sign. We have applied the term **performative** to the speaker's expectation that the listener will react in a specified way. Thus, by definition, every sentence includes a performative.

The Performative

We arrive at the same conclusion if we examine empirically, one at a time, sentences that are actually used by someone. To any given example, we can assign a role that the sentence carries out within a given passage of discourse, or within a conversation between two or more people. Every sentence is produced by a speaker with a definite intention; it is produced to have some specific effect on a listener.

Before passing to a concrete representation of performatives for the first three sentences, we must introduce another important distinction with respect to performatives. Consider the two sentences

(7) I order you to go to class.
(8) I promise you to go to class.

If we ask ourselves what the performatives are for these sentences—what kind of linguistic act the speaker intends to carry out in pronouncing the two sentences—the answer is that in (7) the speaker wants to give an order and in (8) he wants to make a promise. *Order* and *promise* are linguistic acts in the same sense as the linguistic acts of informing, asking and requesting that we examined earlier. But there is a difference between the performatives of sentences (7) and (8) and those of sentences (1), (2) and (3). In sentences (7) and (8) the performative is made explicit, expressed through certain specific English verbs (*order* and *promise*, respectively). By contrast, in sentences (1), (2), and (3) the performatives remain implicit. Certainly the nature of the particular performative is somehow marked even in the superficial form of sentences (1), (2), and (3). The question, (2), differs from the assertion (1) by virtue of a shift in word order and a change in intonation. The command (3) differs from both the question and the assertion through the use of the imperative form of the verb and the deletion of the subject of the verb. But obviously the performative has been expressed more explicitly in sentences (7) and (8), in which we find verbs serving no purpose other than to clarify to the listener the type of linguistic act the listener wants to carry out in uttering the sentence.

We know what sort of representation to give to sentences (7) and (8). These are normal sentence structures in which the predication of the nucleus (*I order* and *I promise*) has a sentential structure as one of its arguments, that is, a nuclear subordinate. Therefore the representation will be

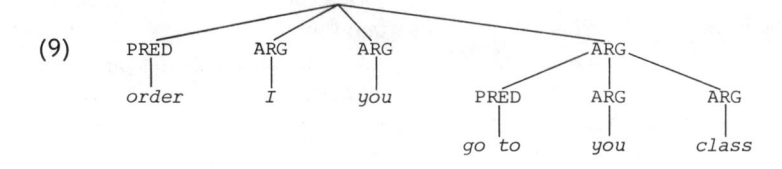

(9)
```
         PRED      ARG    ARG           ARG
          |         |      |              
        order       I     you     PRED   ARG   ARG
                                   |      |     |
                                 go to   you   class
```

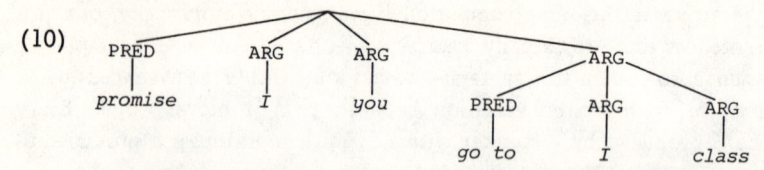

(10)
```
PRED    ARG   ARG        ARG
 |       |     |      ___/|\___
promise  I    you   PRED  ARG ARG
                     |     |    |
                   go to   I  class
```

But we also know that the dominant structures (*I order you X* and *I promise you X*) make up the performatives of the respective sentences, in that they describe the kind of linguistic act that the speaker intends to carry out in pronouncing each sentence.

We will have a more detailed representation of the two sentences if we carry out a componential analysis of *to order* and *to promise*. At this point we shall introduce the component USE, which will also be useful later on. USE is a predicate with three arguments, and stands for the mental operation in which someone X uses something Y for some goal Z. So that from (9) and (10) respectively we can pass on to more detailed representations, which are

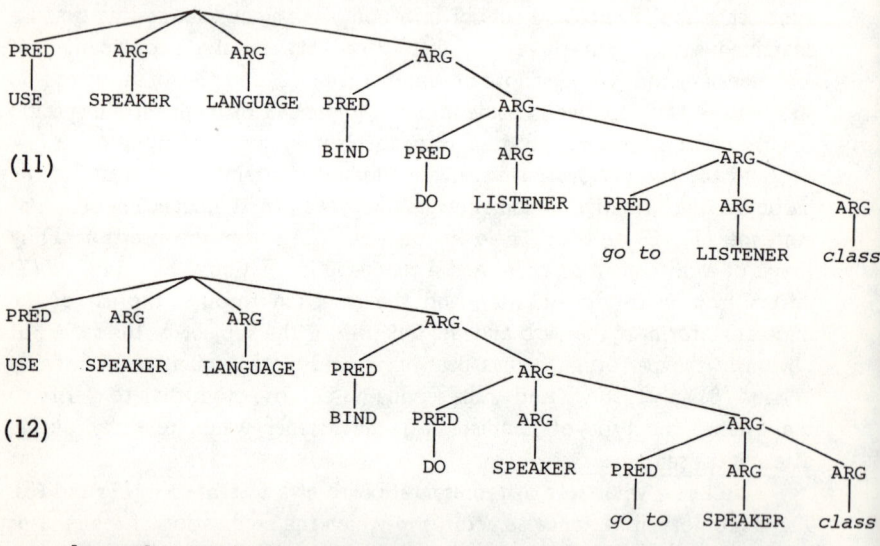

(11)
```
PRED  ARG      ARG          ARG
 |     |        |        ____/|____
USE  SPEAKER LANGUAGE  PRED        ARG
                        |      ____/|____
                       BIND  PRED         ARG
                              |        ____/|____
                             DO  LISTENER  PRED  ARG    ARG
                                            |     |      |
                                          go to LISTENER class
```

(12)
```
PRED  ARG      ARG          ARG
 |     |        |        ____/|____
USE  SPEAKER LANGUAGE  PRED        ARG
                        |      ____/|____
                       BIND  PRED         ARG
                              |        ____/|____
                             DO  SPEAKER  PRED  ARG    ARG
                                           |     |      |
                                         go to SPEAKER class
```

As can be seen from the above, the meaning of *to order* is analyzable as "The speaker uses the language in order to bind the listener to do a certain thing." The meaning of *to promise* is analyzable as "The speaker uses the language in order to bind himself to do a certain thing."

Let us go now to sentences (1), (2), and (3) in which the performative is implicit. Precisely because of these sentences the performative is not expressed in words, we must give a representation directly at the level of semantic components. For the sentence

The Performative

(1) *Frank is going to class.*

we propose the representation

(13)
```
         PRED    ARG      ARG         ARG
          │       │        │           │
         USE   SPEAKER  LANGUAGE    PRED   ARG         ARG
                                     │      │           │
                                   ASSUME LISTENER   PRED   ARG    ARG
                                                      │      │      │
                                                    go to  Frank  class
```

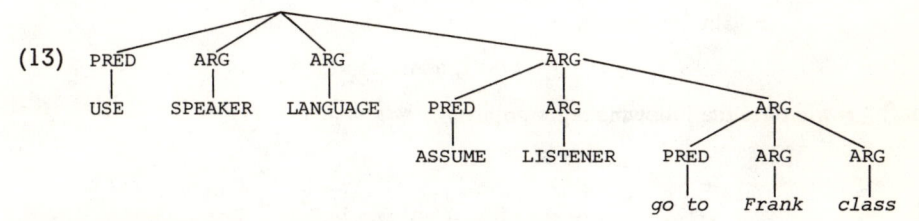

or alternatively, "The speaker uses the language in order that the listener assume that Frank is going to class."

The sentence

(2) *Is Frank going to class?*

will have, by contrast, the representation

(14)
```
  PRED    ARG      ARG           ARG
   │       │        │             │
  USE   SPEAKER  LANGUAGE

                      PRED    ARG       ARG         ARG
                       │       │         │           │
                      USE   LISTENER  LANGUAGE

                                  PRED    ARG        ARG
                                   │       │          │
                                 ASSUME  SPEAKER

                             PRED       ARG                         ARG
                              │          │                           │
                              OR      PRED    ARG    ARG
                                       │       │      │
                                     go to   Frank  class

                                      PRED       ARG
                                       │          │
                                      NEG      PRED    ARG    ARG
                                                │       │      │
                                              go to   Frank  class
```

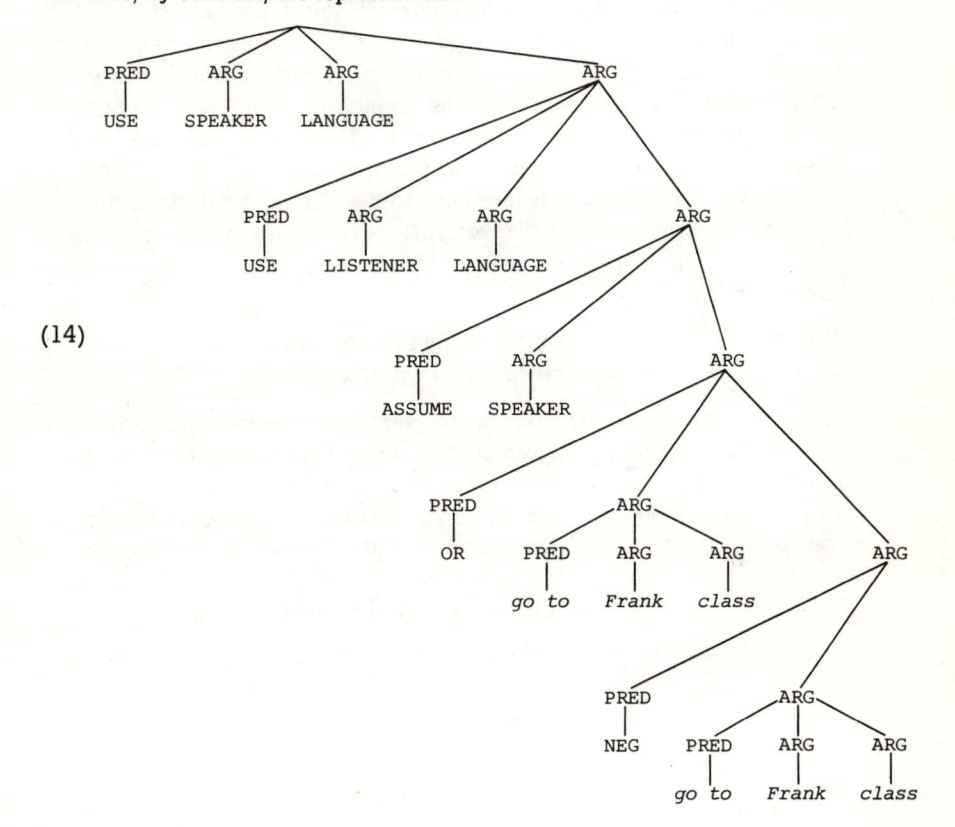

which is paraphrasable as "The speaker uses the language in order that the listener use the language in order that the speaker assume either that Frank is going to class or that Frank is not going to class".

Finally, the sentence

(3) Frank, go to class!

will have the following representation:

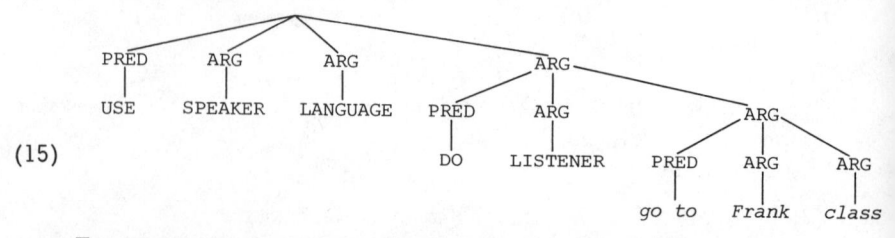

(15)
```
        PRED   ARG     ARG        ARG
         |      |       |         /|\
        USE  SPEAKER LANGUAGE  PRED ARG    ARG
                                |   |     /|\
                               DO LISTENER PRED ARG  ARG
                                            |   |    |
                                          go to Frank class
```

For present purposes, we will overlook the rather difficult question regarding why the same performative intent is sometimes rendered explicit, and sometimes left implicit. At this point it should at least be clear that the analogy holding between implicit and explicit performatives demonstrates that it is correct to represent even the implicit performative as a predicate which takes the proposition as an argument. Therefore the proposition can always be considered the "object" of its performative.

On the other hand, it is necessary to keep in mind that words like *to order* and *to promise* express the performative of the sentences in which they appear only when they are used in the first person present indicative. For example, in sentences:

(16) Frank orders John to go to class.
(17) I promised John to go to class.

order and *promise* are not used in the first person present indicative and hence do not express the performative of the two sentences (16) and (17). It is not difficult to see that the speaker who produces these two sentences is not carrying out the linguistic acts of ordering or promising, but is merely asserting in (16) that Frank carried out the linguistic act of ordering, and in (17) that the speaker himself, in the past, carried out the act of promising. Thus the representations for (16) and (17) will be the following

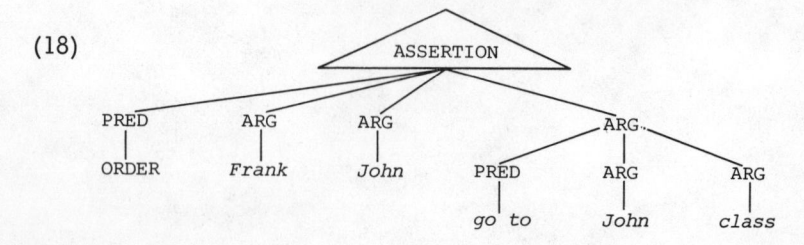

(18)
```
                    ASSERTION
        PRED   ARG    ARG      ARG
         |      |      |       /|\
       ORDER  Frank  John   PRED ARG  ARG
                             |    |    |
                           go to John class
```

The Performative

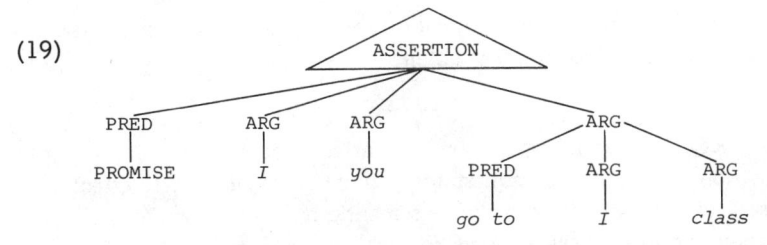

(19)
```
                        ASSERTION
         ┌──────────┬──────┬────────────────┐
        PRED       ARG    ARG              ARG
         │          │      │         ┌──────┼──────┐
      PROMISE       I     you       PRED   ARG    ARG
                                     │      │      │
                                   go to    I    class
```

In language there are verbs which can be used as performatives, in that they are used to express the performative of a sentence, but the same verbs can also be used in a non-performative way, to describe the execution of some linguistic act—in the past, in the future, as it was carried out by some third party, etc. Examples of these verbs, called performative verbs, include *to order* and *to promise* as used performatively in (7) and (8) and as used non-performatively in (16) and (17). The remaining class of verbs, non-performative verbs, can never be used to express the performative of a sentence. An example is the verb *to eat*. In the following sentence

(20) *I am eating.*

I am eating cannot express a performative. Instead, *I am eating* is necessarily the predication of the nucleus of a proposition, while the performative of that proposition is, in (20), a performative of assertion.

We have considered and analyzed only a small number of the performatives within a given language. Other examples of implicit performatives are contained in the sentences

(21)   *Who is waiting in the living room?*
(22)   *What a beautiful dress!*
(23)   *Good luck!*

and other explicit performatives include the following:

(24)   *I congratulate you on your victory.*
(25)   *I advise you not to go.*
(26)   *I warn you that Frank is leaving.*

The variety of possible speech acts within a given language is much greater than these few examples, and we have barely begun a complete and systematic study of this fundamental mechanism of language.

We must also consider the possibility—a frequent occurrence in natural conversation—that a sentence can have a performative value quite different from the one which actually appears on the surface. Thus apparent questions such as

(27)   *Can you pass me the salt?*
(28)   *Why don't you go by train?*

are not actually requests for information, but rather requests or suggestions of possible actions. Similarly, the sentence

(29)   *I need help.*

is not necessarily, as it appears on the surface, the offering of a piece of information, but rather, a request for action. To explain these effects it is necessary to postulate more complex semantic representations for performatives than those we have offered so far, but we shall not go into these problems.

For now, instead of proposing analyses of other performatives or of these special effects, we will concern ourselves with an aspect of the performative that still has to be examined (see Parisi and Puglielli, in press). Consider the sentence

(30)   *Frank has left because the windows are closed.*

As discussed in Chapter 1, when this sentence is given with different kinds of pause and intonation, it can have two different interpretations. In one the speaker is saying that the reason why Frank left is because the windows were closed. Frank was, perhaps, suffocating and therefore had to leave. In this first case the sentence has more or less the same meaning as

(31)   *It is because the windows are closed that Frank left.*

But there is another interpretation for (30), by which *because the windows are closed* is no longer the motive for Frank's leaving, but rather the reason why the speaker arrived at the conclusion that Frank left. In this second interpretation, (30) can no longer paraphrase (31), but rather

(32) *It is because the windows are closed that I conclude that Frank left.*

How are the two different interpretations of (30) represented? The first interpretation poses a few problems. We have an assertive performative, with a proposition composed of a nucleus (*Frank left*) and an adverbial (*because the windows are closed*). So that the representation of (30) is

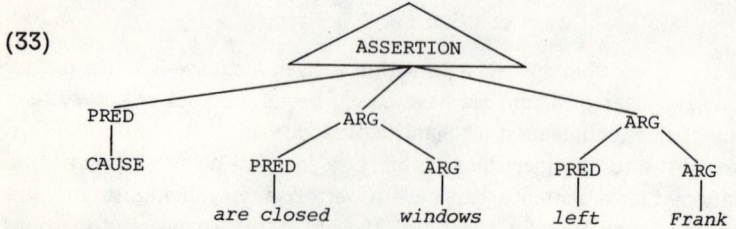

(33)

```
                         ASSERTION
                    /        |        \
                 PRED       ARG        ARG
                  |        /   \      /   \
                CAUSE   PRED   ARG  PRED   ARG
                         |      |    |      |
                     are closed windows left Frank
```

The representation of (30), on the other hand, poses an interesting problem. In (30), *because the windows are closed* continues to be an adverbial, but it is

The Performative

no longer an adverbial of the nucleus of the proposition. Otherwise, the representation of (30) would be identical to that of (31). Furthermore, we know that in (30), *because the windows are closed* does not express the reason for which Frank left. Therefore we cannot use the semantic construction rules available to us so far. However, a brief reflection should give us a sufficiently natural solution for this problem. In sentence (30), *because the windows are closed* expresses the reason why the speaker feels he can assert that Frank left. In other words, *because the windows are closed* is a qualification on the performative, and so can be considered an adverbial of the performative. We need only extend to the performative the same recursive nucleus-adverbial mechanism used earlier, so that the performative also has an obligatory nucleus with optional adverbials. Thus the representation of (30) should be something like the following:

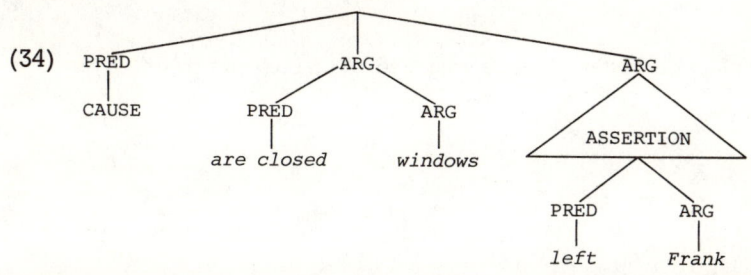

(34)
```
         PRED         ARG                          ARG
          |          /   \                          |
        CAUSE     PRED   ARG                    ASSERTION
                   |      |                      /      \
               are closed windows             PRED      ARG
                                                |        |
                                              left     Frank
```

If we compare the two representations (33) and (34), we can see how they reflect the fact that in (31) the adverbial modifies the nucleus of the proposition (*Frank left*), in that it provides Frank's motive, while in (30) the adverbial in no way affects the proposition, but instead modifies the nucleus of the performative (*I assert . . .*), providing the motive for that assertion.

This means that the class of adverbials can be divided into propositional adverbials and performative adverbials, according to whether they modify the nucleus of the proposition or the nucleus of the performative. A further illustration of this comes from the following:

(35)   (a)   *Frank is probably sleeping.*
                 (b)   ?*Probably Frank is sleeping.*
                 (c)   **Frank is sleeping probably.*
(36)   (a)   ?*Frank is peacefully sleeping.*
                 (b)   **Peacefully Frank is sleeping.*
                 (c)   *Frank is sleeping peacefully.*

Note that we tend to place *probably* before the participle in (35). It is less acceptable when placed at the beginning of the sentence, and totally unacceptable (without unusual intonation) at the end of the sentence. By contrast, the most acceptable placement for *peacefully* is at the end of the sentence, exactly the point where *probably* is least acceptable. This contrast can be explained if we analyze *probably* as a performative adverbial in (35), while *peacefully* is a propositional adverbial in (36). This way, the different surface distributions for these adverbials can be explained with general rules that apply to performative versus propositional adverbials. The only other solution would be to formulate different, arbitrary surface placement rules for every possible adverbial in the language.

Similarly, *now* is a performative adverbial in (37) and a propositional adverbial in (38). An arbitrary system for classifying adverbials would not be able to explain why the same lexical item can function so differently in these two sentences:

(37)   Now, Frank has left.
(38)   Frank has left now.

According to the system we have suggested, the representation of (37) is

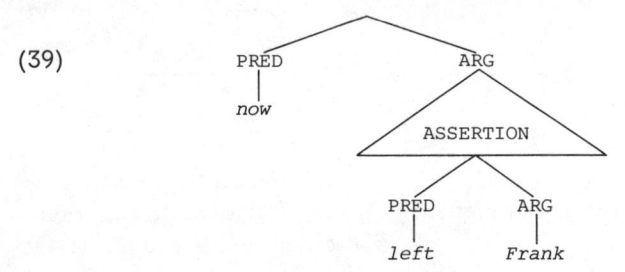

(39)

```
           PRED        ARG
            |
           now
                  ASSERTION
                  PRED    ARG
                   |       |
                  left   Frank
```

whereas the representation of (38) is

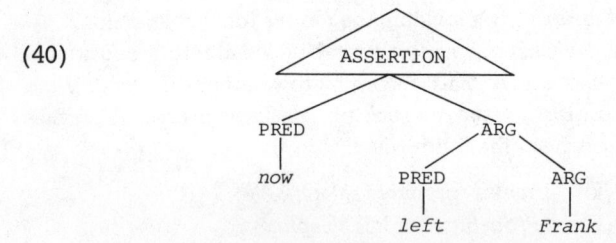

(40)

```
              ASSERTION
         PRED          ARG
          |        PRED    ARG
         now        |       |
                   left   Frank
```

It is therefore quite natural that the nucleus of the proposition in (37) can be qualified by an adverbial of the type *two days ago*, as in the sentence

(41)   Now, Frank left two days ago.

This could not occur for the nucleus of the proposition in (38), which is already modified by the time adverbial *now*, since there would be a direct semantic conflict between the two time adverbials. Thus the expression

The Performative   **121**

(42)   *Frank left now two days ago.

is semantically anomalous.

We will conclude this chapter on the performative by examining a particularly important performative adverbial, the word *and*, important because it permits us to pass from a representation of a single sentence to a representation of discourse.

We have seen up to this point some performative adverbials that are predicates with only one argument, such as *probably* in (35), and *now* in (37). We have also looked at performative adverbials made up of a predicate with two arguments, such as *because* in (35). Such a performative adverbial is, by definition, characterized by the fact that one of its two arguments is the nucleus of the performative. However, there are also performative adverbials in which both of the arguments consist of performative nuclei. Consider the expression

(43)   Frank sleeps and John studies.

If we take these two sentences separately, as in

(44)   Frank Sleeps.
(45)   John studies.

we have two structures that can be easily represented in our model. From the point of view of the performative, we have two assertions, yielding the two configurations

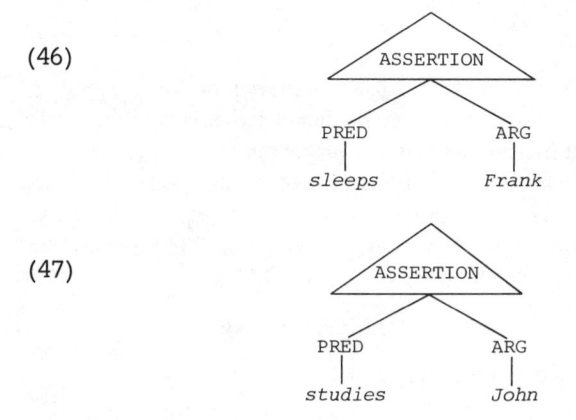

(46)
```
         ASSERTION
         /       \
       PRED      ARG
        |         |
      sleeps    Frank
```

(47)
```
         ASSERTION
         /       \
       PRED      ARG
        |         |
      studies   John
```

What is the difference between using two separate sentences such as (44) and (45), and using an expression such as (43)? It is clear that in using (43), we nevertheless make two assertions, the same assertions made in (44) and (45). But whereas (44) and (45) are separate sentences, in (43) there is a connection between the two assertions, in that the second has been joined to the first. At this point we will introduce the two-place predicate ADD, which serves as a performative adverbial in (43), taking as its arguments the two separate performatives of the sentences that underly (43). The representation of (43) then becomes

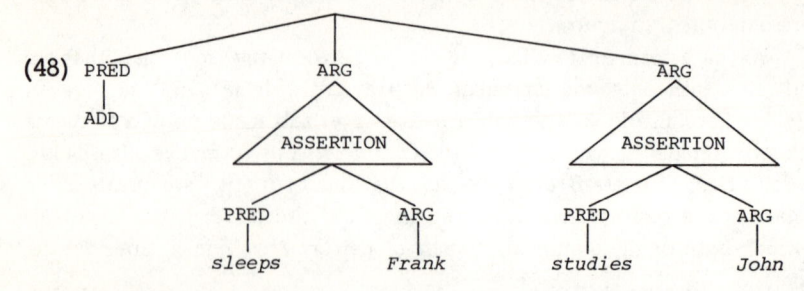

(48)
```
        PRED         ARG                    ARG
         |
        ADD      ASSERTION              ASSERTION
                 /      \                /      \
               PRED    ARG            PRED    ARG
                |       |              |       |
              sleeps  Frank          studies  John
```

Representation (48) captures the essence of the unit that we call **discourse,** the connections that distinguish a set of independent sentences from the set of sentences that form discourse. We have a discourse every time that a performative adverbial takes two or more performatives as its arguments.

This permits us to give a representation to the lexical item *and*, which would be

(49)
```
         PRED     ARG      ARG
          |        |        |
         ADD       X        Y  ⟷  /and/
```

with the further condition that X and Y must contain two performatives.

At this point we can also give a more detailed representation to the nonrestrictive noun modifiers treated in the preceding chapter. As you will recall, these modifiers consist of extra information that the speaker furnishes to the listener regarding a certain *x*, information which we represented earlier as an associated configuration that the speaker adds to the primary configuration of a sentence. Thus

(50)   *I met the janitor, who gave me the keys.*

was represented in the preceding chapter as

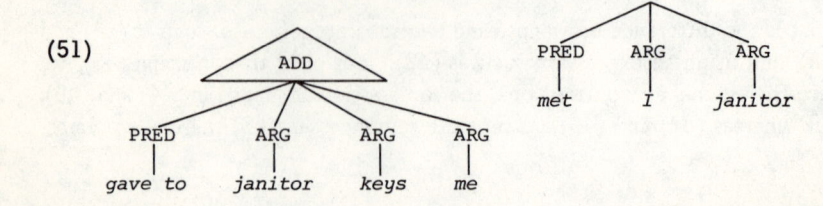

(51)
```
              ADD                       PRED  ARG   ARG
                                         |    |     |
      PRED   ARG    ARG    ARG          met   I   janitor
       |     |      |      |
    gave to janitor keys   me
```

The Performative

But we now know that the primary configuration must be dominated by a performative, which in the case of (50) would be an assertion. A further bit of reflection should convince us that a nonrestrictive clause such as *who gave me the keys* in (50) functions as an assertion which is added to the assertion represented in the primary configuration. So that if we include the triangle notation for the performative dominating the associated configuration, the representation of (50) now becomes

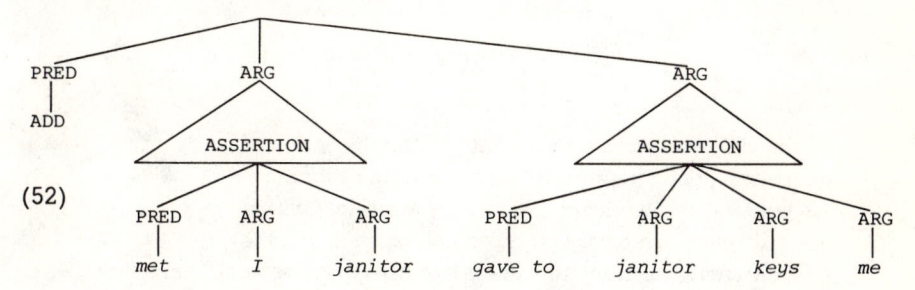

(52)

```
PRED        ARG                                    ARG
 |           △                                      △
ADD       ASSERTION                              ASSERTION
        PRED  ARG  ARG              PRED   ARG    ARG    ARG
         |    |    |                 |      |      |      |
        met   I  janitor          gave to janitor keys    me
```

A test of this relationship is the fact that a sentence such as (50) can be paraphrased with a bit of discourse of the following type:

(53)   I met the janitor and he gave me the keys.

Obviously, when the relative clause is of the restrictive type, this paraphrase will not work. Hence

(54)   I read the book that Mark gave me.

has a different representation than (52) (see the preceding chapter), and cannot be paraphrased as

(55)   I read the book and Mark gave it to me.

How, then, do we represent restrictive noun modifiers like *that Mark gave me* in (54)? The answer should become clearer in the next chapter, on presuppositions.

Presuppositions 7

In the chapter on nominals, we introduced the notion of associated configurations to represent noun modifiers. As you will recall, the configurations associated with a given sentence can be of two types, corresponding to the two different functions that noun modifiers can serve. When a modifier is used to help the listener identify the particular x to which the speaker is referring, then that associated configuration is **presupposed** by that sentence. When, instead, the modifier merely serves to give additional information about an already identified x, then the associated configuration is **added** to the sentence. Added configurations are very common, in the sense that we normally do not speak in isolated sentences but rather in discourse, adding one sentence to another. In the last chapter, on performatives, we saw how to represent the elementary connection which ties one sentence to another in discourse. As a first approximation we can now say that this same connection unites an added associated configuration with the primary configuration.

Similarly, the configurations which are presupposed by a sentence—or, more briefly, its **presuppositions**—are also an important and complex aspect of semantic representation, and therefore of the language function. However, it is an aspect that has not yet been studied sufficiently, and for that reason this chapter will be more of an exploration than a systematic treatment.

Let us begin by examining the use of presuppositions with restrictive modifiers. We said that a configuration is presupposed by a sentence in cases such as those in which the word *the* in front of a noun signals to the listener that the speaker wants him to know which particular x is being discussed. It is the information present in the associated configuration which permits the listener to identify this particular x. Without the associated configuration the sentence is not complete, or more accurately, the linguistic act that the speaker wants to carry out in uttering the sentence is not complete. Hence, in this case and in all others, a presupposition is information not contained in

Presuppositions

the primary configuration of a sentence, but which is necessary for the linguistic act carried out with that sentence to function adequately.

The fact that presupposed information is not contained in the primary configuration can be demonstrated with

(1)   *I met the janitor.*

where the information that permits the listener to understand *which* janitor is not actually mentioned in the sentence. In fact, presupposed information is generally not mentioned in a sentence that uses that presupposition. Sentences such as:

(2)   *I read the book that Mark gave me.*

are an exception, in that the presupposed information (... *that Mark gave me*) is mentioned in the same sentence that presupposes it. On the other hand, sentence (2) illustrates an obvious fact, that when a speaker cannot take for granted that his listener has available the information presupposed by a sentence, then that speaker is required to furnish such information explicitly.

In any case, as we have stated, one of the fundamental aspects of linguistic communication is that the basic unit of communication, the sentence, carries out its communicative function only on the basis of a mass of other information that is presupposed but not explicitly mentioned. The advantage of the mechanism is precisely this: a sentence can, with the help of presuppositional devices, evoke all this specific information in the listener, without requiring the speaker to mention all the presuppositions one at a time.

The greatest advantage of the mechanism of presupposition rests in the great number and variety of presuppositions that are possible for a given sentence. Presuppositions consisting of restrictive modifiers, that is those which permit the listener to identify the particular x to which a noun refers, are only one type of presupposition. In this chapter we will review a number of types of presuppositions, to give an idea of the complexity of this phenomenon. Nevertheless, as we said, many problems remain open to a more complete and systematic treatment.

Consider the three sentences

(3)   *Frank is sleeping.*
(4)   *It is Frank that is sleeping.*
(5)   <u>*Frank*</u> *is sleeping.*

(In sentence (5), *Frank* is underlined to indicate that a strong contrastive intonation or stress falls on that word). With the mechanisms for semantic representation that we have introduced so far, we cannot give these three sentences anything but an identical representation. If we look at the proposition, we find in all three the same predication *is sleeping*, with the same, single argument *Frank*. If we examine the performative, we find that all three sentences have the same performative, an assertion. And yet it is obvious that a grammar which assigned the same representation to all three sentences would certainly be incomplete, since something obviously distinguishes all three, particularly sentence (3) as compared to (4) and (5). If we ask ourselves under what circumstances we would use (3) as opposed to (4) or (5), the difference begins to emerge. To say (4) or (5) instead of (3), there must be a presupposition that someone is sleeping. Therefore in uttering (4) or (5) we limit ourselves to asserting only that this someone is Frank. Such a presupposition is absent from sentence (3). There is, then, a systematic difference between a sentence like (3) and its corresponding cleft version, (4), or between the same sentence with contrastive stress as in (5). To (3) we will give the usual representation

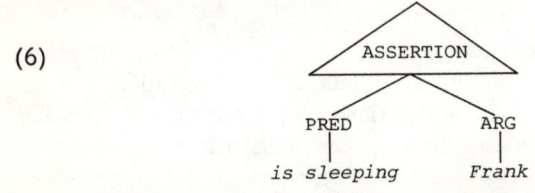

(6)

```
                ASSERTION
               /         \
            PRED          ARG
             |             |
         is sleeping     Frank
```

while to (4) and (5) we will give this representation:

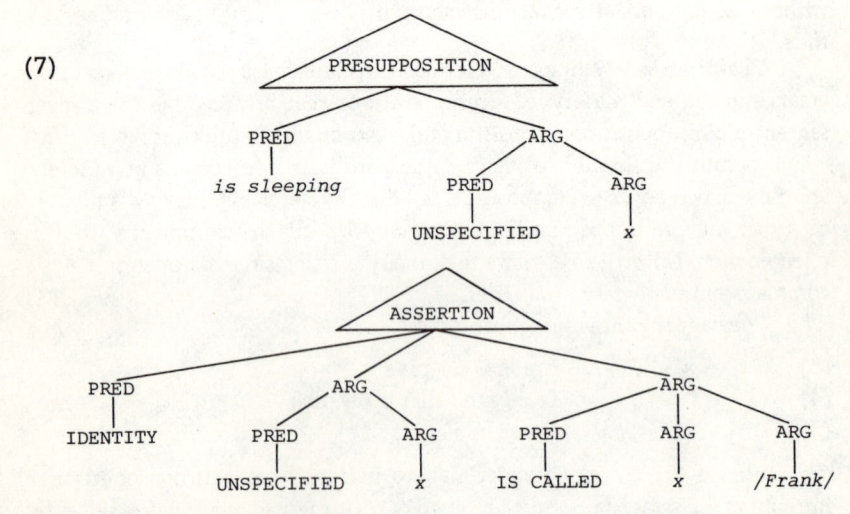

(7)

```
                    PRESUPPOSITION
                   /              \
                PRED               ARG
                 |                /    \
             is sleeping       PRED    ARG
                                |       |
                           UNSPECIFIED   x

                         ASSERTION
              /              |              \
           PRED             ARG              ARG
            |              /   \            /    \
         IDENTITY       PRED   ARG       PRED   ARG   ARG
                         |      |         |      |     |
                    UNSPECIFIED  x    IS CALLED   x   /Frank/
```

The predicate UNSPECIFIED used as a noun—that is, used to create a referent *x*—is the formalization of the concept of "something" or "someone"

Presuppositions

which we have used frequently in the preceding chapters. Note that a predication like *is sleeping* can impose specific conditions on its argument (for example, that it must be animate), and in this case the referent *x* is not completely unspecified, but instead receives some specification from its predicate. The predicate IDENTITY, in the asserted portion of representation (7), is the same predicate that we used in the identity sentences described in the chapter on nominals.

Presuppositions of this type occur also when the performative of the sentence is not declarative, but is, for example, a question. Thus the sentence

(8) *Is Frank sleeping?*

has the representation

(9)
```
              QUESTION
              /      \
           PRED      ARG
            |         |
       is sleeping  Frank
```

while the sentences

(10) *Is it Frank that is sleeping?*
(11) *Is Frank sleeping?*

have the representation

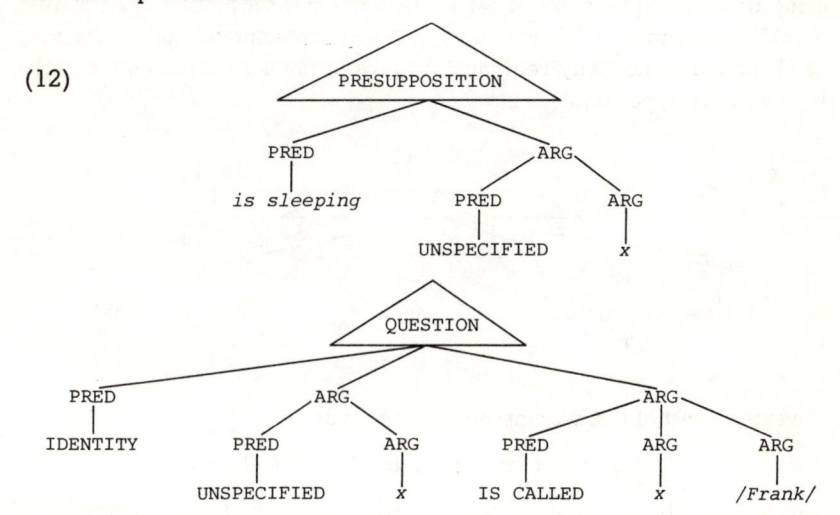

(12)
```
                    PRESUPPOSITION
                    /            \
                 PRED            ARG
                  |             /    \
             is sleeping    PRED    ARG
                              |       |
                         UNSPECIFIED  x
```

```
                         QUESTION
         /                  |                        \
       PRED                ARG                       ARG
        |                /      \                /    |    \
     IDENTITY         PRED     ARG           PRED    ARG   ARG
                       |        |             |       |     |
                  UNSPECIFIED   x         IS CALLED   x   /Frank/
```

It is interesting to observe that, while questions requiring a positive or negative answer may or may not have such a presupposition, all questions requiring more than a simple positive–negative answer do have the same presupposition as cleft or contrastive yes-no questions. Hence a question such as

(13) *Who is sleeping?*

always presupposes that someone is sleeping, and the speaker is simply asking who this someone is.

Let us turn now to another type of presupposition, associated with performatives. In the last chapter we furnished analyses of several performatives. But in fact, these analyses are not complete if we do not keep in mind that every performative carries with it certain presuppositions that regulate its use in normal communication.

Consider the sentence

(14) *Frank is going to class.*

The intention of whoever produces this sentence is to inform the listener of something. Sentence (14), then, has an assertive performative, parapharased in the last chapter as "The speaker uses the language in order that the listener assume X." Suppose now that, later on, the listener finds out that the speaker, when he said sentence (14), did not at all believe that Frank was going to class. Clearly, in this case the listener could justifiably reproach the speaker for having violated a rule of language use. In fact, to utter a sentence such as (14)–that is, to speak in order that the listener assume that Frank is going to class–presupposes above all that the speaker himself assumes that Frank is going to class. Thus a more complete representation of the meaning of (14) includes not only configuration (13) in the last chapter, but also the following presupposition:

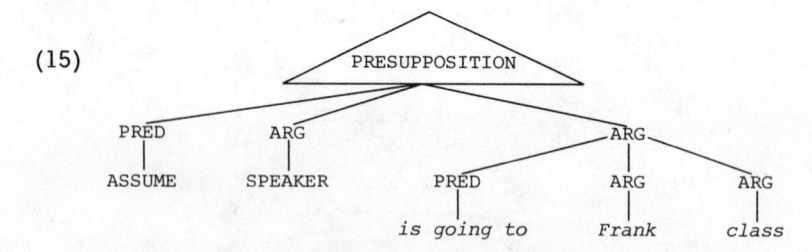

(15)
```
                    PRESUPPOSITION
        ┌──────────────┼──────────────┐
       PRED           ARG            ARG
        │              │         ┌────┴────┐
      ASSUME        SPEAKER     PRED  ARG   ARG
                                 │     │     │
                            is going to Frank class
```

An explicit test of this presupposition is the statement

(16) **Frank is going to class, but I don't believe it.*

which is clearly nonsense. In fact, to say (16) would be to presuppose "I assume that Frank is going to class" and then declare "I do not assume that

Presuppositions

Frank is going to class." We are close to a true contradiction, such as

(17)   *I believe that Frank is going to class, but I don't believe it.

The only difference is that in (17) the two contradictory sentences are both asserted, while in (16) the first is presupposed (in *Frank is going to class*) while the second is asserted. If the speaker does not assume that which he wants the listener to assume—but assumes, in fact, the opposite—we have what is commonly called a lie. Thus, if in saying (16) the speaker is not simply ignorant of whether Frank is going to class (which would also violate the presuppositions of (16)), but actually knows that Frank *isn't* going, we say that he is lying.

Presupposition (15) is not the only one which accompanies the use of an assertive performative. For example, in saying (14), the speaker presupposes that the listener does not already know beforehand that Frank is going to class. In other words, we inform someone of X when we believe that that person is ignorant of X. Otherwise, what is the point of speaking? An obvious example is the fact that one does not normally say to an adult

(18)   *You are called Frank.*

because presumably that adult already knows his name. However, (18) could be used with a small child who is learning to speak. Similarly, the assertion

(19)   *It is raining.*

is not repeated more than once, unless for example the speaker thinks that the listener didn't hear or didn't understand him.

Nevertheless, it does often happen that assertive sentences are used not to inform the listener of something he doesn't know, but to remind him of something that he already knew, or to state the premises of certain conclusions. Thus the coach who calls the team together can begin by saying

(20)   *Next Sunday we're facing the Green Bay Packers.*

—something of which his players are quite aware.

Like assertive performatives, other performatives also have their presuppositions. When information is requested, it is presupposed that the listener might know the response. So that it would make little sense to ask my neighbor what Queen Elizabeth is doing at this precise moment. Also, if I do ask a question, it is also presupposed that I myself am ignorant of the answer. For example, an adult would not normally ask

(21)   *What is my name?*

There are also particular conditions when this presupposition does not hold.

For example, in a classroom the teacher may ask the pupils "How much is two plus eight?" when she does not at all presuppose that she herself is ignorant of the answer. But in fact, it is likely that the performative underlying such "pedagogical" questions is a bit different from the performative of normal questions. Normally we ask X to know X, but a teacher asks X to find out if the pupil knows X.

The first presupposition of questions—that the listener might know the answer—is a particular case of the general presupposition of requests, the presupposition that the listener can do what he has been asked to do. Hence one would not normally ask one's neighbor to make it stop raining. The parallel between the request and the question performative is not a coincidence. In both questions and requests, the speaker uses the language to cause the listener to do something.

However, it is also clear that speakers often intentionally violate the presuppositions of assertions, requests, questions, etc. to achieve certain stylistic effects. We referred briefly to this phenomenon in the last chapter, with reference to "polite" requests that are expressed as questions. For such intentional violations to work, it is clear that both the speaker and the listener must recognize that the normal presuppositions of a particular performative are being violated. Otherwise, communication fails.

Another type of presupposition is contained in the meaning of individual lexical items. Consider the sentence

(22) *Frank is a bachelor.*

said to someone who doesn't know Frank very well. If it later comes to light that Frank is a 7-year-old boy, the listener would have cause for complaining to the speaker. In fact, sentence (22) leads the listener to believe that Frank is an adult, and not a child. This means that, within the meaning of a word like *bachelor*, we can distinguish two parts: an asserted portion (the fact of being unmarried) and a presupposed portion (the fact of being an adult). Hence the representation of the lexical item *bachelor* would be

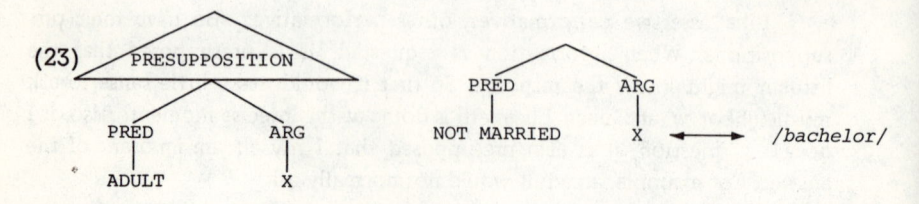

(23)
```
      PRESUPPOSITION                    PRED      ARG
       PRED      ARG                NOT MARRIED    X   ⟷  /bachelor/
       ADULT      X
```

In parallel, the representation of the meaning of sentence (24) would be

Presuppositions 131

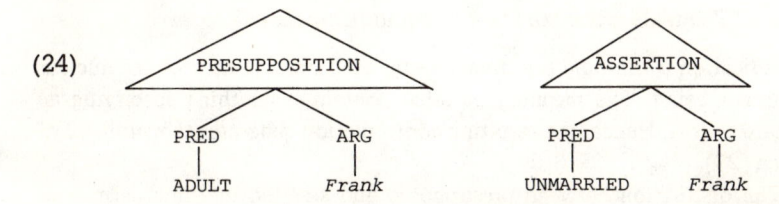

(24)
```
      PRESUPPOSITION              ASSERTION
       /         \                 /      \
     PRED       ARG             PRED      ARG
      |          |               |         |
    ADULT      Frank         UNMARRIED    Frank
```

In other words, in saying that Frank is a bachelor, it is taken for granted that Frank is an adult. If it then turns out that Frank is, instead, a child, then it is not at all clear what *Frank is a bachelor* could mean. A direct proof that to be adult is presupposed by a word like *bachelor* can be found by taking the negation of (22), which is

(25)   *Frank is not a bachelor.*

In (25) we are negating that Frank is unmarried, but it remains true that Frank is an adult. The representation of (25) is

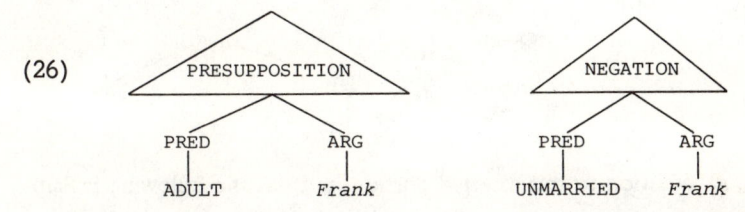

(26)
```
      PRESUPPOSITION               NEGATION
       /         \                 /      \
     PRED       ARG             PRED      ARG
      |          |               |         |
    ADULT      Frank         UNMARRIED    Frank
```

The bachelor example is not in any way an unusual case. All, or almost all, lexical items have a presupposed portion within their meaning. Given the sentence

(27)   *Frank is thinking of coming.*

we are authorized to suppose, even if we don't know who Frank is, that he is at least a human being, simply because only human beings can be arguments of a predicate like *think*. Hence *think* should be represented as

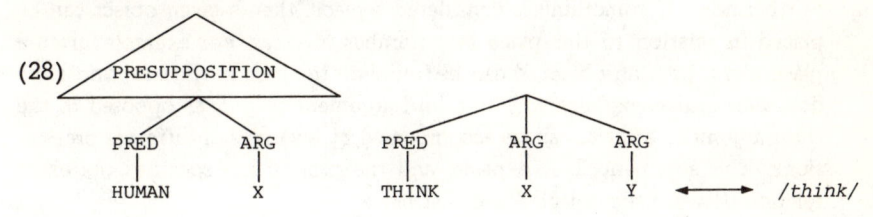

(28)
```
      PRESUPPOSITION
       /         \
     PRED       ARG         PRED    ARG   ARG
      |          |           |       |     |
    HUMAN       X          THINK     X     Y   ⟵ /think/
```

This formulation permits us to explain the strangeness of a sentence considered in the first chapter:

(29)   *The table is thinking that it would be preferable to leave.

The predication *is thinking* presupposes that the first argument of the nucleus is a human being. The meaning of *table* contains something specifying an inanimate object. Hence, the resulting contradiction generates the anomaly of sentence (29).

The distinction between presupposed and asserted meaning permits us to explain another fact that we left unsolved in Chapter 4. There we gave the same representation to the two verbs *give* and *put*. We explained the difference between the two verbs as resting on the fact that *put*, as opposed to *give*, requires conceiving of its third argument as a place. With the concepts introduced in this chapter, we can formulate more precisely the difference between these two verbs. *Put* and *give* have the same asserted portion within their meanings:

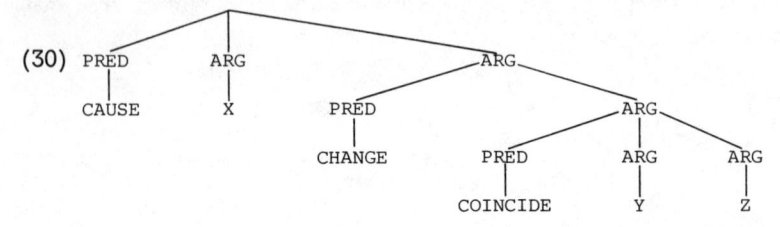

(30)
```
       PRED      ARG              ARG
        |         |          _____|_____
       CAUSE      X         PRED            ARG
                             |         _____|_____
                            CHANGE   PRED    ARG   ARG
                                      |       |     |
                                   COINCIDE   Y     Z
```

However, in addition to this asserted portion, *put* has the following presupposition:

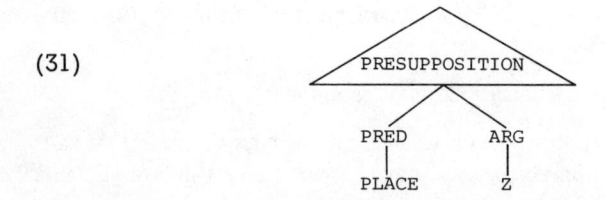

(31)
```
        PRESUPPOSITION
        _____|_____
       PRED        ARG
        |           |
       PLACE        Z
```

Furthermore, if something is considered a place, then a given object can be placed in relation to this place in a number of ways. For example, given a place like a box, an object Y can be found *on the box, in the box, under the box*, etc. Which explains why the third argument of *put*, as opposed to the third argument of *give*, can be accompanied by a variety of different prepositions. The argument Z is a place, and the preposition specifies the exact relation between the object Y and that place.

Lexical presuppositions are extremely common, and are relevant for all classes of words. Consider, for example, these three sentences:

Presuppositions 133

(32) I'm surprised that Frank won.
(33) Clyde deceived me that Frank had won.
(34) I hope that Frank won.

Listening to these three sentences, we can take for granted that the speaker in (32) assumes that Frank has won. while the speaker in (33) now assumes that Frank has not won, and finally, the speaker in (34) assumes neither interpretation. These are the three respective presuppositions of *to be surprised, to deceive,* and *to hope*. Thus, if we want to represent the meaning of these words (and, in parallel, the meanings of the three sentences (32), (33), and (34)), we will have a presupposed and an asserted portion, just as we had for the word *bachelor*.

Consider, in conclusion, the verbs *criticize* and *accuse*, in sentences

(35) Frank criticized Mark for not moving.
(36) Frank accused Mark of not moving.

These two verbs are in a reciprocal relation to one another, in that one asserts what the other presupposes, and vice-versa. Sentence (35) presupposes that Mark did not move, while asserting that Frank said that that was bad. Sentence (36) presupposes that it was bad not to move, while asserting that Frank said that Mark did not move. Hence the lexical representations for *criticize* and *accuse* contain the same semantic material, but distributed inversely between the asserted portion and the presupposed portion.

The Mapping Mechanism 8

In the preceding chapters, we have examined possible ways to represent the meaning of various aspects of a sentence. But, as noted in the first chapter, language is a system that associates sounds and meanings. Therefore, to communicate it is not sufficient to elaborate a given thought in one's own mind. It is also necessary to translate that thought into words. This requires articulating the sounds that correspond to that particular thought—sounds that correspond in the sense that the listener, upon hearing them, will be able to reconstruct in his own mind the speaker's thought as opposed to some other meaning. A situation in which an individual, the speaker, communicates with another, the listener, can be represented graphically as follows:

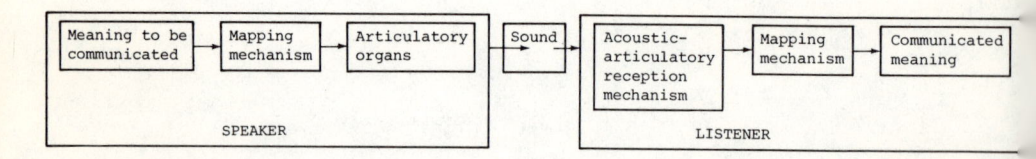

| Meaning to be communicated | → | Mapping mechanism | → | Articulatory organs | → Sound → | Acoustic-articulatory reception mechanism | → | Mapping mechanism | → | Communicated meaning |

SPEAKER   LISTENER

The mapping mechanism would not be necessary if a speaker could present directly to his listener the meanings that he wants to communicate. But listeners do not have direct access to the speaker's brain; the speaker is restricted to a single means of communicating thoughts—the emission of sounds or other signals, directly accessible to the listener, from which that listener can retrieve the speaker's thoughts. Hence an organism that communicates linguistically must have at his disposal, in addition to a mechanism capable of constructing semantic configurations, a mechanism capable of emitting sounds, and, along with this, a system that can give the emitting mechanism highly precise instructions so that for each specific semantic configuration that is constructed there can be a corresponding production of sounds with highly specific characteristics. By "highly specific" we mean that a second organism capable of receiving sounds (the listener) will be able to reconstruct the semantic configuration used to generate those sounds (and no other configuration), by processing the sounds produced by the first organism via the same intervening mechanism.

It is the task of this mapping mechanism to transfer the characteristics of the semantic configuration into the characteristics of the chain of sounds, and vice-versa. To accomplish this efficiently, the mechanism must take a number of factors into account. Above all, it must insure that the chain of sounds will permit the retrieval of *all* the information contained in the semantic configuration—and nothing more. Second, the retrieval of such semantic information must take place as rapidly as possible, requiring a minimum of mental work on the part of the listener. Finally, the mechanism must minimize the risk of misunderstanding (cases in which the listener constructs a semantic representation different from that one intended by the speaker), ambiguity (cases in which the listener constructs two possible semantic representations and does not know which one to choose), and uncertainty (cases in which the listener cannot reconstruct a semantic representation for the sentence he receives). These constraints sometimes work in opposition to one another. For example, the criterion of maximally rapid communication may interfere with the need to avoid misunderstanding. The mapping mechanism will have to be efficient enough to carry out its task in the best possible manner, achieving the optimal compromise among the various constraints taken together.

Let us turn now to describing some characteristics of this mapping mechanism. Unfortunately, research in this area is not far advanced, so that our description of the mapping mechanism will necessarily be both incomplete and imprecise. Above all, like all of the model of language that we are presenting, this description will be subject to revision.

The mapping mechanism can be described in general terms as a list of rules. All mapping rules have the general form

(1) $$A \leftrightarrow a$$

in which A indicates some characteristic of the semantic configuration of a sentence, and a indicates some characteristic of the sound sequence with which the sentence will be expressed. Hence mapping rule (1) must be interpreted as

(2)   If, in the semantic configuration of a sentence, there is a characteristic A, do what is necessary to insure that the sounds expressing the sentence have characteristic a.

The arrow uniting A with a points in two directions because the rule holds true for the listener as well. In the latter case, the rule should read

(3)   If, in the sound sequence that you hear there is a characteristic a, the semantic configuration that you construct to interpret those sounds must have characteristic A.

  The semantic configuration of a sentence contains two types of information. For the sake of convenience (and ignoring the many other meanings that these terms have in linguistics), we will call the first type **content information** and the second type **structural information.** Content information consists of the particular semantic components that are found in the configuration. Structural information regards the relations among these semantic components, and above all information specifying which portion is the nucleus and which is the adverbial, which occurs in a dominant clause and which in a subordinate, which is the performative and which is the proposition, what things are presupposed and what things instead are asserted, asked, commanded, etc. The sum of these two types of information form the total information found in the semantic representation of a sentence—and so all the information that the mapping rules must transfer into sounds. If the listener manages to deduce from the sounds which components the speaker has used, how he has connected one with another, which portion contains the nucleus and which contains the adverbials, what are the dominant clauses and which are the subordinates, etc.—he will have retrieved all the semantic information that interests him, and has thereby understood the sentence.

  Let's take an example. Suppose that the semantic configuration to be communicated is the following:

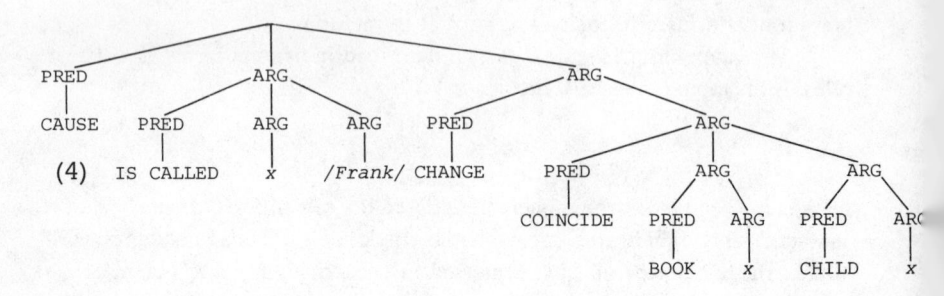

(4)
```
         PRED        ARG              ARG
          |           |                |
      ┌───┴──┐        |          ┌─────┴─────┐
    CAUSE  PRED      ARG   ARG  PRED        ARG
            |         |     |    |      ┌────┴────┐
        IS CALLED    x  /Frank/ CHANGE ARG       ARG
                                        |         |
                                      ┌─┴─┐     ┌─┴─┐
                                     PRED ARG  PRED ARG
                                      |    |    |    |
                                  COINCIDE      
                                     BOOK  x   CHILD  x
```

We suggest that (4) is the semantic configuration underlying the sentence

(5)   Frank gives a book to the child.

(4) is not a complete representation of the meaning of the sentence. It lacks the performative, certain presuppositions, and some aspects of the meaning that are expressed as the present tense of the verb (*gives*) and the articles *a* (*a book*) and *the* (*the child*). Furthermore, the semantic components are only in part truly elementary components, in the sense that no further analysis can be applied. For example, BOOK and CHILD are certainly not elementary components. But these flaws are not critical for present purposes. We would stress instead that (4) contains two types of information. First, it contains certain semantic components and no others: CAUSE, IS CALLED, /Frank/, CHANGE, COINCIDE, BOOK, and CHILD. This is the content information. Second, (4) contains structural information. For example, (4) tells us that IS CALLED (/Frank/) is the first argument of CAUSE, while CHILD is the second argument of COINCIDE and not vice-versa. If it were the other way around, we would have the semantic configuration for the sentence.

(6)   The child gives a book to Frank.

rather than (4). Sentences (5) and (6) have the same content information, but they contain different structural information.

If in the information contained in the semantic configuration we can distinguish between content and structural information, then analogously among the mapping rules we can distinguish between rules which map content information and rules which map structural information. Nevertheless, while the distinction between structural and content information within the semantic configuration is fairly clear, the distinction between rules that map the first type of information and rules that map the second type is only approximate, insofar as a single mapping rule may also project a combination of both types of information. We can at most suggest that there are rules which map primarily structural information and rules which map primarily content information. We will call the first **lexical mapping rules** and the second **syntactic mapping rules**. Hence we will call the system of lexical mapping rules the **lexicon,** and the set of syntactic mapping rules the **syntax.** However, let us keep in mind that the distinction between lexicon and syntax is not absolute. For example, the lexicon, in the great majority of cases, maps part of the structural information as well. *Give* projects not only the components CAUSE, CHANGE, and COINCIDE, but also the particular way in which these are combined (e.g., which component takes the other as its argument). This distinction is useful overall, but may sometimes be difficult to maintain.

138   **The Mapping Mechanism**

Lexical rules and syntactic rules are then distinguished by the type of semantic information that they map or, in other terms, by the type of element *A* in rule (1). In general, we can say that the lexical rules transfer their particular type of information (content) into the particular words used in a sentence. Instead, syntactic rules transfer their type of information (structural) into such relations as the order between words, certain aspects of morphology (e.g., the endings applied to words), and into characteristics like pause and intonation. Nevertheless, as we have insisted, this distinction is approximate. There are cases in which structural information is mapped into sound with a given word (for example, the word *that* indicates the beginning of a subordinate clause, as we shall see shortly). There are also cases in which content information is mapped into sound through morphology or intonation (for example, the verb forms indicating past or future tense express a precise set of semantic components—see the chapter on componential analysis). The semantic configuration of the request performative, for example, is expressed with imperative verb endings, and the question performative is expressed with a particular kind of rising intonation plus a rearrangement of the word order.

Let us return to configuration (4), to examine some concrete illustrations of the way that mapping rules operate to transfer the information in this configuration into the information contained in sounds.

Suppose that the following four rules are found among the lexical rules:

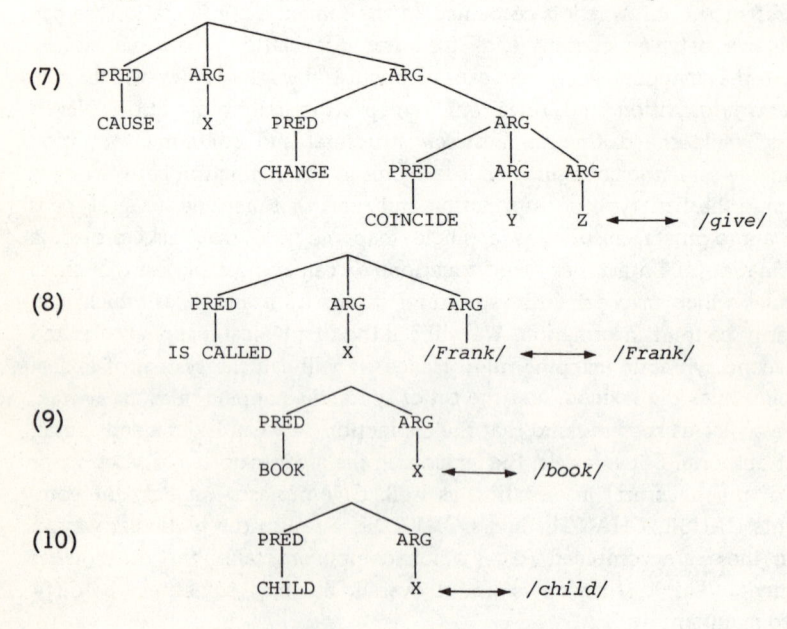

(7)
```
       PRED    ARG         ARG
        |       |           |
       CAUSE    X         PRED    ARG
                           |       |
                         CHANGE  PRED   ARG  ARG
                                  |      |    |
                                COINCIDE Y    Z  ⟷  /give/
```

(8)
```
       PRED      ARG    ARG
        |         |      |
     IS CALLED    X    /Frank/  ⟷  /Frank/
```

(9)
```
       PRED    ARG
        |      |
       BOOK    X   ⟷  /book/
```

(10)
```
       PRED    ARG
        |      |
       CHILD   X   ⟷  /child/
```

The Mapping Mechanism

As should be evident, such lexical rules are the same things that we called *lexical representation* in the chapter on componential analysis. To the left we have a configuration of components, the element A, and to the right the sound into which that configuration must be mapped, the element a. To be more precise, a lexical mapping rule, for example (7), can be formulated as follows:

(7b) In the semantic configuration there is the subconfiguration

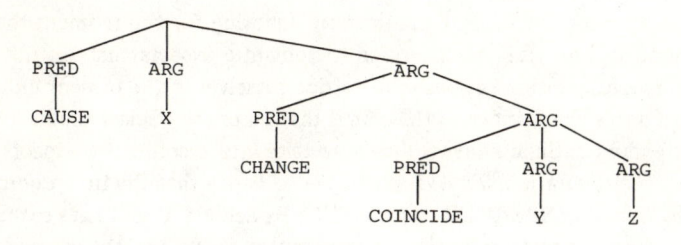

```
         PRED    ARG         ARG
          |                  
        CAUSE    X      PRED       ARG
                         |
                       CHANGE   PRED    ARG  ARG
                                 |       |    |
                              COINCIDE   Y    Z
```

Map this subconfiguration with *give*.

The mapping mechanism, with regard to the lexicon, functions in the following manner. If, within the semantic configuration of a sentence, one finds a subconfiguration (a partial configuration) identical to the configuration corresponding to element A of a given lexical rule, the speaker will select the element a of the rule to express this subconfiguration. By dividing the semantic configuration into such subconfigurations and finding for each one a lexical rule capable of expressing it, without leaving anything outside, the mapping mechanism transfers the content information of that sentence into sound. Configuration (4) could be subdivided as follows:

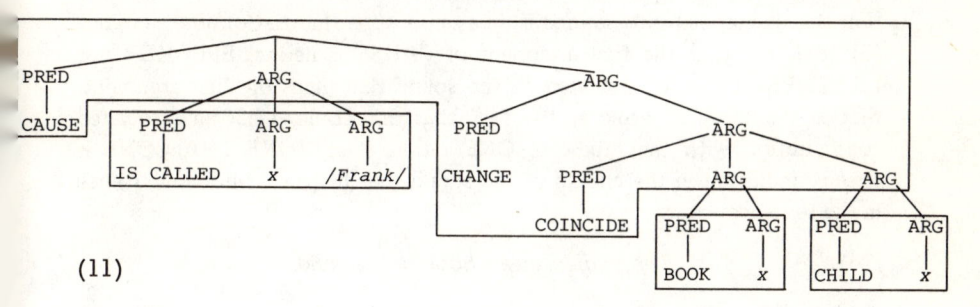

```
PRED      ARG                         ARG
 |
CAUSE  PRED     ARG   ARG    PRED           ARG
        |                     |
     IS CALLED   x   /Frank/ CHANGE  PRED         ARG
                                      |
                                   COINCIDE  PRED  ARG   PRED  ARG
                                              |    |      |    |
                                             BOOK  x    CHILD  x
(11)
```

After this has been done, we note that the four subconfigurations into which we have subdivided (11) correspond to the four lexical rules listed above (rules 7–10). This means that the mapping mechanism can map (11) into the sounds *give, Frank, book,* and *child.*

But let's look at another aspect of the mapping of configuration (4), in particular the way in which the nuclear predication of that configuration is mapped. Following lexical mapping rule (7), we should map this predication with *give*. But we know that the correct sentence is (5), and not

(12) *Frank give a book to the child.*

It is therefore necessary to have rules that assign the proper endings to the sound that maps the nuclear predication. Ignoring for the moment the tense and mood of the verb, which refer to semantic aspects that are not represented in configuration (4), we will restrict ourselves to the present indicative. We need a rule that assigns to the sound that maps the nuclear predication the proper ending *-s*. Such a rule will have to take into account two aspects of the semantic configuration. First, it will have to verify that the first argument of CAUSE is neither SPEAKER nor LISTENER. Second, it will have to make use of a semantic distinction that is not represented in (4), i.e., the presence of an associated configuration in which ONE or MORE THAN ONE (see the chapter on nominals) are predicates of the same x that is the first argument of CAUSE. Hence, the rule that results is the following:

(13) *The nominal which is the first argument of CAUSE is neither SPEAKER nor LISTENER, and has an associated configuration in which ONE is a predicate of the same x that appears in that nominal.* $\longleftrightarrow$ *The sound that maps the nuclear predication ends in -s.*

Applying this rule, we can be sure that the correct sentence is (5) rather than (12).

Rule (13) is a particular type of syntactic rule, in which the information that is mapped into sounds is, in a sense, superfluous. Consider sentence (5): the fact that the first argument of CAUSE is neither SPEAKER nor LISTENER is already indicated in the sound that maps the first argument, that is, *Frank*. Furthermore, the fact that this nominal has an associated configuration with the predicate ONE rather than MORE THAN ONE is already indicated in the ending of the sound that maps that nominal. Hence in the sentence:

(14) *The soldiers give a book to the child.*

another mapping rule has already been applied, formulated as:

(15) *There is an associated configuration in which MORE THAN ONE is the predicate of the same x as the nominal. The sound that maps such a nominal ends in -s.*

The Mapping Mechanism

We might ask why there is such redundancy in the mapping rules, why there is more than one rule to carry the same semantic information into sound. Redundancy seems to exist in languages for at least two reasons. First of all, a certain amount of redundancy is generally useful because there is a greater guarantee that the information will be communicated to the listener, as we know from information theory. An ending may not have been perceived by the listener, for example the *-s* in *soldiers,* so that the ending on *give* (without the *-s*) guarantees that the listener will reconstruct the correct semantic configuration, i.e., MORE THAN ONE predicated of the *x* in the nominal that is the first argument of CAUSE.

Second, there are in most languages sentences in which what is normally redundant information ceases to be so. This can be demonstrated with more evidence in a language like Italian, in which there is more redundancy than in English. In Italian the verb agrees in both number and person with the first argument of CAUSE. Hence, in the sentence

(16)   *I soldati danno un libro al bambino.*
         (The soldiers give a book to the child.)

the verb *danno* (give) has a third person plural ending. But consider two more facts about Italian. First, Italian permits a sentence such as

(17)   *Danno un libro al bambino.*

in which the first argument of *danno,* i.e., *i soldati* (the soldiers), is not mapped. In such cases, only the ending of the verb tells us that the first argument of CAUSE is neither SPEAKER nor LISTENER, and that MORE THAN ONE is a predicate of the same *x* that is that argument. Although such sentences would be ungrammatical in English, it is worth noting that in certain situations speakers will take advantage of the same sort of redundancy—in highly casual speech (e.g., "How was your day?—Oh, got a lot of work done..."), in informal letter writing, and certainly in telegrams.

A second possibility in Italian is the sentence:

(18)   *I due leoni ha ucciso il cacciatore.*
         (The hunter killed the two lions.)

in which the first argument of CAUSE does not precede the predication *ha ucciso* (killed) in the sequence of sounds, but instead follows it. In this case as well, it is only the ending of the verb that tells us that the first argument of CAUSE has the predicate ONE. Hence in this case as well, rule (13) is no longer redundant.

We have indicated the general form that mapping rules take. We have also seen that, among the kinds of information present in the semantic representation of a sentence, we can roughly distinguish between content information and structural information. Content information is mapped mostly (but not always) with lexical mapping rules. Structural information is mapped mostly (but not exclusively) with syntactical mapping rules. With regard to the first type of mapping rules, a description of the mapping mechanism presents few problems. It is primarily a matter of describing the lexicon of the language. In Chapter 4 on componential analysis we presented a series of lexical mapping rules of English. The task is a matter of extending componential analysis to the rest of the lexical items. However, with regard to syntactic mapping rules it is not possible at this point to present many specific rules beyond those illustrated above, particularly since research on the nature of such rules has not progressed very far. We will try instead to indicate a rough outline of the kinds of structural information contained in the semantic configurations of sentences in a given language, and the kinds of syntactic rules that will be necessary to map such information. For each type of structural information, we will also indicate quite briefly the kinds of surface means that the syntactic rules of English use to map that item.

The distinction between nucleus and adverbial is above all a distinction between nuclear predications and adverbial predications. Nuclear predications are recognizable in English because they are always mapped with a verb. This is never true for adverbial predications. Once we have identified nuclear versus adverbial predications, the problem is to identify the nominals that form the arguments of each type of predication, so as to complete the identification of the entire nucleus and the entire adverbial. But before we can identify which nominals belong to which predications, there is one other type of structural information that must be determined, concerning what semantic material belongs to the nominal itself. We have seen that a nominal can be extremely complex, in part because a given noun can take one or more modifiers. The problem, for the mapping mechanism, is to assign given sounds as the modifiers of a particular noun, and thereby establish that it is part of a given nominal. Here one of the primary superficial characteristics used for this goal is the relative proximity of nouns and modifiers. Noun modifiers, in English, tend to precede or occasionally follow immediately the noun that they modify. In English, the two fundamental mapping rules seem to be the following. When an associated configuration is mapped with a verb in the finite mode, the corresponding modifier—a relative clause—*follows* the noun it modifies. When instead the associated configuration is mapped without a verb in the finite mode, the corresponding modifier—an attribute—immediately *precedes* the noun it modifies.

At this point it is possible to map a third item of structural information, the information concerning which nominals are the arguments of a given

The Mapping Mechanism

predication. Note that knowledge of a given lexical item must include knowledge of the number and type of arguments that the predication requires. For example, with a predication like *give*, we know that we must look for three arguments to complete the meaning of the predication. But since a sentence can have several predications and a large number of possible arguments, our problem is to find, among all the nominals present in a sentence, which are the arguments of a given predication and which belong instead to some other predication. In particular, we must determine which nominals are arguments of the nucleus and which belong to the adverbial. Here too the characteristics of the English mapping mechanism tend to involve relative proximity as a means of conveying this information. A nominal tends to be found near the predication of which it is an argument rather than some other predication. For example, if an adverbial has a second argument, other than the obligatory nucleus, that argument follows immediately after the adverbial predication. Since adverbial predications are recognizable for the fact that they cannot ever be mapped with a verb, the nearness of the second argument to that predication keeps it isolated and distinct from the material belonging to the nucleus.

If a predication has more than one argument, then we have the problem of mapping a fourth bit of structural information, regarding the place a given nominal occupies in the predicate. This problem was confronted earlier in a specific case, when we sought a rule that would permit us to distinguish sentence (5) from sentence (6). It is often the case that, when a predicate has more than one argument, some arguments are preceded by prepositions (e.g., *for Bill*, *to Cincinnati*, etc.). In these instances, the preposition indicates the particular place in the predicate that a nominal occupies.

The mapping rules considered so far pertain to the structural information within a single sentential structure. But these rules can be applied recursively to all the sentential structures within a given sentence. For example, if a given sentence has a sentential structure embedded as an argument of the main clause or of the adverbial, the mapping rules apply within both the embedded structure and the dominant configuration. The problem is, however, to keep these sentential structures distinct from one another, indicating which is dominant and which are subordinate. If this problem is not resolved, then even though the mapping rules specify how material is organized within a given sentential structure, the material of one structure may be confused with the material of another. Above all, unless the boundaries are clear it is not possible to reconstruct the precise place occupied by each structure in the semantic representation as a whole.

As we saw in the chapters on the nucleus and adverbial, a subordinate sentential structure can be mapped on the surface in either explicit or implicit form. In the latter case, the structure is clearly marked as a subordinate by the fact that the predication of the nucleus is not assigned the morphological form of finite verbs. However, the problem remains open in those cases in which the structure is mapped on the surface in explicit form, with a nuclear predication that is assigned finite verb endings. When this occurs, it is necessary to find some other way of isolating the sentential structure and assigning it the role of subordinate. The English language uses three surface means for this goal, depending on whether the sentential structure is the argument of the nucleus or of the adverbial, or whether it is a relative clause serving as a modifier.

The first of these superficial means is the word *that*, which is inserted in the chain of sounds in order to indicate to the listener that the sentential structure to follow will be a subordinate. The listener then knows that the next sentential structure must be taken as a block and considered as the argument of another sentential structure, or the modifier of the noun that immediately precedes *that*.

The second of the surface means consists in the use of a small group of words that by their very presence in the chain of sounds mark the sentential structure that immediately follows as an argument of the adverbial or as a modifier of a noun. In the first case, we have the so-called conjunctions: *because, although, if,* etc. In the second case, we have so-called relative pronouns, such as *which, who, whose,* and *whom.*

Finally, the third surface means used in English to mark a sentential structure either as a nuclear argument or as a noun modifier consists in placing the whole structure immediately after that nucleus or noun, without any particular words to mark the beginning of the intended subordinate. When this means is used, the listener has two ways of determining the status of the clause that follows as either a nuclear argument or noun modifier. In the first case, a subordinate sentential structure may follow directly after another sentential structure which has an argument still to be filled. Since the listener knows that there is still an argument missing, he will examine the embedded sentential structure to determine whether it fills that function. In the second case, when one nominal follows immediately after another, the simple juxtaposition of the modifier after the nominal it modifies will require us to interpret that second nominal as the subject of an associated configuration. This is usually the only possible interpretation when one nominal follows another in this fashion, as in the sentence

(19)   *The dog you see in the garden is mine.*

where *you* follows immediately after *dog*. However, if the subject of the associated configuration is the shared nominal to be deleted, then the modifier cannot simply follow the noun it modifies, as in

(20)   *The dog is running in the garden is mine.

For a sentence like (20) to be grammatical, it is necessary to signal explicitly on the surface the presence of the sentential modifier, using the above mentioned word *that*, as in

(21)   The dog that is running in the garden is mine.

We have examined the rough outlines of a mapping mechanism. For all the various subdivisions of the information contained in the semantic representation of a sentence, including both content and structural information, there are rules that apply to each subdivision, transferring it into acoustic information. Particularly for the lexical mapping rules examined so far, notice that each application of a rule (i.e., assignment of a word) is largely independent of the context. The rules operate without particular regard for the other words among which a given word is inserted in discourse (the linguistic context), and with little regard for the concrete situation in which the sentence is uttered by a speaker to a listener (extralinguistic context). In other words, by using the mapping rules introduced so far, the listener can retrieve the appropriate semantic information, and hence understand the sentence, by taking into consideration one at a time the words uttered by the speaker, without worrying about either the linguistic or the extralinguistic context in which those words were uttered.

For example, given the sequence of sounds

(22)   The chair touches the table.

the listener can recover the corresponding semantic structure, which in abbreviated form would be[1]

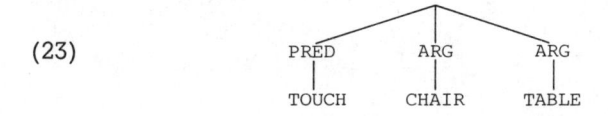

(23)
```
          _____|_____
         |           |           |
        PRED        ARG         ARG
         |           |           |
       TOUCH       CHAIR       TABLE
```

(23) can be derived merely by using the appropriate lexical and syntactic rules, without noting the context in which each word was uttered. We might say that in a sentence like (22), the information which the listener needs can all be found in the sequence of sounds; there is no need to consider the

---

[1] We are ignoring here the semantic structure of articles.

context. If we represent with dotted arrows the operation of mapping rules, then we can represent sentence (22) as follows:

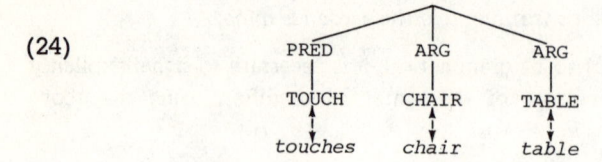

(24)
```
              PRED         ARG         ARG
               |            |           |
              TOUCH        CHAIR       TABLE
               ↕            ↕           ↕
             touches       chair       table
```

This way of mapping semantic information into sounds, using rules that are independent of the context, is not the only way to communicate. An important aspect of the mapping mechanism is that it also includes rules that map some semantic information through use of the context. Consider this sequence of sounds:

(25)   *The chair touches it.*

Obviously, without a well-determined context, the listener cannot derive the appropriate semantic information for (25). If, however, (25) is inserted within a passage of discourse, as with the example

(26)   *Look at the table. The chair touches it.*

then the listener is once again able to derive the semantic representation, which in the particular case of (26) is similar to (22). To understand (25), then, the listener must use a mapping rule that operates by way of the context. We will call the mapping rules that make use of the context **contextual rules**. Non-contextual rules can be represented schematically as follows:

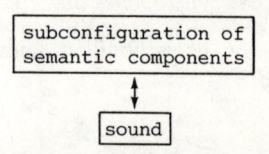

```
        ┌──────────────────────┐
        │  subconfiguration of │
        │  semantic components │
        └──────────────────────┘
                   ↕
              ┌────────┐
              │ sound  │
              └────────┘
```

But contextual mapping rules have the following representation:

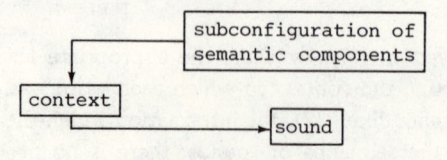

```
           ┌──────────────────────┐
       ┌───│  subconfiguration of │
       │   │  semantic components │
       │   └──────────────────────┘
       ↓
  ┌─────────┐            ┌────────┐
  │ context │───────────▶│ sound  │
  └─────────┘            └────────┘
```

(25) is not an isolated example. There are a variety of contextual rules, which we will examine according to the kind of context that they employ.

For some, the context is found within the very sentence in which the

The Mapping Mechanism

rule operates. Consider the sentence

(27)   *Frank washes himself.*

Let us try to determine the way in which this sentence was mapped, from a semantic representation into the particular sound sequence of (27). The semantic representation of (27) is

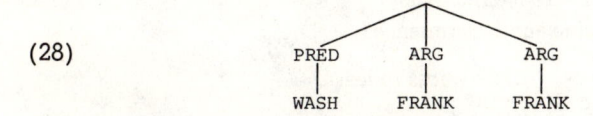

(28)
```
              _____|_____
             |      |      |
            PRED   ARG    ARG
             |      |      |
            WASH  FRANK  FRANK
```

If there were no contextual mapping rules, then the only possible way to represent the mapping of (28) would be

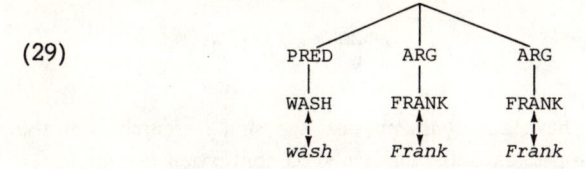

(29)
```
              _____|_____
             |      |      |
            PRED   ARG    ARG
             |      |      |
            WASH  FRANK  FRANK
             ↕      ↕      ↕
            wash  Frank  Frank
```

But such a representation is not correct. In fact, while we can indeed say that WASH is mapped as *wash* and FRANK is mapped as *Frank*, there is no mapping rule in English which would automatically map the second FRANK as *himself*. To be convinced of this, it is sufficient to consider the sentence

(30)   *Bill washes himself.*

where *himself* would map not FRANK, but BILL. In other words, that which *himself* maps will vary within the context. Therefore *himself* must belong among the contextual mapping rules. Such a contextual mapping rule might be the following:

(31)   *If a nominal is coreferential with the subject, and that subject is neither SPEAKER nor LISTENER, and if the subject is a person and a male, then map such a nominal with* himself.

Hence the correct representation for the mapping of (28) is not (29) but

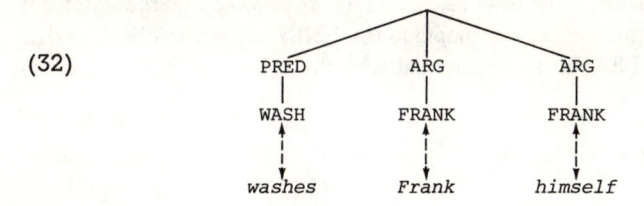

(32)
```
              _____|_____
             |      |      |
            PRED   ARG    ARG
             |      |      |
            WASH  FRANK  FRANK
             ↕      ↕      ↕
           washes  Frank  himself
```

When the listener hears the word *himself*, he will not directly reconstruct FRANK, but must instead pass through the context. He will find the subject nominal in the chain of sounds (*Frank*) and from this recover the semantic representation FRANK. At this point, through rule (31), he will know that the subject nominal is identical to the argument he is seeking for *himself*. The process functions in the opposite direction from the speaker's point of view, hence the arrows in (32) are bidirectional.

Let us now examine another sentence:

(33) *Clare wants to leave.*

which has the semantic representation

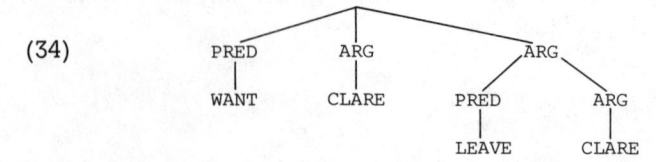

(34)
```
           PRED    ARG       ARG
            |       |       /    \
           WANT   CLARE   PRED   ARG
                           |      |
                          LEAVE  CLARE
```

In this case too, we have an argument—i.e., the single argument of the predicate LEAVE—mapped onto the surface via a contextual mapping rule. The correct representation for the mapping of (34) would be

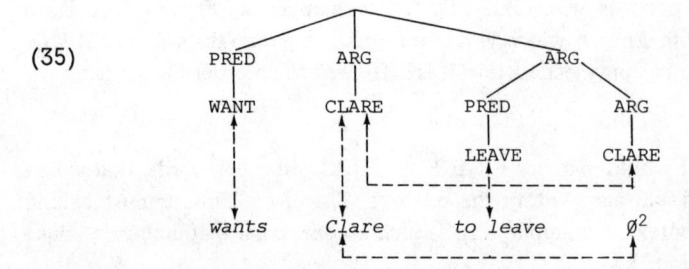

(35)
```
           PRED    ARG       ARG
            |       |       /    \
           WANT   CLARE   PRED   ARG
                           |      |
                          LEAVE  CLARE

          wants   Clare   to leave   ∅²
```

where the argument of LEAVE, which is CLARE, is not mapped with a normal non-contextual mapping rule, which would produce the sound *Clare*, but rather with a contextual mapping rule that refers back to the argument of the higher predicate WANT. In other words, given a sentence like (33), the listener knows that the individual who leaves is the same person as the individual who wants. How does he know this? What would be the statement on the right of this contextual mapping rule? What signals the listener that the argument of LEAVE is coreferential with the argument of WANT is the

---

² This symbol means "no sound."

The Mapping Mechanism

infinitive form of the verb LEAVE, i.e., *to leave*. The mapping rule could be formulated as

(36) *If there is a subject nominal of a subordinate sentence that is co-referential with one of the arguments of the nucleus, map this nominal with ϕ and add the infinitive morpheme to to the left of the verb that maps the predicate of which this nominal is an argument.*

Let us turn now to some other contextual rules, which operate on a wider context than the one contained in the immediate sentence. First we will examine some rules that operate on coordinate semantic structures, structures united by the predicate ADD. Consider the sentence

(37)   *Mary drinks wine and Carl water.*

which has the following semantic representation and (in short form) mapping:

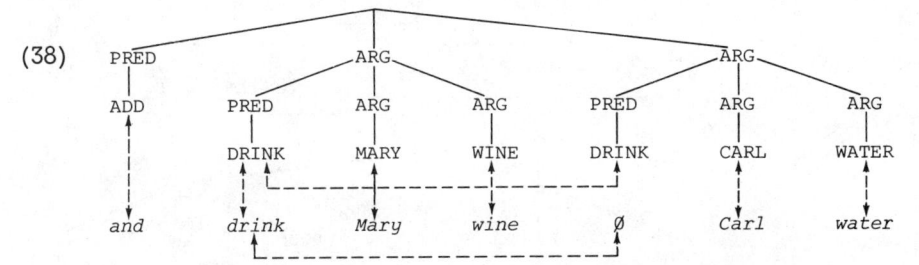

(38)
```
        PRED ────────ARG────────        ────ARG────
         │         ╱    │    ╲          ╱    │    ╲
        ADD     PRED  ARG   ARG      PRED  ARG   ARG
         │       │     │     │        │     │     │
         │     DRINK  MARY  WINE    DRINK  CARL  WATER
         ↓       ↓     ↓     ↓        ↓     ↓     ↓
        and    drink  Mary  wine      ∅    Carl  water
```

The mapping rule for coordinate structures could be expressed as

(39) *Given two structures united by the predicate ADD, if there are one or more subconfigurations which are present in both these structures, map the second of these identical subconfigurations with ϕ.*

This rule is formulated in more general terms than are needed for sentence (37) alone. In (37) what is shared by both structures is the predication DRINK. If, instead of speaking only of predications, we have used the more general concept of subconfigurations, it is because we can have one single rule valid not only for sentences such as (37), but also for many other coordinate sentences, such as

(40)   *Frank speaks slowly and clearly*
(41)   *Frank drinks wine and beer.*
(42)   *Frank and Mary drink wine.*

which have, respectively, the following representations:

(43)

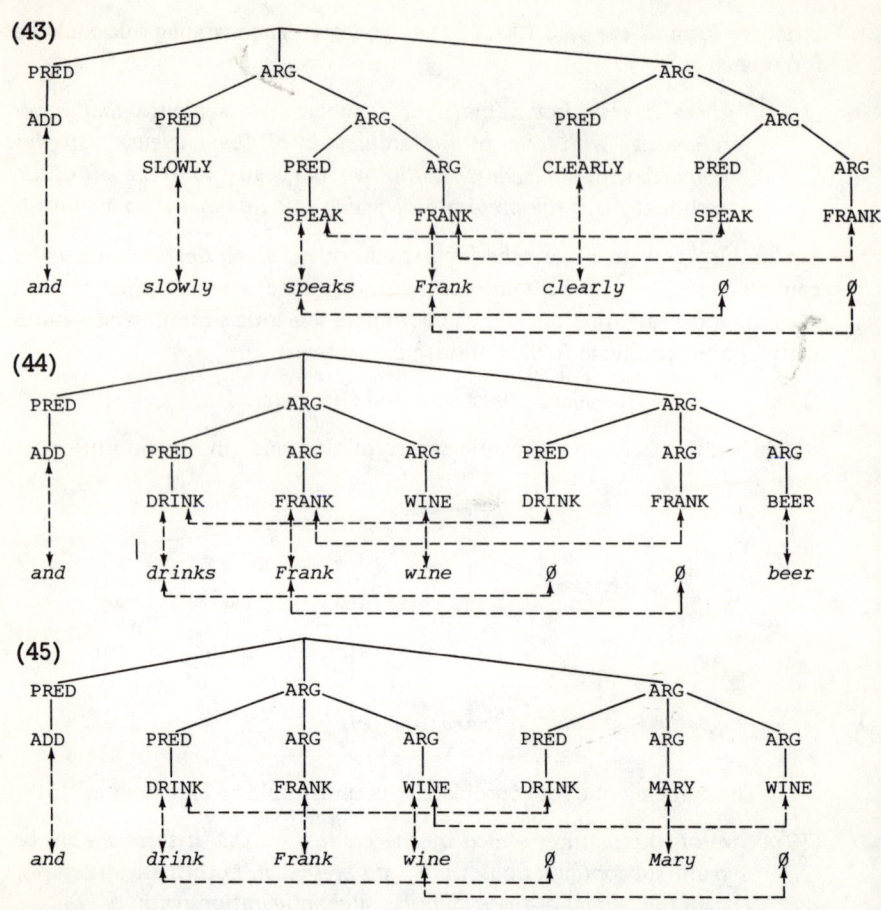

```
         PRED ─────── ARG ─────────────────── ARG ──────────
ADD    PRED       PRED ──── ARG        PRED       PRED ──── ARG
 │      │          │         │          │          │         │
 │    SLOWLY     SPEAK      FRANK     CLEARLY    SPEAK      FRANK
 │      │          │         │          │          │         │
and   slowly    speaks      Frank     clearly      ∅          ∅
```

(44)

```
         PRED ─────── ARG ─────────────────── ARG ──────────
ADD    PRED    ARG    ARG        PRED    ARG    ARG
 │      │       │      │          │       │      │
 │    DRINK   FRANK   WINE      DRINK   FRANK   BEER
 │      │       │      │          │       │      │
and   drinks  Frank   wine        ∅       ∅     beer
```

(45)

```
         PRED ─────── ARG ─────────────────── ARG ──────────
ADD    PRED    ARG    ARG        PRED    ARG    ARG
 │      │       │      │          │       │      │
 │    DRINK   FRANK   WINE      DRINK   MARY   WINE
 │      │       │      │          │       │      │
and   drink   Frank   wine        ∅     Mary    ∅
```

The last example is particularly interesting, in that it illustrates how, given a general rule that the verb must agree in number with the subject, the subjects of the two coordinate structures function as a single plural subject, so that the verb has the plural ending (*drink*, instead of *drinks*). This poses a problem regarding why the plural ending appears in some cases when the subject has the component MORE THAN ONE (see mapping rule (15)), and other times when there are two singular subjects in coordinate structures. It would be preferable to have a single condition in semantic representation which determines the mapping of the plural verb ending. We might offer the hypothesis that the predicate MORE THAN ONE is not elementary, but always contains the predicate ADD. Hence the pluralization rule would be sensitive to the presence of the predicate ADD.

Another unresolved difficulty consists in the fact that rule (39) does

The Mapping Mechanism 151

not apply in all possible coordinate structures. Consider this representation:

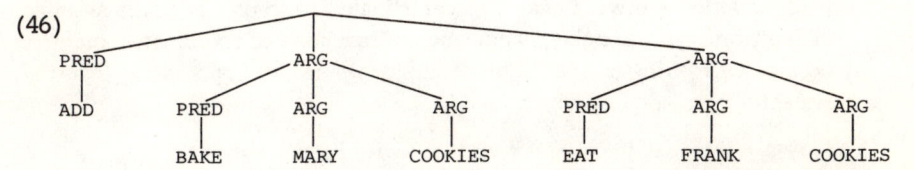

(46)
```
           PRED          ARG                    ARG
            |         ╱   |                 ╱    |
           ADD     PRED  ARG    ARG      PRED   ARG    ARG
                    |    |      |         |     |      |
                   BAKE MARY  COOKIES    EAT  FRANK  COOKIES
```

On the basis of rule (39), this representation should be mappable with the sentence

(47)   *Mary bakes cookies and Frank eats.*

Instead, the correct mapping of (46) must be

(48)   *Mary bakes and Frank eats cookies.*

which maps the first of the two coreferential arguments with ϕ instead of the second, as rule (39) would dictate. A still better mapping of (46) would be

(49)   *Mary bakes cookies and Frank eats them.*

where the second coreferential argument is mapped with a different contextual rule, concerning the pronoun *them* (see below). In some cases, this second solution is the only possible one. Hence the structure

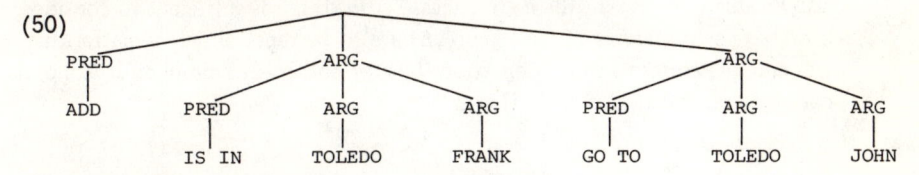

(50)
```
           PRED          ARG                    ARG
            |         ╱   |                 ╱    |
           ADD     PRED  ARG    ARG      PRED   ARG    ARG
                    |    |      |         |     |      |
                  IS IN TOLEDO FRANK     GO TO TOLEDO JOHN
```

cannot be mapped with either

(51)   **Frank is in Toledo and John is going.*

or

(52)   **Frank is in and John is going to Toledo.*

but only with

(53)   *Frank is in Toledo and John is going there.*

mapping the second argument via another contextual rule, concerning the sound *there* (see below). These and other similar cases indicate that rule (39) needs to be modified.

Mapping with ϕ—that is, a reduction typical of coordinate structures—has a precise semantic explanation. It apparently depends on the presence of the semantic component ADD which, as noted in the chapter on performatives, underlies the word *and*. This component is also present in the meaning of the word *with*, and the phenomenon of reduction of coordinate structures occurs with *with* as well. For example, we might hypothesize that the semantic representation of

(54) *Frank went out with Peter.*

has the following form:

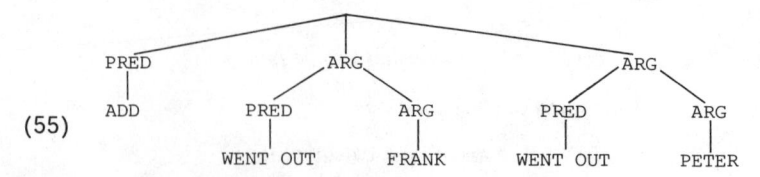

(55)

```
           PRED        ARG              ARG
            |         /  \             /  \
           ADD    PRED   ARG       PRED   ARG
                   |      |          |     |
                WENT OUT FRANK   WENT OUT PETER
```

But a structure such as (55) is also the one underlying

(56) *Frank and Peter went out.*

It is true that in this way we capture the similarities in meaning that undoubtedly exist between (54) and (56), in that they are both assigned the same representation. But we must also recognize that the two sentences are not perfectly synonymous. So that, in addition to the resemblances, we must also be able to represent the differences. To do this, it is sufficient to consider how the performatives of (54) and (56) are to be represented—a matter that was simply omitted in representation (55) for purposes of simplicity. A more complete representation of (54) is

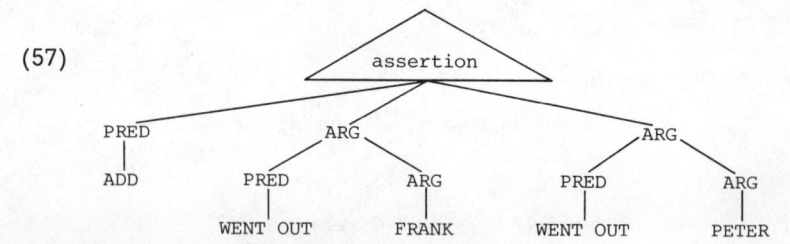

(57)

```
                      assertion
           _____|_____
          PRED     ARG             ARG
           |      /   \            /  \
          ADD  PRED   ARG       PRED   ARG
                |      |          |     |
             WENT OUT FRANK   WENT OUT PETER
```

whereas the representation for (56) is the following:

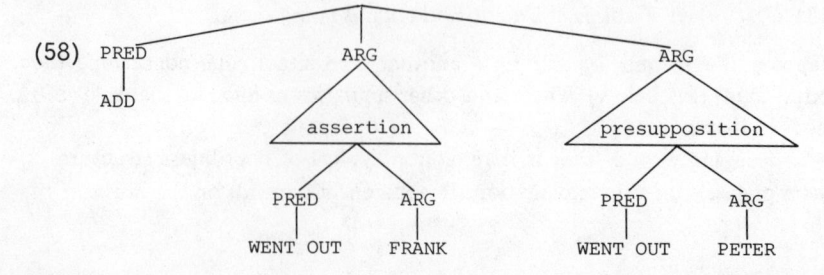

(58)

```
      PRED        ARG                    ARG
       |         /   \                  /   \
      ADD    assertion              presupposition
             /      \                /         \
           PRED     ARG           PRED         ARG
            |        |             |            |
         WENT OUT  FRANK        WENT OUT      PETER
```

The Mapping Mechanism

In other words, (54) is a sentence, whereas (56) is a discourse unit. More particularly, in representation (57), and therefore sentence (54), ADD is a propositional adverbial. But in (58), and so discourse (56), ADD is a performative adverbial. At the level of mapping, this difference has a precise effect: ADD as a propositional adverbial is mapped with the word *with* and obligatorily requires reduction (*with Peter*), while as a performative adverbial it is mapped with the word *and*, and reduction is left optional. The fact that reduction is optional in the latter case is illustrated by the fact that we can have

(59)   *Frank left and Peter left.*

as a mapping of (57).

The contextual rules operate on even more "distant" contexts than those examined so far. Recall the example

(25)   *The chair touches it.*

which, as we noted, has the representation (24):

(24)
```
           PRED      ARG      ARG
            |         |        |
          TOUCH     CHAIR    TABLE
```

Whereas TOUCH and CHAIR are mapped, respectively, by *touches* and *chair* via normal mapping rules, TABLE is mapped with the word *it* via a contextual rule. As we noted, this rule operates via a context that may extend to previous discourse.

(26)   *Look at the table. The chair is touching it.*

The semantic representation of (26), plus an approximation of its mapping, would be the following:

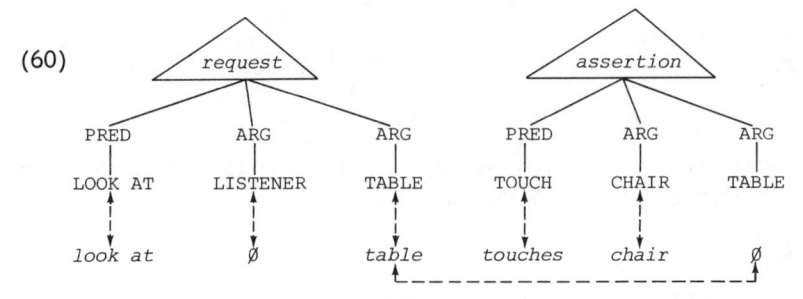

(60)
```
          request                              assertion
    PRED     ARG       ARG           PRED      ARG      ARG
     |        |         |             |         |        |
   LOOK AT LISTENER   TABLE         TOUCH     CHAIR    TABLE
     ↓        ↓         ↓             ↓         ↓        ↓
   look at   ∅        table         touches   chair     ∅
                        └─────────────────────────────┘
```

If we want to give a first approximation for the mapping rule for the word *it*, we might say

(61) *If there is a nominal that is coreferential with another nominal, where*

that nominal is singular in number and is neither masculine nor feminine, and the identity of the first nominal is retrievable from the context, map that nominal with it.

It is interesting that in rule (61), and in other similar rules, there is consistent reference to **retrievable contexts**. In the preceding contextual rules, the context through which mapping passed was always defined by the rule in some precise fashion. For example, in the rule for *himself* treated in (31), reference was necessarily made to a nominal within the sentence. In the rule for mapping the subject of an embedded sentence, (36), the context is one of the arguments of the nucleus. In rule (39) for coordinate structures, the context is one of the elements in the first of the two coordinate structures. By contrast, in rule (61), the context through which mapping must pass is much less defined. Any context will do as long as it is "retrievable" by the listener, i.e., as long as the listener, on the basis of the elements at his disposal, can identify the antecedent efficiently, without errors, rapidly, without uncertainty, without a great deal of mental efforts, and so forth. Hence, it is not necessary that TABLE be the object complement of the sentence in which it is embedded (*Look at the table.*), nor is it necessary that such a sentence have an imperative performative. However, if there are two nominals that the listener could retrieve as the interpretation of *it*, then the rule may not apply. Hence the passage of discourse

(62)   *Look at the table and the bench. The chair touches it.*

is unacceptable for an efficient mapping mechanism. On the other hand, the referral of rule (61) to a retrievable context generally does mean that a more precise context was not available. Thus the sentence

(63)   *The dog washes it.*

is not acceptable as a mapping of the structure

(64)
```
        ┌──────┼──────┐
       PRED   ARG    ARG
        │     │      │
       WASH  DOG    DOG
```

because a more precise rule, similar to (31), applies to these more precise circumstances, mapping (64) into the sentence

(65)   *The dog washes itself.*

Further on we will examine some representations in which rule (61) cannot

The Mapping Mechanism

apply, even though there is one nominal coreferential with another. For example, we cannot have

(66)   *The dog that I saw it is a mastiff

nor

(67)   *The dog I saw it is a mastiff

but only

(68)   The dog that I saw is a mastiff

In such cases there is an appropriate rule that has priority over (61).
    A rule similar to (61) operates in the mapping of the sentences

(69)   Let's go into the living room. The children are playing there.

The semantic representation and mapping of (69) are

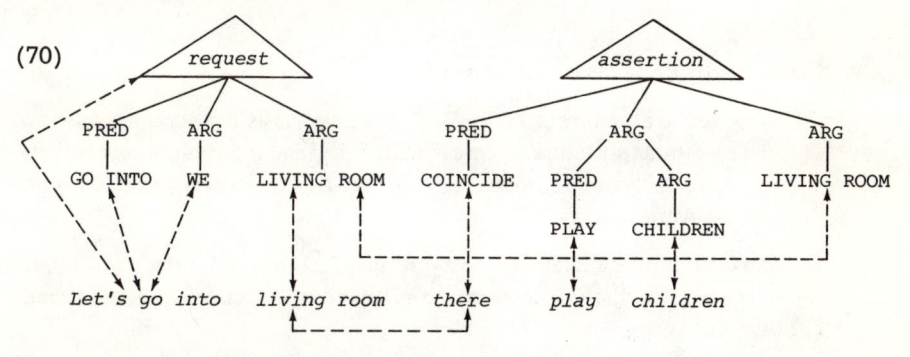

(70)

```
         request                           assertion
       /    |    \                      /     |      \
    PRED   ARG   ARG              PRED      ARG         ARG
    GO INTO WE  LIVING ROOM    COINCIDE   PRED  ARG   LIVING ROOM
                                          PLAY  CHILDREN

    Let's go into  living room    there    play  children
```

The contextual rule for the word *there* (in the sense of a place pronoun) is approximately the following:

(71)   *If there is a predicate COINCIDE that has as an argument a nominal coreferential with a nominal situated in another retrievable context, map COINCIDE and this nominal with the word there.*

    A third example of a rule of this type occurs in the sequence

(72)   The children are noisy. Nevertheless, John is staying home.

which has the following representation (and approximate mapping):

(73)

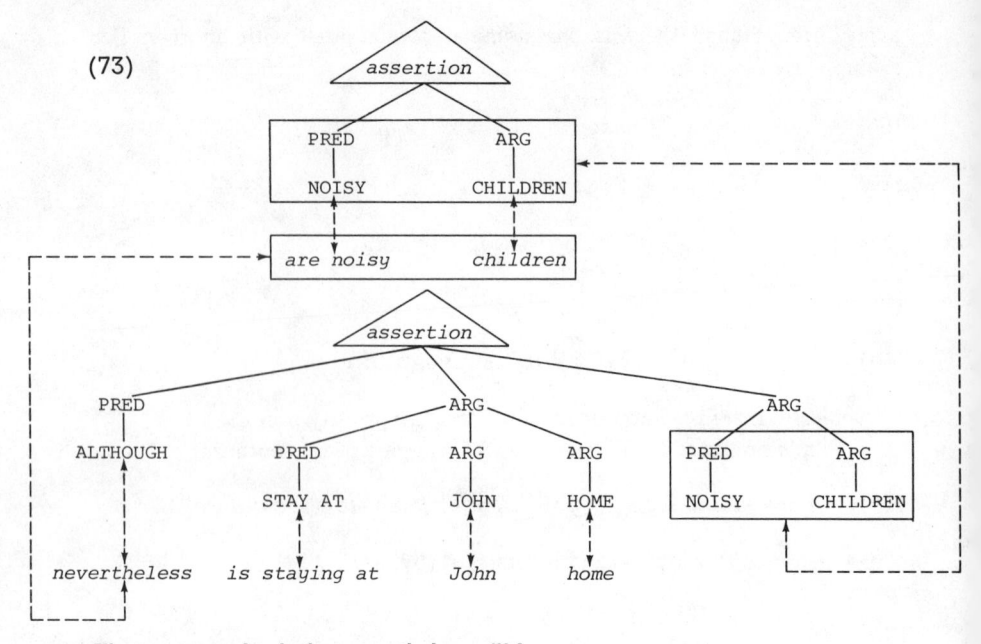

```
                           assertion
                          /         \
                      PRED           ARG
                       |              |
                     NOISY         CHILDREN

                    are noisy      children

                           assertion
                     /        |          \
                  PRED       ARG          ARG
                   |        /   \        /    \
              ALTHOUGH   PRED   ARG   ARG   PRED    ARG
                   |      |      |     |     |       |
                        STAY AT  JOHN HOME  NOISY  CHILDREN

              nevertheless  is staying at  John  home
```

The contextual rule for *nevertheless* will be

(74) *If there is a predicate ALTHOUGH which has as a second argument a sentential structure identical with a sentential structure recoverable from the context, map ALTHOUGH and its second argument with the word* nevertheless.

Let us now look at one last group of contextual rules, which are important because they operate in the mapping of associated configurations. The sentence

(75) *The book on the table is mine.*

has the semantic representation

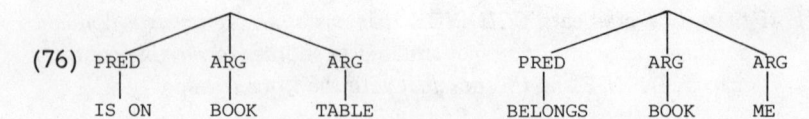

(76)
```
     PRED    ARG    ARG           PRED    ARG    ARG
      |       |      |             |       |      |
     IS ON   BOOK   TABLE         BELONGS BOOK    ME
```

where the structure on the right is the primary configuration and the one on the left is an associated configuration that is the modifier of a noun appearing in the primary configuration.[3]

---

[3] We have omitted the performative structure because at this point we are not interested in whether the associated configuration is restrictive or nonrestrictive.

The Mapping Mechanism

The mapping of (76) occurs in the following way:

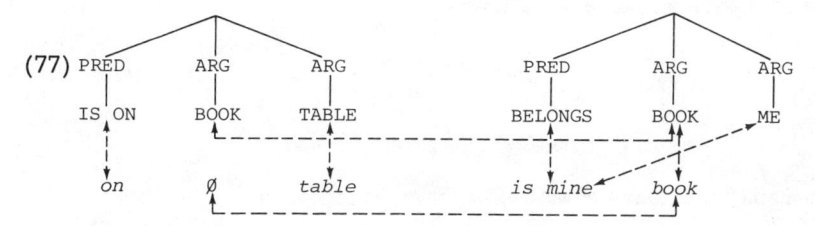

(77)
```
     PRED    ARG    ARG           PRED     ARG    ARG
      |       |      |              |       |      |
     IS ON   BOOK  TABLE         BELONGS   BOOK    ME
      |       |      |              |       |      |
      on      ∅    table         is mine   book
```

In an associated configuration there is always a nominal which is coreferential with a nominal in the primary configuration. Such a nominal is mapped with ∅. This may sometimes not occur, in that the element IS can be mapped explicitly with *is* for both configurations, according to the normal mapping rule for IS. In such cases, it becomes necessary to introduce the word *that* into the chain of sounds. Hence configuration (76) can be mapped like (75), or alternatively as

(78)   *The book that is on the table is mine.*

The reason for introducing *that* is obvious enough, if we consider that otherwise the chain of sounds would be extremely difficult to interpret, as in

(79)   **The book is on the table is mine.*

As noted earlier in this chapter, the function of *that* is precisely to separate one sentential structure from another on the surface.

Configuration (77) can be mapped as (75), as (78), and less often in a third fashion:

(80)   *The book which is on the table is mine.*

where the same problem of separating the associated and primary configurations on the surface is solved by using the word *which*.

The contextual rules noted so far, at least as interpreted here, have one thing in common: The context used for interpretation is always linguistic, the rest of discourse within which the target sentence is located. But as we said at the beginning of our discussion of contextual rules, these rules can operate either via a linguistic context or through a nonlinguistic context, the concrete physical–social situation in which the sentence is uttered. Consider the sentence

(81)   *Take it!*

used while pointing to a book. In saying this sentence the speaker wants the listener to do something, i.e., to take the book. This means that he has in mind a predicate with two arguments, the predicate TAKE and the two arguments LISTENER and BOOK. Omitting the performative, the semantic representation would be the following:

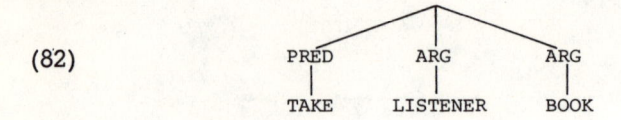

(82)
```
          PRED      ARG       ARG
           |         |         |
          TAKE    LISTENER   BOOK
```

To map (82) onto sentence (81), we have the following:

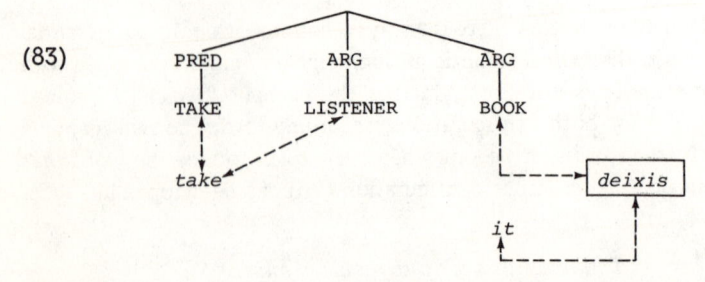

(83)
```
          PRED      ARG       ARG
           |         |         |
          TAKE    LISTENER   BOOK
           |                   |
          take                 └----→ deixis
                    ↑                   ↑
                    it ←----------------┘
```

The label **deixis** is used to indicate the use of the nonlinguistic context in the operation of mapping. The word **deixis** is derived from the Greek term for "pointing"—and often involves precisely that. This contrasts with the use of the linguistic context, which is called **anaphora** instead of **deixis**.

In reality, the semantic representation of (81) is still more complex, in that the sentence uses deixis to map not only the noun BOOK, but also the restrictive noun modifier that permits the listener to know which particular book is being discussed. Hence a more complete representation of (81) would be the following:

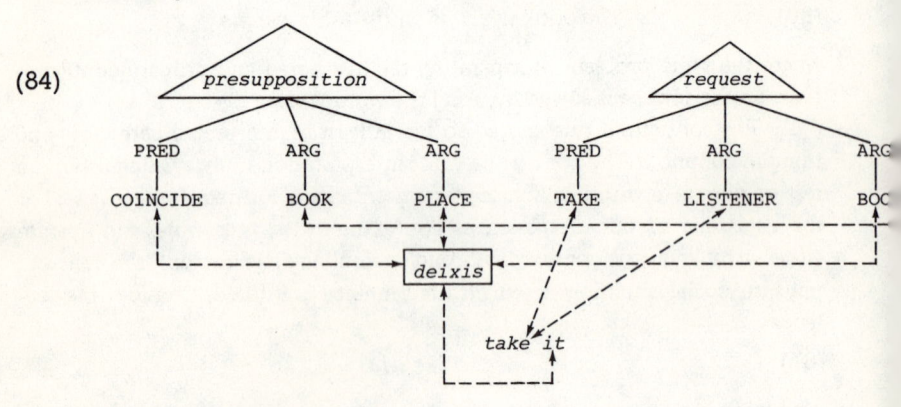

(84)
```
       presupposition                    request
    ┌──────┼──────┐              ┌──────┼──────┐
   PRED   ARG    ARG            PRED   ARG    ARG
    |      |      |              |      |      |
 COINCIDE BOOK  PLACE           TAKE LISTENER BOOK
                 |
               deixis
                 |
              take it
```

By contrast, in the sentence

The Mapping Mechanism

(85) 　　　　　　　　*Take this book!*

the noun is mapped with normal mapping rules, and only the restrictive modifier is mapped deictically. Hence the representation of (85) would be

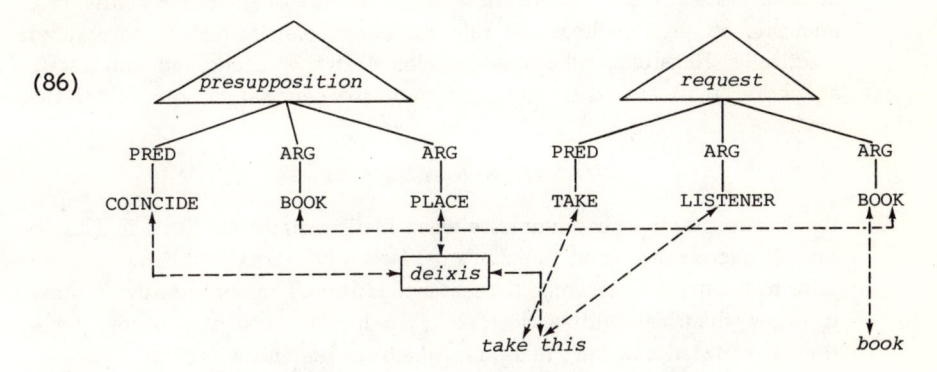

(86)

```
              presupposition                    request
           /        |        \              /      |       \
         PRED      ARG       ARG          PRED    ARG      ARG
          |         |         |            |       |        |
       COINCIDE   BOOK      PLACE         TAKE   LISTENER  BOOK
          ↑         ↑         ↑            ↑       ↑        ↑
          └─────────┴─────→ deixis ←───────┘       ↑        ↑
                              ↑↑                            |
                           take this                       book
```

In fact, *this* actually contains more than one semantic component, including elements of the type NEAR THE SPEAKER, which distinguish *this* from *that*, which contains FAR FROM THE SPEAKER.

It should be evident if we compare this example again with example (25) that there are many contextual mapping rules which use the same word to map either through a linguistic context or through a nonlinguistic context. Thus *it* uses the linguistic context in (50) and the nonlinguistic context in (81). In the same fashion, *there* uses the linguistic context in the sequence

(87)　　　　　　*Frank arrived in Rome. There he met Luigi.*

and the nonlinguistic context in the sentence

(88)　　　　　　　　　*Frank slept there.*

while pointing to a bed. *So* uses the linguistic context in the sequence

(89)　　　　　*They drank and laughed. So passed the night.*

and the nonlinguistic context in

(90)　　　　　　　　　*You must do it so.*

said while trying to give a practical demonstration of how to slice salami. *He* passes through the linguistic context in the sentence

(91)　　*Mary saw Frank and understood immediately that he was guilty.*

and passes through the nonlinguistic context in

(92)   *He is tall.*

said while indicating a friend in the room. Examples like these can be multiplied indefinitely. The vast majority of contextual rules can be applied in both cases. Exceptions are those that are used only or prevalently in a linguistic context, such as the rule for *nevertheless*, which is never used deictically. Regarding rules that are almost always deictic and only rarely anaphoric, there are cases like *recently* and the personal pronoun *I*. With the sentence

(93)   *Mark visited New York recently.*

the speaker wants to communicate when Mark visited New York, and to do this he chooses a deictic mapping rule. *Recently* means essentially "slightly prior to the moment in which the sentence is uttered" and obviously, in order to know when Mark visited New York, the listener must base his interpretation on knowledge of the situation in which the sentence was heard.

Another case of a rule that is almost always deictic regards the word *I*. Consider the sentence

(94)   *I believe that Frank will come.*

Independently of the context, using only the words that form the sentence, the listener knows that the first argument of BELIEVE is the person who utters the sentence, the speaker. But to identify precisely who the speaker is in this particular case, the listener must turn to the nonlinguistic context, basing his interpretation on knowledge of who was speaking at that moment—knowledge that is not furnished with the words of the sentence.

At this point we might ask why, beyond the normal mapping rules, we also find contextual mapping rules. There are no doubt many reasons, but we will consider only two. In the first place, the use of the deictic context (e.g., saying "This is mine" while pointing to a book on a table instead of saying "The book on the table is mine") seems to require less conceptual elaboration. Deictic mapping rules are often used (and perhaps are indispensable) in the first sentences of very young children, probably because it is less taxing to their more limited capacities. Second, anaphoric contextual rules offer the advantage of economy (i.e., not repeating words), which is one of the criteria for an efficient mapping mechanism (see beginning of chapter). Nevertheless, such "economy" can also run counter to the criteria of speed and efficiency, if the passage through the context is too long and tortuous for the listener. Or else, it may leave the listener in a situation of uncertainty if it is not immediately clear which part of the context must be used. To alleviate this kind of risk, every contextual mapping rule must furnish—independent of the

The Mapping Mechanism

context—a few general indications of the type of semantic material to be recovered. This leaves to the context only the task of furnishing the specific material corresponding to these indications. Such "clues" furnished by contextual rules permit and facilitate the recovery of the rest of the semantic information by the listener.

Consider again the sequence

(95)   Mary looks at the table. The chair is touching it.

To reconstruct the second argument of *touch*—the antecedent of the word *it*—the listener passes through the context, in this case the context contained in the previous sentence *Mary looks at the table*. But the word *it* already tells him, independently of the context, that he must seek a nominal of neuter gender. Thus the listener can recover the nominal *table* from the preceding sentence instead of, erroneously, the nominal *Mary*. The opposite holds in the sequence

(96)   The dog looks at the table. The chair is touching it.

In the case of (96), both the dog and the table would satisfy the requirement of a neuter gender nominal that might be the antecedent of *it*. Hence, there is the risk of confusing the listener.

What holds true for *it* holds true for most contextual mapping rules. For example, *who* tells us, independently of the context, that we must look for a human antecedent. *Recently* tells us that we must try and identify the time of utterance and not, for example, the place in which the conversation is taking place. This is also the case for those contextual mapping rules (like several noted earlier) in which a nominal is mapped by leaving a place unfilled in the chain of sounds as a signal that certain semantic material must be sought in the context. So that in

(97)   Bill wants to leave.

the argument of *to leave* is recovered by the listener through the context even though it does not appear directly in the chain of sounds. In fact, in (97), the very fact that a word is missing signals to the listener to seek the missing term in the context (in this case the preceding linguistic context). This is the meaning of the symbol ϕ that we have used in preceding contextual rules. It is the particular combination of the *empty slot* and the kind of material surrounding it that furnishes to the listener some clue as to the kind of material that must be recovered to complete the semantic representation of the sentence. Therefore, even with so-called zero markings, information is present to help the listener, directing him to particular kinds of contexts and not to others.

A Comparison with Traditional Grammar

As we stated in the first chapter, the linguistic model presented in this volume is closely related to generative-transformational linguistics. Transformational grammar represents an effort to return to the objectives and concepts of traditional grammar, in particular the approach to linguistics that preceded so-called "modern linguistics" in the nineteenth and twentieth centuries. We are in complete agreement with this point of view. It is for this reason that we would like to devote this final chapter to a direct (if brief) comparison between the linguistic model presented in this book, and the linguistic model of traditional grammar.

One of the fundamental characteristics of traditional grammar is the elaboration of two groups of concepts, pertaining to the grammatical analysis and the logical analysis of sentences, respectively. The concepts found within grammatical analysis are the so-called "parts of speech": noun, verb, adjective, pronoun, article, preposition, conjunction, adverb and interjection. The concepts that pertain to logical analysis are subject, predicate, complement, attribute, and a few others. How are these concepts dealt with in our model?

Let us begin with the concepts used in logical analysis, i.e., subject, predicate, complement, and so forth. As we noted at the end of the chapter on the nucleus, in our model there is no term corresponding to the concept of *complement*. This traditional concept obscures a distinction of fundamental importance for our model: the assignment of an argument to either the nucleus or the adverbial. Hence in the sentences

(1)   *John eats the apple.*
(2)   *Frank sleeps in the study.*

the apple and *in the study* are both complements in traditional grammar. We prefer to consider *the apple* as part of the nucleus, as an argument intrinsic to

A Comparison with Traditional Grammar

the semantic nature of the verb *to eat*. By contrast, *in the study* is outside the nucleus, and hence in an adverbial. It is an optional element with respect to the nucleus rather than an element required by the semantic nature of the verb *sleep*. This distinction cannot be made with the traditional concept of "complement." It is true that some traditional complements, such as the object complement, are found only within the nucleus and never within the adverbial. In this respect, our model overlaps with more traditional analysis. But it is also true that other complements can be found within either the nucleus or the adverbial. In these latter cases, the decision depends not upon the nature of the complement itself, but on the semantic structure of the nuclear predicate. In the chapter on the nucleus, we offered examples in which the same place complement forms part of the nucleus of a sentence with one verb, and part of an adverbial in a sentence with a different verb (e.g., *Mary knits/puts the sweater in the kitchen*).

On the other hand, traditional grammar meets numerous and often unresolvable problems with the classification of complements into classes like object, indirect object, locative, etc. This taxonomy is quite foreign to our model, and hence we escape many of these problems. Classes like object and indirect object have nothing to do with the **structure** of the semantic configuration, i.e., division into predicate–argument, nucleus and adverbial, etc. Instead, these classifications reflect the **content** of the sentence, the particular semantic predicates present within a given configuration.[1] In other words, the fact that a given argument is traditionally classified as a complement of manner (e.g., *with pleasure*), place (e.g., *at home*), instrument (e.g., *with a knife*), etc., depends on the particular semantic predicates expressed by the proposition dominating that complement, or by the nominal within that complement, or by the verb upon which the complement depends, and so forth. Lists of possible complement types (sometimes referred to as cases) can be extended, diversified, or detailed as much as we like, given the considerable variety of semantic predicates and their possible combinations. Thus it seems more economical to us to analyze them directly at the level of semantic predicates, without attempts to group these predicates into ad hoc "taxonomies" or lists of cases.

But the fundamental reason why we exclude the concept of complement from our model is that it is contrasted with the concept of "subject." The very fact that only one role of "subject" is assigned in a given sentence privileges the nominal that is given this role. We feel, instead, that at the most elementary level of semantic representation the so-called "subject"

---

[1] For this use of the expressions *structure* and *content*, see the chapter on mapping rules.

is only one argument among others, on the same plane as the complements of traditional grammar. This is probably one of the most fundamental differences between our model and traditional approaches. As we insisted throughout this book, this does not mean that the concept of subject disappears entirely from our grammar. It would be impossible to eliminate it, since every sentence (at least in English) necessarily contains a nuclear argument that agrees with the verb in the nucleus in both number and person. We will use the term **subject** to indicate that argument of the nucleus that is chosen to agree with the verb.

Let us turn now to a third concept in traditional logical analysis, the predicate. To distinguish this concept from our notions of **elementary predicate** (or **semantic component**) and **predication** (a configuration of semantic components—or even a single component—which make up the meaning of a lexical item), we will call this former concept **traditional predicate**. The traditional predicate corresponds in our model to the predication of a nucleus when the sentential structure is mapped as an explicit sentence.

The discussion could be closed here. Nevertheless, we must stress that incorporating the concept of predication into our model makes it a rather different thing from the traditional notion. By using the term of "nuclear" predication, we automatically assume that there are other types of predications, in particular adverbial predications and those predications which are nouns. In this way we can capture the fundamental nature of all words (i.e., as predications) while at the same time demonstrating the different roles that these predications can serve in the semantic configuration of particular sentences.

Second, we can capture the relationship between **predication** and **predicate**, that is, between the level at which semantic—cognitive material is already organized to form the meaning of a word (the **predication**) versus the underlying level of elementary semantic material (**components** or **predicates**). In essence, our model permits a more unified view of the mechanism of language, from the elementary semantic—cognitive units to the organization of sentences and, beyond that, to the organization of discourse. This unity is provided by a recursive process, the continual reapplication of the fundamental mechanism of predicate/argument. However, this continual reapplication does produce discontinuities, insofar as it generates units at increasingly higher levels. The elementary units (**predicates** or **components**) generate combinations (**predications**) which correspond to the meanings of words. These higher units in turn generate predicate—argument combinations (**nuclei, adverbials, subordinate sentential structures**), which in turn are combined to generate **propositions** and **performatives**. The combination of a proposition

A Comparison with Traditional Grammar

with a performative generates a **sentence**. The combination of sentences generates a unit of **discourse**. Thus the human mind can generate extremely complex semantic–cognitive structures, such as passages of discourse, through the use of a single elementary mechanism which is applied recursively, the mechanism of predicate and argument.

Despite the homogeneity of the system as a whole, the individual units can be kept separate during both comprehension and production, because they are organized hierarchically into progressively higher levels. This hierarchical arrangement means that a passage of discourse is not immediately divided into a configuration of elementary semantic components, but is first divided into a configuration of sentences. A sentence is not immediately reduced to a configuration of components, but to a combination of a performative with a proposition. A proposition is not merely a configuration of elementary components, but a combination of a nucleus and an adverbial. And so forth.

Let us now turn to the place occupied in our model by the traditional concept of **attribute,** including restrictive and nonrestrictive relative clauses. These attributes and relative clauses are all noun modifiers, which are configurations associated with the primary configuration of a sentence. The difference between attributes and relative clauses is that, in the case of attributes, the predication of the associated configuration appears on the surface as an adjective. With relative clauses, on the other hand, the predication in the associated configuration appears as a particular type of sentential structure. The same mechanism of associated configuration also gives rise to expressions such as *on the table* in the sentence

(3) *The book on the table is mine.*

In all these cases, we have a configuration associated with the primary configuration of the sentence.

As for the traditional concepts of subordination and coordination, we already know how these are treated in our model. Traditional subordinates include nuclear and adverbial subordinates on the one hand, and relative clauses on the other. We prefer to keep these two structures distinct, so that nuclear and adverbial subordinates are found **within** the proposition, whereas relative clauses are configurations **associated** with the proposition and so are found **outside.** With regard to coordination, it is the product of particular kinds of adverbials, called discourse adverbials, that take two performatives (and hence two sentences) as their arguments.

Finally, the traditional concepts of **sentence** and **paragraph** are translated into our concepts of **sentence** and **discourse.** Our concept of sentence renders explicit the fact, largely ignored within traditional treatments, that the basic unit of linguistic communication is an **act** with which a speaker intends to communicate something. Hence each sentence must also carry with it an indication of the type of communicative intention formulated by the speaker, as well as the specific content of that intention. In our terms this means that a sentence must be made up of a performative and a proposition (taking proposition in our sense of the term). The larger unit called **discourse** (the analysis of which has barely been mentioned in this book) consists fundamentally of a set of sentences related to one another through the use of performative adverbials, and other adverbials that refer back to information provided earlier in discourse. Since such operations are recursive—i.e., can be repeated to form ever larger units—there are no inherent limits to the size of a discourse structure.

Obviously, for all the hierarchical language structures mentioned thus far, we must not conclude that the actual process begins with the smallest units and combines them to form larger units. On the contrary, there exists a level of planning for discourse and for sentences, which makes use of a series of "subprograms" that then construct the smaller units that articulate the structure of a sentence or discourse passage.

Let us turn now to the so-called **parts of speech**. The assignment of all words to a determined grammatical category is one of the fundamental procedures of traditional grammar. The role of **noun** or **verb** or **adjective**, etc. is viewed in this approach as though it reflected intrinsic properties of the word. Hence, in the lexicon each item specifies not only a phonetic form and a meaning, as in our model, but also a grammatical category to which the lexical item belongs. This is, in fact, the system used in standard dictionaries.

Examining the role of the traditional grammatical categories within our model, we must above all conclude that such roles are much less important that in traditional grammar. This does not mean that these categories do not correspond to some aspect of the language mechanism, but that in comparison with other more important aspects of language (i.e., those considered in the preceding chapters) the so-called **parts of speech** are only a reflection—partial, indirect, and often distorted—of semantic structure.

In our model, in fact, there are no parts of speech in the sense of intrinsic properties of words. In the lexicon items are equal, in that they are all predications. This common characteristic is more fundamental than all the distinctions into nouns, verbs, adjectives, and so forth. Something equivalent to grammatical categories arises only within the semantic representation of a sentence, i.e., in correspondence to the diverse functions carried out by individual subconfigurations within the total configuration. The same subconfiguration corresponding to a lexical item could carry out different functions in different sentences. Thus we need not assign that configuration a "part of speech" as an intrinsic property.

On the other hand, it is fairly clear why traditional grammar did conceive of parts of speech as the intrinsic properties of words. The particular function carried out by a lexical item within a sentence must be indicated on the surface through the application of some syntactic mapping rule. Suppose that a given language uses the position of words in a sentence to carry out this function. Or suppose that in another language, that same function is carried out by accompanying each word with a particular form detached from that word. In either language, we would be much less likely to try to attribute a single grammatical category to the words involved in that function. But in still other languages, the same function may be indicated by incorporating a suffix as a morphological part of that word. In this last case, there would be a much stronger temptation to consider the grammatical function as an intrinsic property of the word itself. Let us consider an example. In English many words traditionally called adverbs are characterized by the ending *-ly: swiftly, deeply,* etc. These occur frequently as adverbial predications. But there are a great many languages in which these same so-called **adverbs** are morphologically indistinguishable from so-called **adjectives**. In such languages, the structural information relative to being the predication of an adverbial is mapped onto the surface by the particular position assumed by the word, or perhaps through some information in the context, or through still other surface mechanisms. In this kind of language, we would not conclude that there exists a grammatical category of **adverb**. Evidently, by postulating these grammatical categories or parts of speech, we allow ourselves to be influenced by the particular mapping rules of the language we happen to be studying. This has often occurred in traditional grammars. For example, many older models were strongly influenced by the peculiar characteristics of Greek and Latin, such that research into less known languages often involved a search for Latin-like case relations, and so forth. If we assign parts of speech on the basis of the mapping mechanism of a given language, we risk attributing a universal value to the surface characteristics of a particular language. Or alternatively—as is the case in American tradition of Bloomfieldian structural linguistics—we analyze a language into parts of speech solely on the basis of purely "formal," surface characteristics, and abandon altogether any effort to characterize the universal human language mechanism. This last, structuralist approach occasionally comes up in traditional models as well, for example when the parts of speech are divided into **variable** and **invariable,** or when a given part of speech or category is defined by the simple fact of preceding some other part of speech, as is the case with prepositions. In our model, instead, the equivalent of parts of speech are not **categories** assigned to words as intrinsic properties, but **functions.** These functions can, at least in principle, be carried out by any semantic subconfiguration corresponding to one or more lexical items, depending on the nature of the total configuration within which that structure is found. So that we no longer ask ourselves "To what grammatical category does this word belong?," but rather, "What is the function served by this word within this sentence?"

There is another important difference between our model and the parts of speech of traditional grammars. The fact that parts of speech are considered sentence-functions instead of word-categories means that we need not restrict these functions to single words, but can instead extend the function to a structure made up of several words within a given sentence. Hence, whereas the concepts of noun, adverb and adjective are applied to single words, the concepts of nominal, adverbial and noun modifier can be applied either to single words, or to any group of words that carries out these functions.

Having clarified the general difference between our approach and the traditional approach as to the problem of parts of speech, we can now turn more specifically to the way in which individual parts of speech are treated in our model.

As we have seen, in our model all words are of equivalent status at the lexical level: they are all predications. The differences in function appear later, at the level of semantic representation of a sentence. A first, fundamental distinction can be made between predications having as an argument something which is not otherwise identified linguistically (and therefore used for the precise purpose of introducing this something into communication) versus those predications whose arguments are already independently identified linguistically. We have called the first **nouns** and the second **predications in the strict sense.** The fundamental distinction, then, lies between nouns and predications in the strict sense. This distinction cannot be found in traditional grammar, although it is implicit in the tenet sometimes advanced that the fundamental grammatical distinction lies between nouns and verbs. But in this proposal, the category of verb is more restricted than our concept of predication in the strict sense. In our model, this last category does exclude nouns, but it includes, in addition to verbs, adjectives, adverbs, prepositions, and conjunctions. All these parts of speech are defined in our

A Comparison with Traditional Grammar

model as predications whose arguments are already linguistically identified.

By contrast, our category of nouns does cover more or less the same area as the corresponding category in traditional grammar. We define the concept of noun quite differently, but nevertheless we do capture an essential element implicit in older models.

Further distinctions can be made within the category of strict predications, in particular the distinction between predications of the nucleus and predications of the adverbial. Nuclear predications correspond roughly to verbs and to adjectives, while adverbial predications tend to cover the traditional concepts of prepositions, conjunctions and adverbs. A further distinction within adverbial predications would contrast predications with only one argument (which would necessarily be a nucleus) with predications with two or more arguments. The first group corresponds roughly to the so-called adverbs, while the second corresponds to prepositions and conjunctions. Finally, when the second argument of the adverbial predications (the first argument being the nucleus) appears on the surface as an explicit sentential structure, we have conjunctions. When the second argument does *not* appear as an explicit sentential structure, we have prepositions.

This series of distinctions can be summarized as follows:

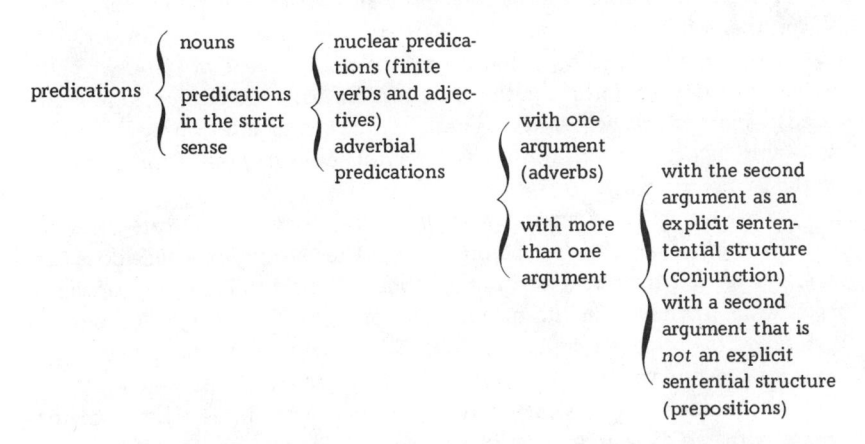

predications
- nouns
- predications in the strict sense
  - nuclear predications (finite verbs and adjectives)
  - adverbial predications
    - with one argument (adverbs)
    - with more than one argument
      - with the second argument as an explicit sentential structure (conjunction)
      - with a second argument that is *not* an explicit sentential structure (prepositions)

The correspondence between traditional grammatical categories and possible distinctions in our model, as represented above, are only approximate, and offered purely for their heuristic value. In the first place, we know that such correspondences sometimes do not hold up. For example, in the sentences

(4) *The book is on the table.*
(5) *Frank has gone to Cincinnati.*

on and *to* are two prepositions for traditional grammar, but they are not adverbial predications in the semantic representation that we assign to these sentences. Instead, they are predications of the nucleus or parts of such predications. Similarly, in the sentence

(6)   *John resigned from the committee, like Frank did the day before.*

like is an adverb for traditional grammar, but for us it is an adverbial predication with two arguments instead of one. *Vice president* is a noun for traditional grammar in the sentence

(7)   *Frank is vice president of the company.*

But in this sentence, *vice president* does not fall under our definition of nouns, serving instead as a predication in the strict sense.

In the second place, as noted earlier, the traditional taxonomy classifies isolated words, while our functional categories can include either single words or groups of words. Hence in sentence (5), the nuclear predications is *has gone to*; for the traditional grammar this phrase includes two categories, a verb and a preposition. Finally, the scheme shown above is also insufficient in that there are traditional categories (e.g., interjections) that are not included at all.

For us, the distinction between verb and adjective is purely semantic, unlike the structural distinctions referred to in the scheme. Underlying adjectives, there is probably always a semantic component of state, which is absent in most verbs (although this is a question that must be studied in more detail). The past participle has, instead, a semantic component of completion—although this adverb form also deserves more study (see Parisi, in press, on the past participle).

We have not yet considered two other fundamental categories of traditional grammar—articles and pronouns.[2] The category of article does not receive a unified treatment within our model. There is an important language mechanism, discussed in the chapter on nominals, that is signalled on the surface by the so-called **definite article**. This is the mechanism of identification, for the listener's benefit, of the particular *x* to which the speaker refers. But this function can be signalled on the surface even in the absence of the article with words such as *this, that, I,* or *you.* Proper nouns also serve this same function when used to identify elements, as in

(8)   *Frank has arrived.*

---

[2] The category of *interjection* is sufficiently doubtful within traditional grammar itself that we need not consider it here, although the phenomena covered by that term deserve greater study.

A Comparison with Traditional Grammar

But proper nouns do not serve this function when they identify no particular element, as in

(9) *A certain Frank has arrived.*

By contrast, the so-called indefinite articles signal that the speaker cannot or does not intend to help the listener identify the particular *x* to which he refers (see the chapter on nominals). However, this function can also be carried out with words that are not traditionally considered articles, such as *some* and *any*.

As for the pronoun, we have already considered this device at length in the chapter on mapping rules, in particular with regard to contextually-based mapping rules. The category of pronoun is quite heterogeneous in comparison with other traditional categories. We can explain this heterogeneity by attributing pronouns to the mapping mechanism rather than, as with the other categories, to the level of semantic representation. As such, the so-called pronoun is only one aspect of a much wider phenomenon, by which semantic material is brought to the surface indirectly, by passing through the context. It is this general phenomenon, in all its manifestations, that is of greatest interest in our model. The pronoun is only one particular aspect of this mechanism.

Traditional grammar proposes a series of subdivisions within major categories. Let us examine some of these briefly.

For nouns, the distinctions between proper and common, singular and plural, are treated more or less completely in the preceding chapters. The distinction between abstract nouns and concrete nouns, on the other hand, does not seem to be particularly useful for a description of linguistic competence.

Within the category of adjectives, we find the subcategory of possessive adjectives. For our model, these adjectives are predications with two arguments, similar to the semantic material underlying the *'s* termination. In such predications, the second argument is filled with the component SPEAKER (*my*), or the component LISTENER (*your*), and so forth. (See sentence (75) in the preceding chapter.) Demonstrative adjectives (i.e., *this* and *that*) are also predications with two arguments, in which the predication is the semantic component COINCIDE and the second argument is brought to the surface via the context, either linguistic or nonlinguistic (see, for example, sentence (85) in the preceding chapter). Interrogative adjectives appear when the sentence has the performative of questioning, and in particular when the listener is asked to identify something (see chapter on presuppositions). The interrogative adjective (e.g., *whose*) serves to indicate what is being asked while the rest of the sentence is presupposed. Indefinite and numeral adjectives consist of a rather heterogeneous group, within which we can discern the operation of semantic components of quantity, and occasionally (as in the case of *some* and *many*) the same sort of function discussed with regard to indefinite articles, i.e., the nonidentification of a particular x to which the speaker refers. Finally, traditional grammar offers a class of **qualifying adjectives,** a wastebasket category serving to group all adjectives that are not otherwise classified.

The subcategories for pronouns are somewhat similar to those for adjectives. The only difference is that the so-called pronouns map one argument through the context where that same argument is mapped noncontextually by a corresponding adjective. For example, in the adjective *my* the first argument of the predication is brought to the surface by a direct mapping, as in

(10) *My book is on the table.*

In the corresponding pronoun *mine*, the same element (the argument *book* in sentence (10) is brought to the surface by reference to the context, as in

(11) *Mine is on the table.*

The same sort of analysis applies for demonstrative, interrogative, and indefinite pronouns compared with their corresponding adjectives.

There are two further categories of pronouns, which have no corresponding adjectives—personal pronouns and relative pronouns. Personal pronouns pose no particular problems. They are predications used as nouns which have as a predicate the component SPEAKER, LISTENER, and so forth, plus an operation identifying some particular speaker, hearer, etc. by passing through the context. (See, for example, sentence (94) in the previous chapter). Relative pronouns, which are also discussed in the chapter on mapping rules, are used to bring to the surface a nominal contained within an associated configuration that is coreferential with a nominal contained in the primary configuration.

Further traditional subdivisions are those within the categories of preposition, conjunction, and adverb. In these cases, the distinctions are almost always purely semantic, based on particular semantic components that are mapped by specific prepositions, conjunctions and adverbs. For example, locatives like *on* and *under* are so classified because of some sort of place component within their semantic structure. Categories like these pose no problems for representation beyond the usual problems involved in an adequate componential analysis of the lexicon.

A Comparison with Traditional Grammar 173

This completes our examination of the correspondence between traditional grammatical categories and mechanisms in our model. In general, the parts of speech lose much of their importance. In a sense, our model amplifies logical analysis to a point where a separate grammatical analysis or "parsing" becomes superfluous. Some categories and subcategories disappear altogether, others are modified radically, while still others remain in the sense that they are translated directly into the concepts introduced in the preceding chapters. But even in the latter case, the traditional categories are just some of the possible distinctions that can be recognized, and they do not seem to have any special value.

Before concluding this comparison, we would like to consider two final points.

First, we have seen how the concepts of logical analysis and grammatical analysis are treated within our model. But there are also certain aspects of our model that receive no treatment whatsoever in traditional grammar. Therefore our model not only modifies the older grammar, but also expands and completes the old view. The first aspect is the componential analysis of the meaning of words. We propose a means of analyzing and representing the meaning of words in such a fashion as to integrate this representation into the analysis of the sentence as a whole. Since both the lexicon and the sentence are made up of predications, the study of the lexicon becomes part of the study of grammar. A second aspect regards the presence in our model of performatives and presuppositions. These mechanisms permit a systematic treatment of sentences for what they really are: communicative acts that take place in a context of intentions and shared knowledge. A third aspect is connected with both the first and the second: the introduction into the grammar of the *encyclopedia*, the collection of world knowledge connected with the lexicon. Thus the model is on the one hand open to the study of the relationships between the linguistic competence and the general cognitive competence of speakers. On the other hand, it captures language as it is actually used, as a means of communication between organisms.

We would like to underscore a second difference between our model and traditional grammar. Our model should be more complete, consistent, and unified as compared with traditional grammar. Moreover, it should be able to identify more linguistic universals than is the case with traditional grammar and should thereby acquire a greater explanatory power. But the most important distinguishing characteristic of our model with respect to traditional grammar is a methodological one. It is the systematic recourse to empirical data to verify and modify every aspect of the model itself. Traditional grammar, at least as we know it today, is static, offered without justification, and hence arbitrary. This determines its other negative characteristics, as the purely label value of many of its concepts or their being only juxtaposed without forming any unitary system. By contrast, the necessity of justifying every aspect of the model with empirical data from many different sources (native linguistic intuitions, language acquisition of children, historical change, laboratory experimental data, clinical data, etc.) makes our model a basically dynamic one, that is, something that can be constantly modified and improved. The systematic recourse to the empirical data increases in principle the explanatory power of a grammar and its capacity of being understood, used, and taught.

Glossary

Adverbial An optional part of a sentential structure which takes the nucleus as one of its arguments.

Argument The object of a mental operation.

Associated configuration (or noun modifier) A sentential structure, which is not part of a given proposition, but which has a nominal that is coreferential with a nominal in that proposition.

Content information Information regarding the semantic components that are present in a semantic representation.

Contextual mapping rule A rule of the mapping system which transfers semantic information into sounds and vice versa through the use of the context (linguistic or nonlinguistic).

Discourse A semantic configuration made up of two or more sentences connected by a discourse adverbial.

Discourse adverbial An adverbial that takes two or more performatives as its arguments.

Elementary predicate (or semantic component) A mental operation which cannot be decomposed into simpler operations.

Encyclopedia All knowledge associated with a lexical item but not contained as part of the intrinsic meaning of that lexical item.

Lexical mapping rule (or lexical item) A rule of the mapping system which transfers primarily content information into sound and vice versa.

Lexicon The set of lexical mapping rules.

Mapping mechanism The system of rules which serve to transfer semantic information into phonetic information and vice versa.

Nominal Any argument of a predication that is not the nucleus of the sentential structure in which it is found.

Noun A predication used to construct an argument that has not yet been linguistically identified.

Nucleus The obligatory portion of a sentential structure.

Performative A semantic configuration which specifies the type of communicative intention of the speaker. The performative consists of an obligatory portion, its nucleus, and optional portions, its adverbials.

Performative adverbial An adverbial that forms part of a performative.

Predicate A mental operation carried out on one or more things.

Predication A semantic configuration which is the meaning of a lexical item.

Predication in the strict sense A predication that is not a noun.

Presupposition A semantic configuration which consists of information necessary for the listener to understand a sentence, but which does not in itself form part of the proposition or the performative of the sentence.

Proposition A semantic configuration which specifies the content of the communicative intention of a speaker and which, when dominated by a performative, constitutes a sentence. The proposition consists of an obligatory portion, the nucleus, and optional portions, the adverbials.

Propositional adverbial An adverbial that forms part of a proposition.

Sentence The minimal unit of linguistic communication, consisting of a proposition dominated by a performative plus possibly a set of presuppositions and associated configurations.

Sentential structure A semantic configuration which could be used as a proposition.

Structural information Information regarding the relations among components as they are arranged in a semantic representation.

Subordinate sentential structure A sentential structure which constitutes the argument of a nucleus or of an adverbial.

Syntactic mapping rule A rule of the mapping system which transfers into sound primarily structural information and vice versa.

Syntax The set of syntactic mapping rules.

Bibliography

Antinucci, F., & Parisi, D. Early Language acquisition: A model and some data. In C. Ferguson & D. I. Slobin (Eds.), *Studies in child language development.* New York: Holt, 1973.

Antinucci, F., & Parisi, D. Early semantic development in child language. In E. H. & E. Lenneberg (Eds.), *Foundations of language development,* Vol. I. New York: Academic Press, 1975.

Boyd, J., & Thorne, J. P. The deep grammar of modal verbs. *Journal of Linguistics,* 1969, 5, 57–74.

Bach, E. Nouns and noun-phrases. In E. Bach & R. Harms (Eds.), *Univerals in linguistic theory.* New York: Holt, 1968.

Fillmore, C. J. The case for case. In E. Bach & R. Harms (Eds.), *Universals in linguistic theory.* New York: Holt, 1968.

Fillmore, C. J. Verbs of judging: an exercise in semantic description. In C. J. Fillmore & T. Langendoen (Eds.), *Studies in linguistic semantics.* New York: Holt, 1971.

Gordon, D., & Lakoff, G. Conversational postulates. In *Papers from the seventh regional meeting,* Chicago Linguistic Society, 1971.

Grice, H. P. Logic and conversation. In P. Cole & J. L. Morgan (Eds.), *Syntax and semantics* (Vol. 3). New York: Academic Press, 1975.

Lakoff, G. *Irregularity in syntax.* New York: Holt, 1970.

Lakoff, G. Linguistics and natural logic. In D. Davidson & G. Herman (Eds.), *Semantics of natural language.* Dordrecht: Reidel, 1972.

Leech, G. *Toward a semantic description of English.* Cambridge: Cambridge University Press, 1969.

Lenneberg, E. H. *Biological foundations of language.* New York: Wiley, 1967.

Luria, A. R. *Le funzioni corticali superiori nell'uomo.* Florence: Editrice Universitaria, 1967. Translated into English as *Higher cortical functions in man* (Basil Haigh, tr.). New York: Basic, 1966.

McCawley, J. Lexical insertion in a transformational grammar. In *Papers from the fourth regional meeting,* Chicago Linguistic Society, 1968.

McCawley, J. Where do noun-phrases come from. In R. Jacobs & P. Rosenbaum (Eds.). *Readings in English transformational grammar.* Waltham, Mass., 1970.

Parisi, D. The past participle. *International Journal of Italian Linguistics,* in press.

Parisi, D., & Antinucci, F. Early Language development: A second stage. In F. Bresson (Ed.), *Current problems in psycholinguistics.* Paris: CNRS, 1974.

Parisi, D., & Puglielli, A. Hopping adverbs. In *Proceedings of the 11th International Congress of Linguists.* In press.

Ross, J. R. On declarative sentences. In R. Jacobs & P. Rosenbaum (Eds.), *Readings in English transformational grammar.* Waltham, Mass., 1970.

Searle, J. *Speech acts: an essay in the philosophy of language.* Cambridge: Cambridge University Press, 1969.

Index

A

Adjectives, 167, 171–72
Adverbial predicates, 36, 142
Adverbials, 32–40
  recursion and, 39
Adverbs, 167
Anaphora, 158
Argument, 17–24
Associated configuration, 97–98
  contextual mapping rules and, 156–57
Attribute, 165

B

Before, 82

C

Chomsky, Noam, 8
Complements, 31, 163–64
Component analysis, 41–85
  encyclopedia, role, 83–85
  lexical meaning, role, 83–85
  of must sentences, 64–71
  prepositions, 78–82
Content information, 136–37, 142
Contextual rules, 146–61
Coordination, 165
Count nouns, 107

D

Definite article, 170
Deictic mapping rules, 160
Deixis, 158
Demonstrative adjectives, 171
Deontic must, 68, 71, 72
Diachronic differences, 13
Dialectal differences, 13
Discourse, 122, 165, 166
During, 80–81

E

Encyclopedia, 83–85
Entailment, 5–6
Epistemic, 69, 71
Epistemic can, 74
Epistemic will, 75

G

Grammar, 1–14

I

Idiolectal differences, 13
Indefinite articles, 171
Intention, 77
Interrogative adjectives, 171–72
Invariable, 168

L

Language
  cerebral structure and, 1–2
  model of, 2–8
  universals of, 10

Lexical mapping rules, 137–40
Lexical meaning, 83–85
Lexical representation, 139
Lexicon, 137–38
Linguistic competence, 2–3

M

Main clause, 27
Mapping mechanism, 11, 134–61
   contextual rules, 146–61
   deictic rules, 158–60
   lexical rules, 137–40
   syntactical rules, 137–38
Mapping rules, 19
Mass nouns, 108
Modal verbs, 64–65
   can, 72–73
   have to, 72–73
   may, 67–68, 70–71
   must, 64–71
   shall, 77–78
   will, 75–77
Model, 2–3
Must, analysis of, 64–71

N

Neurosciences, language and, 1–2
Nominalization, 95–97
Nominals, 86–109
Nonrestrictive modifiers, 102–103
Noun modifier, 99
Nouns, 99
   count nouns, 107
   mass nouns, 108
Nuclear predicates, 36, 142
Nuclear subordinate, 31
Nucleus, 15–31

P

Paragraph, 165–66
Parsing, 15–16, 30–31
Parts of speech, 166, 167
Performative, the, 110–23
Permissive may, 71, 72
Personal pronouns, 172

Possessive adjectives, 171
Predicate, 34–35, 45
Predicate configuration, 45
Predication, 45, 164
Predications in the strict sense, 168, 169–70
Presuppositions, 124–33
Projection, *see* Mapping mechanism
Pronoun, 171, 172
Proposition, 111
Psycholinguistics, 2
Pure nominals, 95

Q

Qualifying adjectives, 172

R

Recursion, 26–28
   adverbials and, 39
Redúndancy, 141
Referents
   count noun, 107
   mass nouns, 108
Relative pronouns, 172
Restrictive modifiers, 102–103
Retrievable contexts, 154

S

Semantic components, 44, 45, 106
Semantic configuration, *see* Predicate configuration
Sentence, 165
Sentential structure, 27
Structural information, 136–37
   mapping mechanism and, 142–43
Subject, 30, 164
Subordinate clause, 27, 28, 29
Subordination, 165
Syntactic mapping rules, 137–38, 140
Syntax, 137

T

Traditional grammar, 162–74
Traditional predicate, 164
Transformational grammar, 162